The Way of a Gardener

THE WAY OF A Gardener

A LIFE'S JOURNEY

Des Kennedy

GREYSTONE BOOKS

D&M PUBLISHERS INC.
Vancouver/Toronto/Berkeley

Greystone Books
An imprint of D&M Publishers Inc.
2323 Quebec Street, Suite 201
Vancouver BC Canada V5T 4S7
www.greystonebooks.com

Library and Archives Canada Cataloguing in Publication
Kennedy, Des
The way of a gardener : a life's journey / Des Kennedy.

ISBN 978-1-55365-417-9

1. Kennedy, Des. 2. Gardeners—British Columbia—Denman Island (Island)—
Biography. 3. Authors, Canadian (English)—20th century—Biography.
4. Environmentalists—Canada—Biography.
5. Sustainable living. I. Title.

SB63.K45A3 2010   635.092   C2009-906846-X

Editing by Susan Folkins
Cover and text design by Heather Pringle
Cover photograph by Allan Mandell
Printed and bound in Canada by Friesens
Printed on acid-free, FSC-certified paper that is forest friendly
(100% post-consumer recycled paper) and has been processed chlorine free
Distributed in the U.S. by Publishers Group West

We gratefully acknowledge the financial support
of the Canada Council for the Arts, the British Columbia Arts Council,
the Province of British Columbia through the Book Publishing Tax Credit,
and the Government of Canada through the Book Publishing
Industry Development Program (BPIDP) for our publishing activities.

Mixed Sources
Cert no. SW-COC-001271
© 1996 FSC
FSC

For my brothers, Ger, Brendan, and Vincent

And most especially for Sandy

CONTENTS

PREFACE

And this our life, exempt from public haunt,
Finds tongues in trees, books in running brooks,
Sermons in stones, and good in everything.
I would not change it.
WILLIAM SHAKESPEARE, *As You Like It*

I AWAKEN TO A RESTLESS, MOVING darkness. A high wind is soughing through big conifer trees all around me. The roar is like that of ocean combers heard from a distance or the rumble of a slow-moving freight train. It is a wind from the southeast rummaging through the tree canopy. Slender culms of black bamboo rattle fretfully against the screening of the little summerhouse where my partner and I are lying. We sleep out here for as much of the year as weather allows, exposed to the movements and sounds of the night. Earlier I was awakened by the extravagant hooting of barred owls calling to one another through the woods. Raucous, haunting, antiphonal cries, back and forth, they're as cryptic by night as the calls of ravens are by day. The oracular chorus completed, the soundscape is reclaimed by the rising wind and I drift back into uneasy sleep.

Later in the night there comes a sudden banging on the wooden steps leading up to our little sleeping chamber. Startled awake, I have an instant sense of attack, of danger. But then I make out, not ten feet away, the form of a deer, a small doe, frozen in fear. She must have struggled up the steps and now stands on the deck, unsure of her next move. The deer and I stare at one another in the pale moonlight, and when I hiss disapproval at her, she disappears in a single graceful bound from the deck to the lawn below. The moon is almost full, riding high above the treetops, fast-moving clouds streaming across it like a dancer's veils. Mercury moonlight spills down through our little clearing, illuminating the house and gardens below. The scene is hopelessly romantic, evoking memories of moonlight shining on the landscapes of poems I loved as a boy. Then I sink again into the dream world.

In the pearl gray light of predawn, I pull back the down comforter and rise reluctantly from the warm bed, leaving Sandy to sleep a while longer. I dress quickly in shiveringly cold clothes and grope my way down broad wooden steps into the garden. The overnight deer has nibbled at the late blooms of Madame Isaac Pereire, a sumptuous pink rose growing at the bottom of the steps. Her petals are scattered on damp earth like fragmentary memories of a long-ago love affair. But the deer's damage is minimal; time is what takes the greater toll now, time and the retreat of warmth and light, for we are on the dark side of the autumnal equinox, when night and day were momentarily equal. The elements of darkness daily grow stronger against the retreating light.

I stand for a moment on the flagstone pathway that curves gently through the garden to the house. The night wind has dropped away, leaving in its wake a misty hush across the woodlands. The pungent smell of damp earth and rotting leaves is in the air. Stripped of its high summer finery, the garden is all shapes and textures now— fountains of airy grasses, the shiny ovular surfaces of clipped shrubs. Splashes of color from red crabapples and cotoneaster berries and lush pink cushions of sedum flowers. A Persian parrotia, one of the first trees to flaunt its autumn foliage, is a Joseph's coat of mingled crimsons and purples.

I am sixty-four years old, standing in half-light on a cold stone path in a garden glistening with memories and pleasures. I laid the stones for this path several decades ago while we were creating the garden from scratch amid eleven acres of woodland on a small island off Canada's west coast. For sure this has been a path less traveled, far removed from the frenzied energy of commerce, the jostle of attainment and achievement. I've remained profoundly attached to this particular place, moved by it, inspired by it for decades. It is in its way as cordial as any place on earth—blessed with a benign climate that permits us to grow much of our own food, amid a richly diverse ecosystem whose plants and animals provide an ongoing engagement, and within a community of mostly caring and creative people. No matter how alluringly other options tantalize, no matter what compelling cause may require attention, the place that I share with the woman I love, this haven of natural beauty and spiritual sustenance, remains the fundament. Thomas Merton, the Trappist monk who was one of my early heroes, wrote in *Thoughts in Solitude*: "When we find our vocation—thought and life are one." That's a unity I frequently feel, although in my own case I'd add place, too—that thought and life and place are one.

The days, the seasons spin past at an accelerating rate, and I want to stop them, hold them, squeeze every last drop of satisfaction out of them. Already it's abundantly clear to me that there will not be sufficient days ahead to accomplish all that I wish to do, or to savor fully all that might be savored. I've arrived, unexpectedly, at that point in life when it's appropriate to reflect upon essential questions: Why am I here? How did I become who I am? Where am I going? Does any of this have meaning?

To address such personal matters publicly does not come easily to me, for I was raised to consider self-absorption, and certainly self-congratulation, unseemly, something done by braggarts and poseurs, people who were "full of themselves." Holy Mother Church taught that pride was the deadliest of sins; humility required that we go quietly and modestly about our daily rounds, maintaining a diminished opinion of ourselves as sinners and pilgrims. Nor did respectable people air their dirty laundry in public; private business was to remain private. As the old Irish dictum had it: Whatever you say, say nothing. Behavior that has now become an accepted, indeed exalted part of the cultural landscape—the vulgar chest-thumping of new money, public disrobing by the emotionally bankrupt—was not the way of decent people. And so I proceed with my story under the keenest awareness of how slender a fault line separates candor from exhibitionism.

Intimate readings of a life may be of interest to others for various reasons. Perhaps the writer has been personally swept up in great historical events or been associated with gifted and famous persons. Or maybe the memoirist is a public personality—an actor or artist or star athlete—whose breezy reminiscences of life in the locker room or the green room are sure to captivate and possibly titillate. Perhaps religious conversion has inflamed the writer with fervent desire to spread the Word, or the great tragedy of war or pestilence has blighted the author's life or the lives of those nearby.

My story tends more toward reflection in solitude and silence than to the clash of civilizations or the roar of the crowd. I flatter myself to think that my stony path has run through mostly holy ground, that the small signs and wonders glimpsed along the way speak more of peace than of war, more of beauty and enduring love than of those forces that seek to destroy them. It seems to me that many a life encompasses twists and turns across terrain that the traveler does not recognize or fully understand. An account such as this one—of a journey that begins and ends in wonderment—is at best a descriptive outline of certain stepping-stones across one particular bit of strange terrain. But come along with me now, if you will, for I do have a few peculiar tales to tell.

1

SANCTUARY

The country is holy: O bide in that country kind,
Know the green good,
Under the prayer wheeling moon in the rosy wood
Be shielded by chant and flower and gay may you
Lie in grace.

DYLAN THOMAS, *"In Country Sleep"*

DURING THE EUPHORIC AND TRAGIC days immediately following the Second World War, precisely one month after the atomic bomb attack on Hiroshima, I emerged into this world, specifically into the capable hands of a worthy English midwife. My birthplace was a century-old stone building located on a hill above Woolton Village in Merseyside, a suburb of Liverpool. The cobweb of crooked streets in which the village was enmeshed evoked a decidedly ecclesiastical tone: Saint Mary's Crescent, Monk's Way, Bishop's Crescent, and Abbey Crescent. Church Road, where I was born, boasted two places of worship: a Methodist church in the village and, partway up a hill, Saint Peter's Church of England. Our home was farther up still, at Knowle Park, a Roman Catholic convent and school for orphan girls where my father was farm bailiff. From the very beginning, everything was God. Merseyside, I later learned, was a Stone Age place, its countryside dotted with hill forts, barrows, stone circles, ancient crosses, and magical wells. Whether by accident or design, fate had dropped me into a spiritual hotbed.

Our living quarters were part of an old sandstone block building—I imagine it was the coach house of a former grand estate—that also housed the nunnery's laundry, storage areas, and barns. One entered from the road through a Romanesque stone archway into a cobblestone courtyard. A faded photograph shows my father as a young man, my older brother, Ger, and myself at about age three standing in the courtyard posing solemnly for the camera. A flock of inquisitive ducklings is gathered at our feet. In the background a solitary turkey observes us like a suspicious old bachelor.

I retain only hazy memories of my first five years spent at Knowle Park, just a few dim glimpses, one of them around the excitement of seeing my father spearing rats with a pitchfork while a big collie barked and dashed after the scattering rodents. The chubby little fair-haired fellow in old photos doesn't feel like me at all. I have almost no recollection of how it was to be that child—was I fretful, happy, difficult? How did I view my parents and brothers? Over half a century and many miles removed from the reality, it's almost as though that little person was a chrysalid or larva that later metamorphosed into the being I think of as myself.

My older brother, named for Saint Gerard Majella, was nineteen months older than me, and my younger brother Brendan, named for the Irish monk and renowned navigator, was born fifteen months after me. I was never quite clear who Saint Desmond might have been and remember this causing me anxiety later on, as having a patron saint was a matter of some importance. It turns out that there seems not to have been a Saint Desmond at all, and despite a few early ventures toward sanctity, I was destined not to become the first. Besides the lack of sacred patronage, I suffered the anomaly of having vividly red hair, apparently triggered by a recessive gene that had popped up as a consequence of Danish raiders menacing the Irish coast in the dim mists of history. Our youngest brother, Vincent, was born after the family left Knowle Park.

My father was a robust little Irishman from County Down. His family had lived in Newry until his parents separated when he was fourteen, with his father going his own way and his mother taking her two daughters elsewhere. My dad was on his own, forced to make his way in life. He'd strapped a few garden tools to his bicycle and cycled off across the Irish countryside, picking up whatever small jobs he could. Eventually, like so many before him, he left Ireland for a better chance at work to be found in Liverpool.

My mother's people were Irish too, with a splash of Spanish, although she was born and raised in Liverpool, which was where she and my father met. Her parents had not approved of my father's courtship, apparently considering him an unreliable provider. Harsh words were exchanged, including on their wedding day, and the rift was never healed. I didn't really know any of my grand-parents and we had only fleeting contact with various aunties, uncles, and cousins. I remember no large family gatherings convened to celebrate or to mourn. We were not a clan in any sense. The adults we saw most of were Sister Anthony, a nun from the convent who was quite devoted to us, and my mum's friend Mrs. Richter, a portly little lady who lived down the hill from us, on the lip of Woolton quarry, from which had come the sandstone blocks that composed our house and much of the village.

One thing is certain amid the misty half-remembering of those first few years of life: that I began in a green and pleasant place of trees and fields, barnyard animals and ancient stone buildings, infused by the whispering piety of nuns. There I absorbed a sense of the sacred and of sanctuary, from the Latin *sanctus,* meaning sacred. In the Christian tradition a sanctuary was a holy place or piece of consecrated ground set aside for the worship of God or of one or more divinities. But it also became a place in which, by the law of the medieval church, a fugitive from justice or a debtor was immune from arrest. Thus it was a place of refuge also, a retreat both sacred and safe.

There was no question that danger lurked all about us. Hitler's war had only just ended and Luftwaffe bombs had flattened whole sections of Liverpool. I remember the city pocked with heaps of rubble where buildings once had stood. Even with Hitler dead in his bunker, we were not safe. Across Church Road from our home the high stone walls of an abandoned estate were said to enclose neglected woodlands in whose depths tramps occasionally took shelter. Tramps were men of despicable habits and appetites, and God only knew what vile and filthy acts they'd perform on little boys who disobeyed their parents and ventured into those forbidden woods.

Gypsies sometimes lurked nearby as well, devious characters known for snatching unsuspecting children and carrying them off so they never saw their parents again. Whenever there was an encampment of Gypsies on nearby common land, I tingled with a fearful fascination over these exotic and dangerous people, their odd habits of dress, their strange horse-drawn wagons. They were everything that we were not: itinerant, disreputable, irreligious, tribal, mockingly defiant of society. The men worked as tinkers coming door to door to repair leaking pots and pans and, it was thought, to reconnoiter for what might be pilfered. When the Gypsies broke camp and left, I felt a surcease of danger and simultaneously a sadness I didn't understand because they were gone away.

That the outer world was a breeding ground of evildoers was a conviction that I absorbed, like oxygen, from as long ago as I can remember. An instinctive distrust of strangers became second nature to me, a conviction that people at large were greedy and selfish, eager to take advantage of honest folk like ourselves. More than half a century later I'm still extricating tendrils of that foul inheritance from unexplored recesses of consciousness. I no longer blame my parents for it, for they in their turn had inherited it, the narrow, secretive, gossip-ridden character of Irish peasantry. Neither they nor I had any conception that the real foe, the saboteur of the soul, lies within each of us, and from that dark truth there is no sanctuary.

But everything has two sides, and while there might well lurk the likelihood of catastrophe beyond our little plot of holy ground, I must have intuited that there was safety and loveliness to be savored within it. The instinctive distrust of the unknown, the other, was balanced by a love of my parents and brothers and something else as well—I think an incipient love of solitude and seclusion, a delight in the natural world, in plants and creatures, extremes of weather, starry nights, and landscapes of surpassing beauty. I believe a sense of wonderment was also planted in my soul back then, an intuition of the power and beauty that trembled in everything.

BUT THIS LOVELY sense of being shielded by chant and flower was not to last, for our family was driven out of Knowle Park when I was about five years old. My father had quarreled with the mother superior of the convent. Affable and gregarious most of the time, particularly with people outside the family, my dad was not by nature a quarrelsome person. But when he thought himself ill-treated or misused in some way, he dug in and wouldn't budge. He lacked all skill at compromise or conciliation, and his stubborn sense of outrage at some perceived injustice—perhaps an Irishman's legacy born of six centuries under John Bull's boots—is one of my own more troublesome inheritances.

I don't know what the quarrel concerned but it resulted in his losing his job and our losing our home. A disaster in the land of the landless. A horse-drawn cart pulled up in front of our dwelling one morning. My parents piled our few meager household goods onto the cart and my two brothers and I climbed on as well. Because we didn't own a car and I'd never ridden in one, to do so would have seemed far more remarkable than was riding on a horse-drawn cart.

The horse trudged down Church Road pulling the cart. In my mind's eye the scene is reminiscent of something out of Catherine Cookson: the honest and hard-working farm bailiff and his young family unfairly driven from their home to face a cruel world. We clopped past Saint Peter's Church, in whose graveyard the bones of the as-yet-uncelebrated Eleanor Rigby lay, and down into the village of Woolton. The cart creaked to a halt in front of a two-story brick house, the last of a strip of dismal row houses on Allerton Road in the heart of the village. The house fronted onto the road, staring at a matching row of houses opposite. Next door to us sat the Woolton Public Baths, a squat brick building that held a little swimming pool and washing facilities for those who lacked full bathrooms at home. Across the street from the baths, on the corner of Quarry Road, the Grapes pub and hotel catered to sinners, drunks, and adulterers. A huge stone church up on High Street loomed directly behind our house. We'd moved from the shadow of a nunnery to the shadow of a Congregational church. On Sunday mornings the village resonated with the ringing of bells from its four churches.

But there was not a blade of grass to be seen anywhere on our street, nor any flowers. Trees could be glimpsed only in the distance. Expelled from a green and pleasant place, we'd come to a crowded neighborhood of bricks and stone. Through our small domestic drama, my family was re-enacting the industrialization of

Olde England, moving from pastoral to urban life, for Woolton had already by then been swallowed up as a part of greater Liverpool.

I think a sense of my father's failure hung in the air after our move to the village. Surely it was his stubbornness and pride that had brought us down to this. I wonder now what he felt at the time, and what my mother felt. A more melancholy character, my mother endured life's blows with a resignation that was equal parts stoic and ironic. "The exilic condition comes naturally to a certain kind of Irishman," wrote Anthony Burgess in his preface to *Modern Irish Short Stories,* and I suspect that my father, having experienced exile at a young age, was less fazed by our changed circumstances. No doubt anxious to prove himself a more worthy provider than my mother's family had judged him, he got a job working on the Liverpool buses, first as conductor and later as driver, and we settled into life as village folk. (Twenty years after our expulsion from Knowle Park I would suffer an uncannily similar experience when I was ejected from the monastic life I'd chosen. Like my father, I tangled with religious authority and paid a heavy price. I think of it now as a family specialty, getting up the snoot of religious tyrants and being pitched out onto the street for our efforts.)

But our familial piety wasn't the least bit dampened in the process and, as I reached school-going age, I became a church-going marvel. I can still picture myself rising every morning in a little upstairs bedroom of that row house, dressing quickly and setting out on foot down Allerton Road with my brother Ger while the village still lay hushed in the secrets of morning. Reverently we'd enter Saint Anne's Catholic Church with our little black missals in hand for attentively following the saying of Mass. The highlight was to rise together from the pew where we knelt and make our way up the aisle to kneel at the communion rail to await the approach of the priest murmuring in Latin as he lifted from a golden chalice and placed on each of our tongues the sacred wafer, the Body of Christ. As we had fasted all night and morning, this was our first nourishment of the day.

An old photo, taken on the afternoon of my First Holy Communion, shows me dressed in a white shirt and short pants, white shoes and socks, my hands joined as in prayer in front of my breast, smiling thinly like an earnest young angel. I'm still astonished by the innocence and purity of the image.

After Mass we'd walk back home for a bowl of hot porridge cooked by our mum, with creamy milk from the bottles delivered every morning by the milkman, and sugar sprinkled on top. Then Ger and I would catch the double-decker bus that would carry us down Menlove Avenue to Saint Anthony of Padua School in Mossley Hill. There we learned our catechism from the good nuns:

"Who made me?"

"God made me."

"Why did God make me?"

"God made me to know Him, love Him, and serve Him in this world and to be happy with Him forever in the next."

That was the lesson we learned first: Postponement is the prerequisite for Paradise. Knowing, loving, and serving God are the purposes of this life. Happiness will follow death. Meanwhile we are walking through a vale of tears. This belief system was drilled into us so relentlessly, both at home and in school, we accepted it without question. Just as we accepted that the Protestant kids we passed on the way to our school, and they on their way to theirs, would never be allowed to enter into Heaven. Which was how we could justify having snowball fights with them on the rare occasions upon which it snowed. We disliked and distrusted Protestants on principle—I remember once being taken to a Protestant Christmas party by a kindly lady, and being terrified throughout that the Protestants would surely do something vile and sinful before the party was over. Jews were thoroughly despised; one gentleman who operated a jewelry shop in Woolton Village was invariably referred to as "the old Jew boy." No other ethnicities were ever seen in the village. In many ways we Catholics occupied a parallel universe to the one all around us. We had a sense of ourselves as the elect, bound together as God's chosen people, indifferent to the cares of this tarnished world and yearning toward the glory of the hereafter.

On Sunday morning our family would go to Mass en masse, my parents and we boys kneeling chronologically side by side in a pew. The lavishly embroidered vestments of the priest, the exalted singing of the choir and rumble of the pipe organ, the heady scent of incense and guttering of multiple candles—High Mass was by far the closest thing we knew to spectacle.

Fear and guilt, those twin pillars of Irish Catholicism, underpinned our cosmology. Fear of the future, of falling from grace, was bred like superstition into our young bones. Expect the worst, always. I learned from my mother to fear the bailiffs, coldhearted men who'd put your possessions out on the street if you were evicted for failing to pay the rent. Or, even more fearfully, the Black Maria, the sinister prison van that would haul you away to jail for whatever transgressions you'd committed. More terrifying still, we learned that you could identify the Devil when disguised as a man by looking to see if he had cloven feet. At seven or eight years old I was glancing furtively at the feet of old men I passed on the street, convinced that one of them might well be the Devil in disguise. As well I learned to be alert for any sign of a great crucifix that would spread across the sky, tremendous and ominous, indicating that the end of the world was at hand.

Against these terrors we clung to our faith. We kids mastered the memorization of "Our Father who art in Heaven ..." and "Hail Mary, full of grace ..." and "Glory be to the Father ...," each repeated mantralike in the saying of the Holy Rosary. And we learned that each of us had a guardian angel, a spiritual companion who hovered close by, ready to protect us from evil. I didn't dare disbelieve this, but nor did I ever think of my guardian angel as actually there. I never spoke to it, called it by name, or thought of it as a companion.

ONE OF MY most vivid childhood memories is of the fear and anxiety that filled our house in Woolton Village while my mother was giving birth to her fourth and last child. She lay in labor in a bed specially installed in the front parlor. A midwife was in attendance, and eventually a doctor was called in. We kids were banned from the room, mystified by what was going on, but aware of our dad's distress and an awful apprehension of disaster. The labor was long and difficult—a breech birth, I think—and the baby eventually was pulled into the world by forceps. For the following days Mother lay weak and exhausted, and it was uncertain whether she would recover from the ordeal. But she did, and we kids had a new little brother named Vincent. What nobody realized at the time was that he'd been born almost completely deaf.

Our mother suspected early on that his hearing was impaired, but she was told by the family doctor—a seedy-looking and incompetent old gent, in my memory—that his hearing was normal and that he was "acting out," choosing for some peculiar reason of his own to ignore sounds. In working-class Britain the pronouncement of a doctor was almost as sacred as the word of a priest and not to be questioned. But for years thereafter there remained alive within our family a suspicion, deficient only in any shred of evidence, that the old quack's incompetence with his forceps might have played a role in damaging the emerging baby's ears.

My brothers and I were all impeccably obedient little kids. Disobeying, defying, or talking back to our parents wasn't even considered. The prevailing ethos of the times—that children should be seen, not heard—was reinforced in our case with an absolute religious stricture that one's parents must be obeyed unquestioningly. Our mother was largely responsible for maintaining discipline, and she managed to do so without raising her voice and only very rarely administering a frustrated slap on the bottom. She was, however, masterful in instilling fear of the dreadful things that would happen to disobedient children, not the least of them the ominous "You just wait 'til your father gets home!" One time in a fit of childish rage I punched my fist through a pane of glass in the back door and spent the afternoon in terror awaiting the wrath of my dad upon his return from work. I remember him replacing and puttying the glass, but not that I suffered any punishment. Squabbling or bickering among us kids was not tolerated. In hindsight I find it remarkable how my mother succeeded in keeping four energetic boys under such firm control, employing instinctive skills that were at least as potent as the ministrations of any child psychologist or supernanny.

I don't think that back in those days I was ever really conscious of being poor. The British class system, still clinging to its bigotries and privileges in the postwar years, remained reasonably efficient at isolating each stratum of society, so that comparisons were maintained within one's class rather than with persons of superior or inferior social position. My mother prided herself on always having us kids look well dressed, clean, and tidy. "Oh, look at the tide mark on that neck!" she'd chide if a face wash had left a line between washed and unwashed skin. The other kids we knew in Woolton were more or less like us, although some were more obviously clothed in hand-me-downs, wiping dripping noses on their sleeves, sporting ridiculous haircuts done by their dads. One of our favorite games was playing "Wet Molly" in the brick-walled alleys behind our house. The Wet Molly was a water-soaked rag. Whoever was "it" had to take the Wet Molly and chase after the other kids until close enough to hit someone with the thrown rag. Whoever was hit would become "it" and take up the chase. Equipment costs for this game were extremely low.

Our house was heated, inadequately, only by a coal fire in a fireplace. In wintertime we huddled around the kitchen hearth and mostly lived within a few feet of its warmth. With neither radio nor television to entertain us, on winter nights we kids would be diverted by gazing at the blue, green, and orange genies dancing among glowing coals. On Christmas Day or the solemn occasion when the parish priest came for his annual visit, a fire would be lit in the front parlor too. For lighting we had gas lamps, and I think there were still gas lamps on the streets, lit each evening by the village lamplighter.

Finally the great day arrived when electricity came into the house, putting an end to the evening lighting of gas lamps and the lack of broadcast entertainment. Uncharacteristically, we were the first family on the block to get a television, conferring upon us an instant popularity among neighbors wanting to watch. Like the rest of the neighborhood, we had no indoor toilet in the house and no hot running water. I remember being terrified of having to go outside in the evening down a dark brick passageway to the ancient outdoor toilet behind the house. For our weekly bath on Saturday night, my parents would heat big kettles of water on the coal fire and pour hot water into a tub in which we'd bathe consecutively, starting with the youngest.

Frugality was bred into our bones. The bus ride to and from school cost a couple of pennies each day, so Ger and I would on occasion walk home in order to save the fare, not for ourselves but to give back to our mum. "Oh, aye," she'd tease us, "but what about the cost of wearing out your good shoe leather with all that walking?"

"We walked on the grass wherever we could, to save leather," Ger assured her, and I nodded. Never wasting money and contributing however we were able to the family coffers were unquestioned values to us. Largely because of my mother's wit, these economies were considered not something shameful that poor people were compelled to do, but rather something terribly clever that smart people did. One time my dad brought home a large, flat wooden crate of glazed pears, a luxury item we'd normally never have in the house. He'd been given it because one corner of the crate had been gnawed by rats, but the remainder was perfectly fine. For the next little while we dined like princes on glazed pears.

My father kept a flock of chickens in a small barn in the backyard, and I was morbidly fascinated by how he could expertly kill a chicken with a quick snap of its neck. Every year he'd have a local farmer drop off several big sacks of parsnips from which he'd make his parsnip wine. We kids would help keep the wine cellar stocked too by harvesting clusters of blue elderberries from vacant land, hauling shopping bags full of them back to the house for our mum's elderberry wine. We'd secure an enormous and rare treat by occasionally weaseling a couple of pennies from our mum so we could go to the little store around the corner and purchase a bottle of ginger beer.

There was no crushing sense of deprivation in any of this, and we were capable of what passed for extravagance, especially at Christmastime. We'd have the splendid treat of going into the city to see the captivating Christmas scenes on display in the department store windows, to meet Father Christmas and go to a theater to watch in wonderment a pantomime, none finer than *Peter Pan* with Tinker Bell and Peter flying miraculously above our heads. Somehow excellent presents and stuffed stockings always awaited us on Christmas morning, and Christmas dinner remains vivid with nostalgic affection. It seemed the grandest affair, carried on in the seldom-used front parlor at what was by our standards an elaborately laid table. We had roast turkey and stuffing, mashed potatoes with gravy and brussels sprouts. Always a homemade

Christmas cake with marzipan icing and Christmas pudding with brandy and soft sauce. We older boys were permitted a thimbleful of wine. All of this was better than Dickens ever dreamed of.

The inescapable school Christmas pageants were sometimes less successful, and I achieved a personal worst in my early thespian career when I was cast to play the feature role in a re-enactment of *Good King Wenceslas*. The rest of the class was to sing the carol while another kid, playing the page, and I as king would act out the requisite coming hither and going forth through the rude wind's loud lament. Preparations were proceeding brilliantly until about a week before the night of the pageant when I developed an enormous boil on the back of my neck. Red and painful pus-filled lumps, boils were not uncommon afflictions, and I remember a number of times suffering from my father's attempts to "bring the boil to a head" by applying a scorching hot mustard plaster. Unhappily for the pageant, my kingly costume included both a ruff and a crown. The ruff, rubbing against the agonizing boil, caused me to tilt my head forward, which in turn caused the crown to slip off my head. I think I acted out the whole scene with my head facing straight down and one hand clamping the crown to my head, leaving the other arm free to point toward yonder peasant, the miracle of preheated footsteps and all the rest.

Nobody we knew owned a car. A holiday would be a one-day outing by train to Blackpool or the Chester zoo or the seaside at Rhyl in Wales. But these were splendid expeditions, rife with adventure and excitement, like the time when Mrs. Richter came along with us only to have the sea wind lift her dainty little hat off her head and send it skittering along the beach with all of us boys in hot but futile pursuit. As with everywhere else, dangers lurked along the shore. There were deadly riptides and undertows ready to suck us out to sea. One time my father showed us an enormous jellyfish stranded above the tide line. He nudged it quickly with the point of his shoe and we all jumped back as the creature flicked out venomous tentacles. "One sting of those and you'd be paralyzed," he warned us. The thick grasses growing in the sand dunes were capable of slashing bare legs like rapiers. We viewed with dread a notorious stretch of quicksand where it was said a horse and cart and its unwary driver had all been fatally swallowed up in a matter of minutes. In later years my mother would marvel, "I can't believe you chose to live on an island that you have to take a ferry to get to," because, she said, as a child I'd wept uncontrollably and fought against getting aboard the ferry to cross the Mersey River. Fear of water prevented my learning to swim, even with a swimming pool next door, just as fear of heights kept me firmly on the ground while Ger and his pals would clamber recklessly in treetops. One thing I could do in those days was run, run like the wind, run like the great Roger Bannister, whose "Miracle Mile" and subsequent victory over the Australian John Landy in the "Mile of the Century" in 1954, in the far-distant city of Vancouver, swelled our English schoolboy hearts with pride. An old photograph shows myself and Ger, along with ten other comical-looking lads in short pants and fallen socks, proudly posing as the Saint Anthony of Padua track team with our captain holding a large plaque signifying our triumph over the other parochial schools of the district.

What I loved best about outings away from town were the woodlands and patchwork fields and old castle ruins we'd pass on the train. I vividly remember a school outing we took to a medieval site, a sacred place whose ancient stone buildings held the relics of saints as well as marvelous swords encrusted with jewels. These spoke to me of another time and place, sacred and mysterious in a way that our own lives weren't.

In Woolton Village I found grasses and trees again in Woolton Woods, a park just up the hill from our house. It had open fields we kids could run in and a woodland with wide pathways through it.

In autumn my brothers and I would gather up huge piles of leaves and bury ourselves inside them, becoming leaf people. Tree children. Somewhere beyond the trees there was an area of gardens with a large floral clock as its centerpiece. Though first dazzled by it, I came to dislike the clock, its fussy Edwardian ingenuity. The woods and fields were what called to me. At eight years of age I was already confronted with primitive forms of the timeless questions of how nature, art, and gardening intersect. There was an artificial cuckoo sound that I associate with the clock. I remember hearing the cuckoo sound while walking with my parents through the woods to see the gardens. "Oh, listen! Do you hear the cuckoo?" said my parents, laughing. But I soon figured out it wasn't a real cuckoo and I resented its fake intrusion into the woods. I wanted a living cuckoo to be singing from the trees. I wanted the mystery and wildness of a real wood with real creatures in it, not a park with high palings all around it and a foppish floral clock at its center. Why would you want a clock in a woodland anyway, a place that should be too primal to be measured or divided, a place, as John Fowles wrote in *The Tree,* "teeming, jewel-like, self-involved, rich in secrets just below the threshold of our adult human senses." My child's heart knew instinctively the secrets of trees, and already back then I may have set my sights upon living among them.

Then, suddenly, a seismic shift. Just as we'd left the fields and trees and animals of Knowle Park five years earlier, now a second great change was about to occur: a decision had been made that our family would leave England entirely, leave behind the crowded houses of Merseyside and everything we'd known there, to start a new life in Canada.

2

THE NEW WORLD

We could never have loved the earth so well
if we had had no childhood in it.

GEORGE ELIOT, *The Mill on the Floss*

I N 1954 MY FATHER LEFT my mother and us four boys in
Woolton and sailed off to the faraway land of Canada. The
plan was that he would find work and save every penny
toward buying a house to which we would all move in a year or
so. Not everyone approved of the scheme. One of the teachers at
our school voiced what others were likely thinking: that this was
reckless foolhardiness on his part, that he was bound to fail as other
dreamers had failed before him, and that he'd be back in no time
with his grand dreams crushed and his tail between his legs.

But at home we entertained no doubts. As my mother wrote to
my dad during their long separation: "the boys still go [to Mass]
most days. They are all keeping well and talking of Canada and I
get tired of their questions. They do try to be as good as they can.
I am sure you will be very glad to see them all again ...We shall
be glad to get word from you to cross, we'll lose no time in getting
out of this place." All my hopes and yearnings were of leaving

grimy old Merseyside for the wild excitement of what people still called the New World. The Canada I dreamed of moving to was a vast land of forested wilderness. Television helped stoke the fantasy. One of our favorite shows on the BBC at that time was called *The Cabin in the Clearing,* in which a pioneer couple and their brave daughter, Alice, were repeatedly menaced by wild animals and besieged in their isolated log cabin by murderous Shawnee Indians. I fantasized being with them in the wilderness, protecting pretty Alice from the perils that beset her. One evening, after much pleading, our mother allowed us kids to stay up past our normal bedtime to watch a TV special featuring "the singing rage Miss Patti Page." Fetchingly dressed in a buckskin outfit, perfectly pert and blond and American, she seemed to me the most beautiful woman imaginable singing the most heartrending songs I'd ever heard. And she lived across the ocean, in the land where our father already was and we would soon be.

Finally, in early 1955, a letter arrived with the joyous news we'd awaited so long—our dad had bought a house! He enclosed several small black and white snapshots of what looked to us like an imposing wooden home on a considerable estate. As my mother had promised, we lost no time in disposing of our possessions and preparing to leave in the first week of May, even though this meant abandoning school before our terms were completed. The mid-fifties were the final days when transatlantic liners still were a cheaper alternative to airline travel, so we would take a boat to Canada. Berthed at the Liverpool docks, the Cunard Line ship seemed to me a truly magnificent ocean liner. My earlier fears over boarding the Mersey ferry were long gone, and as the great vessel was pulled away from the wharf and made its way out into the Irish Sea I was filled with a thrilling sense of adventure. As twilight descended, my brothers and I stood at the stern of the boat and watched the twinkling lights of Liverpool slowly fade and vanish into the darkness. We were leaving once and for all; the past was behind us and ahead lay unimagined possibilities.

Everything was changed on that voyage. There was no Mass to attend in the morning, or any school all day. We ate our meals in a plush dining room, served by an acerbic waiter. Not long into the voyage, our mother succumbed to seasickness that confined her to her bunk. We kids were free to roam, make pals with other kids, and get into whatever mischief offered itself, mostly by poking around areas of the ship we were not supposed to enter. Though our mum tried her best to maintain some discipline, we were experiencing a freedom we'd never known before, unhampered by any realization of how temporary a state of affairs this was. The latter part of the voyage involved much watching for icebergs and a collective anxiety that we not suffer the same fate as the *Titanic*.

Then the great excitement of first sighting land. We gathered at the railings and made out on the far horizon a low gray smudge. Cruising up the Saint Lawrence River offered a stunning validation of all my expectations. Forests and farms stretched away from either shore. Wooded hillsides rose beyond. Kids paddled out in canoes to wave greetings to us and ride the wake of our great ship's passing. What a brilliant, wild, wide-open place we'd arrived at!

We disembarked at Montreal and took a train to Toronto. Again, I thrilled to mile after mile of woodlands, farms, lakes, and rivers. We pulled into Union Station in Toronto and wandered together into the waiting crowd. Suddenly a man burst forward and clasped us all in his arms. It was our dad, though he seemed almost a stranger, it had been so long since we'd seen him.

When we got to our new home it was in fact not a country estate, and certainly no cabin in a clearing, but a modest little two-story clapboard house on a city lot in the town of Weston on the outskirts of Toronto. But, wonder of wonders, there were trees growing on the lot, our very own trees—a row of scraggly evergreens out front and several big shade trees in the backyard. The whole neighborhood seemed dominated by enormous spreading trees. Although we were in a new country, with neither relatives nor friends, this appeared to me a far more green and pleasant land than the dreary treeless streets of Woolton Village we'd left behind. Paradoxically, our emigration seemed to me more coming home than exile. Of course, at nine years of age, admiring the few scrawny trees growing around our new home, I had no real idea of what might lie ahead of me. But I think I did have some nascent sense of having answered the call of trees, that the long journey we had just completed had taken me partway toward a destination I did not yet understand.

IT WAS MID-MAY of 1955 when our transplanted family finally got settled in Weston. The school year had little more than a month remaining, but Ger, Brendan, and I were enrolled straightaway at Saint John the Evangelist Catholic School, operated by an order of nuns called the Faithful Companions of Jesus. I think there was some initial confusion as to how our English standards fit with Canadian grades, but I ended up in the grade 4 class under the tutelage of a dour lay teacher named Mrs. Kavanagh. As far as the grade 4 class was concerned, I was the new kid, an immigrant who talked funny and had peculiar red hair. A "limey." (My mother explained that calling us limeys only served to expose the ignorance of those using the term: the applicable pejorative for a Liverpudlian would be "Scouser," from our distinctive dialect called "scouse.") Almost straightaway, we had a little class field day of sorts and in the feature event, the less-than-a-hundred-yard dash across the playground, I finished in a dead heat for first with a startled Wally Somebody who was the most gifted athlete in the class. Few accomplishments could have more effectively established my credentials. In my eagerness to fit in, I quickly adopted whatever local slang I could, which may have won favor with my classmates but certainly didn't with Mrs. Kavanagh. Twice I was held in after school and compelled to write on the blackboard fifty times, on one occasion "Geez is not a word" and on another "Ain't is not a word."

But I had not fallen from grace; far from it. In fact our church-going intensified. The school and adjacent church were about a mile from our house, a pleasant walk along tree-lined streets. My brothers and I would walk to Mass every morning before school, though hardly any other kids did this. We couldn't receive Holy Communion, because we'd eaten breakfast before setting out, but on Saturdays we'd walk to Mass in the morning, when we could take Communion, then back home for breakfast, and return to church for confession in the afternoon. On Sundays my father would drive the family to Mass in the morning and some of us boys would walk back to church for Benediction on Sunday evening. There'd be lots of kids at Sunday Mass, since it was a mortal sin to miss it, but none at Benediction—they'd all be at home watching Walt Disney on TV while we'd kneel in the deserted church with a few old ladies groaning away at turgid hymns like "Tantum Ergo Sacramentum."

We were genuine little saints, my brothers and I. One of our favorite pastimes was to play at saying Mass. We'd create a little makeshift altar in the house from whatever props we had at hand and dress ourselves as priest—a prized role that almost always fell to Ger, who was the primary instigator in the business—and altar boys, then go through the entire ritual, raising our make-believe Host, ringing the bells and all. Holy Mother Church remained at the core of our lives.

Soon we were released for summer vacation, which stretched for an eternity compared with the short English school holidays we'd known. That was the summer of Davy Crockett—the Disney version of America's greatest frontiersman was everywhere, on television and in movie theaters. Three different versions of "The Ballad of Davy Crockett" played repeatedly on radio. Kids were wearing coonskin caps and moccasins. Naturally this fed right into my pre-existing frontier fetishes, and I soon had a pair of moccasins myself. Jim Bowie, Kit Carson, Daniel Boone—I couldn't get enough of them. I devoured Western comic books and TV shows. I acquired a miniature ranch and used to spend hours arranging its fences and buildings and moving around the small figures of cowboys and Indians engaged in endless dispute.

The public schoolyard across from our house had a softball diamond, and frequently on the long, warm summer evenings a crowd would gather for a men's fast-pitch game. These were fabulous events, the players men of immense strength and skill, the uniformed umpire as authoritative a figure as any priest or policeman, the crowds of wives and girlfriends raucous in their running commentaries. I'd experienced nothing like it before: the determination of a batter digging in, the lightning-fast pitch and smack of the ball into the catcher's mitt, the time-honed chants of the players—"Hum, baby, hum!" "You got him, you got him!"—repeated like incantations. This was a game I wanted to play.

I WAS NOT aware at the time of how precarious our financial situation was. Something had gone wrong with the house purchase and, I only learned much later, we had almost lost the house and our investment in it. My father worked at two jobs. He'd leave home late in the evening to work the night shift as a maintenance man on the Toronto subway system known as the TTC. Returning home in the morning, he'd have breakfast and then go to a nearby nursery where he'd work in the greenhouses for another four or five hours, or if there was no nursery work, he'd pick up day-laboring jobs from the labor exchange. In the afternoon he'd work at our place.

In very short order, to my dismay, the trees on our property that I'd prized so much upon arrival had been chopped down to make way for gardens, and within a year or two the front yard was a full English cottage garden while the yard out back was chockablock with fruits and vegetables. My dad would sleep for a few hours in the late afternoon and evening and then begin the work cycle all over again. At the TTC he'd take any special shifts available—on Christmas Day or New Year's Eve—because of the extra pay involved. In all the years I was at home my parents never took a vacation anywhere.

My brothers and I learned from an early age how not to be noisy. Dear old Mum had a very limited tolerance for what she called "bedlam," which would be anything much louder than the sound of snow falling. If I'd tried to raise four active boys within the confines of a small house I'm sure I'd have adopted a similar approach. Plus there was the wrath of a sleep-deprived dad to consider; if we kids were around the house and made any sound at all that awoke him from his slumbers, it was rather like facing a grouchy bear emerging from hibernation. We became adept at creeping and whispering, and came to think of noisy people as depraved.

For the first few years we were identifiably poor amid the modest affluence of our neighbors. In contrast to England, here almost everybody owned their own house; some even had a summer cottage up at Lake Simcoe or on Georgian Bay. Everyone owned a car. A few days before our first Christmas in Canada, there came a rapping on our front door. Two men, volunteers from the parish, had come to deliver a Christmas hamper. We kids were thrilled at all the unaccustomed treats stuffed into the bushel basket, but my parents were mortified. They told the Good Samaritans that we didn't need or want the hamper, that there must be poor people in the parish who deserved it far more than we. There was a terrible awkwardness as we all stood in our little front room, the adults contending over disposition of the hamper, we kids not saying a word. I retain no memory of whether the hamper was finally refused or reluctantly accepted, delight in its treats tainted by the shame that was attached to them. The hamper proclaimed our poverty, that we were a charity case, and this was bitterly intolerable.

As soon as we were old enough, we boys began contributing to the cash flow. Ger and I started with a large paper route when I was about eleven, delivering the old *Telegram* and eventually switching to the rival *Toronto Star*. Spring through fall we'd haul our papers on a wagon and in winter on a sleigh. Like our fellow paperboys we took great pride in knowing how to bundle a paper tightly against itself so you could chuck it from sidewalk to front door without its opening up on impact. Within a year or two we each had our own route, and Ger soon graduated to being assistant on the truck that dropped off each delivery boy's bundles.

The daily rounds of a paperboy were full of perks and perils— I was bitten by dogs and flirted with by girls, and I gained fascinating glimpses into the homes and lives of my customers. I opened my own bank account and derived immense pleasure from its accumulating capital. My first paper route ran down what we called Main Street, the heart of old Weston and now called Weston Road. Here I got to deliver to a mortuary and to a shop that sold scandalous-looking ladies' lingerie. I was equally intrigued by prosthetic devices in one of the shops I served, and treated kindly at the local police station where the cops would occasionally show me their guns.

Best of all, the route brought me into close proximity to the Humber River, which ran through a deep valley more or less parallel to Main Street. This was the kind of wild area toward which my inner Davy Crockett yearned. I spent many a summer afternoon, either alone or with school chums, poking around the willow-cloaked valley bottom and fishing for big suckers in the river's pools. A century earlier the Humber had powered a sawmill and later a flour mill, both of which played a major role in the town's development. But the mills were long gone and so was most everything else along the valley, because it had been one of the areas hardest hit by Hurricane Hazel, the deadliest hurricane in Canadian history, which struck in October of 1954. Almost a foot of rainfall within forty-eight hours had sent a wall of water roaring down the Humber that swept away everything in its path, including one whole block of homes in which thirty-two sleeping residents were killed within an hour. The floodplain was subsequently designated off limits for development, and the resultant ribbon of wilderness through the city fit my predilections perfectly.

SHORTLY AFTER EACH new school year began I would get swept up in World Series fever. This was the golden age of baseball, before expansion and multimillion-dollar contracts. I joined my schoolmates in thrilling to the exploits of Mickey Mantle and Willie Mays and Hammerin' Hank Aaron. We became passionately attached to one team or another. To be sitting in a classroom while the Series games were being played mid-afternoon was pure torture, rendered even more torturous by a sympathetic teacher occasionally providing a scoring update. Within a year or two I'd uncharacteristically become one of the bad boys who'd sneak a miniature transistor radio into the classroom and furtively listen to the game through a cleverly concealed earpiece. And why not? There was nothing in the curriculum, scarcely anything in the universe, of greater consequence than that the Dodgers—the great Jackie Robinson, Pee Wee Reese, Gil Hodges, Duke Snider, and the other Bums—took the 1955 Series over the Yanks in seven games. Or that the following year the excellence of Mantle, Yogi Berra, and

Whitey Ford and Don Larsen's perfect game powered the Yankees to the title in another thrilling seven-game series.

I began my own career playing first base on the class soft-ball team. Dipping into the profits from my newspaper route, I purchased a first baseman's mitt upon which I lavished obsessive attention. I repeatedly worked oil into its soft leather. I placed a ball inside the glove's deep pocket and tied the glove tight around it overnight. I carried my glove wherever I could, repeatedly pounding my right fist into its pocket. Although there was no coach on hand, I worked diligently at my craft, fielding hot grounders and pop-ups, charging the bunt, stretching from the bag to shave a millisecond off a throw from the infield.

When the bitter Toronto winter set in, I was forced to become a sports spectator. Most of my peers were already adept at ice-skating, which I'd never tried because at that time it was virtually unknown in England. For the first winter or two I wobbled around on the neighborhood outdoor rink, but I realized that, no matter how hard I worked at it, I'd never skate as fast as Wally Somebody. I compensated by developing a fierce attachment to the Toronto Maple Leafs hockey team. And what a team! George Armstrong, Frank Mahovlich, Tim Horton, and Johnny Bower. Punch Imlach was our mastermind. Throughout the dark winter months my spirit rose and fell with each victory or defeat. The Saturday-night Leafs game on TV with Foster Hewitt calling the game seemed, sacrilegiously, of far greater consequence than Sunday-morning Mass.

My dad maintained a peculiar enthusiasm for professional wrestling, delighting in the antics of gentlemanly Whipper Billy Watson, barrel-chested Yukon Eric, and the dastardly Miller brothers. He sought to encourage a similar enthusiasm in us kids, and we'd sometimes watch wrestling on TV with him, during the course of which he'd remind us that he could have gotten into professional wrestling himself if only he'd been a few inches taller. The only sporting event

I can remember him taking me to was an evening of wrestling at Maple Leaf Gardens. In the feature match the Nazi-cloaked and eminently detestable Fritz Von Erich sought to apply his evil hold "the Claw" to the virtuous abdomen of Whipper Billy. In the same vein I recall a much-hyped grudge match involving the preening Gorgeous George, who, if he was defeated, would have his flowing blond tresses shaved from his head in the ring. Compared with the genuine heroics of the Leafs, the artificial nonsense of wrestling held only a fleeting appeal for me.

I look back fondly on those first several years in Weston, days of innocence and exploration, when the new world to which we'd journeyed was still an unfamiliar and intriguing place. I loved the family outings we'd sometimes take on summertime Sundays, to the conservation areas at Caledon Hills, Boyd Park, and Heart Lake, or—best of all—the long drive north to Midland where we'd visit the Jesuit Martyrs' Shrine overlooking Georgian Bay and do some fishing in the Wye River. I loved the smell of summer heat, the singing of cicadas in the trees, obtaining prize conkers from the horse chestnuts that grew in front of our school, chumming around with the neighborhood kids, the fantastic icicles that hung from our eaves in winter. I fell ridiculously in love with my grade 5 teacher, a darling young woman who made no secret of her preference for Wally Somebody and his pal Harry Curtis, both of them handsome and wholesomely Canadian. Then she broke all our hearts by announcing one day that she was going to get married and change her name and not teach anymore. Shortly thereafter, another rude shock: at the conclusion of grade 5 my brothers and I and a few other kids at Saint John's would be transferring to a brand-new Catholic school about to open in North York, an adjacent Toronto suburb. I had no way of knowing it at the time, but the days of innocence were already drawing to a close.

3

WHAT DRAGONS
DEVOUR

Education is an admirable thing, but it is well to remember
from time to time that nothing worth knowing can be taught.

OSCAR WILDE, *"The Critic as Artist"*

T HE PARISH OF SAINT BERNARD lay largely in the wilds
of North York, but stretched just far enough across Jane
Street and into Weston to include our block. To begin with,
the parish had neither church nor school, just a small and rather
squalid hall that served as the church, and this is where we attended
Sunday Mass. The surrounding area included undeveloped fields
that were being rapidly turned into residential subdivisions and
shopping centers, primarily to accommodate an influx of Italian
families. A spanking new and hopelessly sterile brick school was
plopped down in the middle of a field alongside an enormous
new church and rectory. The school was stocked with kids like
ourselves who'd previously attended various other schools on the
perimeter of the parish. We were mostly strangers to one another.
What was brilliant for the first few weeks was that the schoolyard

was a prairie of tall grasses within which various clandestine activities could be carried on. But pretty soon the grasses were trampled down and we had a schoolyard like any other.

Our principal was a diminutive but formidable nun named Sister Rosalie, from the same convent of Faithful Companions of Jesus as the nuns at Saint John's, but most of the staff were lay teachers. The parish priest, a crusty old curmudgeon named Father Marshman, regularly prowled around the school and did his best to put the fear of God in everyone. But it was an uphill struggle. Perhaps it was the newness of the place, its rawness, the lack of any tradition, the eclectic mix of kids, but there seemed from the outset to be a sulking disrespect simmering just below the surface, a kind of incipient lawlessness that might break out at any minute. Some of the older boys smoked cigarettes and blasphemed extravagantly; a couple of girls were whispered of as known sluts. One lout used to entertain himself by seizing smaller boys by the nipple and squeezing hard enough to cause a bruise, telling them he'd given them "a purple titty." Sister Rosalie, who brooked no insolence, had her hands full with this lot. A large leather strap hanging in her office warned of retribution for any misbehavior. Only once was I ever sent to the principal's office for some infraction I no longer recall. When I entered her office and explained my transgression to her, she looked at me as though I'd disappointed her awfully. "Hold out your hand," she said dispassionately, as she picked up the strap. I pulled up my sleeve and extended my right hand. She lashed my palm hard several times. I felt a fiery pain after each lash. "Now the other hand." She lashed my left palm the same way. "All right, go back to your desk." Although my hands were stinging as fiercely as if I'd stuck them into a hornet's nest, the greater pain I felt was in having let the principal down. I knew poor Sister Rosalie held high hopes for me, and I had betrayed her expectations, shown myself no better than the worst louts of the class. But also, perversely, I experienced a moronic little swagger of satisfaction at my badness and at my courage under the lash of the murderous strap.

However, the infraction was an anomaly for, like my brothers, I maintained my piety even in the unencouraging environment of the new school. I excelled in class and took satisfaction in scoring top marks, winning spelling bees and the like. Singled out as both pious and bright, I was forced into a public-speaking role I didn't really want, so that whenever a visiting dignitary addressed our class—a priest from the overseas missions, perhaps, or someone from the police warning us about the hazards of train tracks—it fell to me to rise and thank them for their presentation.

Fine literature singled me out as well. So far as I can remember, my first public poem was penned in the eighth grade. It concerned itself with a trout. My imaginative life had by then sashayed away from the Wild West, replacing cowboys with a fixation on trout fishing. I pored eagerly over old fishing magazines. I obtained a fiberglass rod with spinning reel and spent long hours perfecting the techniques of casting. My favorite event when the school visited the Royal Agricultural Winter Fair in Toronto was watching expert anglers cast plugs into circular targets floating at the far end of a long tank. My tackle box held a jumble of barbed hooks, leaders and lead shot, spinners and flashers, and, most absorbingly, flies. I studied the difference between wet and dry flies, stared longingly at displays of delicate flies in the neighborhood sporting goods store and practiced making my own flies, inexpertly gluing random clots of feathers onto hooks. No wily trout ever would, or did, attempt to eat one of these, though I cast them expectantly into the upper reaches of the Humber and Credit and whatever other streams I could. The thrill of an elusive trout flashing silver in a little brook excited a poetic impulse in me, as it had in Yeats before me. Sister Rosalie read my poem aloud to the grade 8 class. I had become a poet.

But I was still consumed with sports, devoting myself to track and field and fastball. By the time I was in grade 7, playing first base was no longer sufficient. Recognizing that the diametrically opposed ambitions of pitcher and hitter are at the heart of baseball, I set myself to become a pitcher. I worked on my pitching with fanatical single-mindedness and eventually was elevated to school pitcher, the player upon whose prowess the glory of the school largely rested in contests against other schools. Although I couldn't conceptualize it at the time, I was intrigued by how aspects of psychology, intimidation, and momentum attend each pitch.

I'm uncertain whether I developed a fervid competitiveness through playing sports, and particularly pitching fastball, or whether I possessed the attitude all along and athletics merely gave it a publicly sanctioned platform. I do know that loving to win and hating to lose became an abiding mindset, later spilling over into political and environmental issues in which I became involved, my own little personalized reworking of the nineteenth-century maxim that "The battle of Waterloo was won on the playing fields of Eton."

BY THE LATE fifties, my old heartthrob Patti Page was yesterday's darling and the schmaltz of the Four Lads and the Mills Brothers had similarly faded. We kids were swept up in the breakout mania of rock 'n' roll and its pantheon of stars—Bill Haley, Little Richard, the Big Bopper, Fats Domino, Buddy Holly. Parents everywhere were outraged. I can remember my mother being not the least bit pleased when she overheard me listening on my little transistor radio to Brian Hyland's "Itsy Bitsy Teenie Weenie Yellow Polka Dot Bikini." But even we kids were engaged in earnest debate over whether the "clean" songs of Pat Boone and Ricky Nelson weren't preferable to the lewd wigglings of Elvis or the sinister leer of "the Killer," Jerry Lee Lewis. A gang of disreputable greasers used to cruise our neighborhood in a big flip-top along the sides of which were painted leaping flames in tribute to Lewis's scandalous "Great Balls of Fire."

During these fraught times, walking to Saint Bernard's school every day along Jane Street, I passed a little music store that had outside its front door a rack containing free handbills listing the Top 40 tunes for that week. The list was a matter of intense interest and considerable discussion among my classmates. Did the blatant teenage pathos of "Tell Laura I Love Her" justify its rating? Did Sheb Wooley's "The Purple People Eater," topping the charts in '58, even deserve to be on the list, it was so spaz? I think the list was compiled by CHUM Radio, Canada's first Top 40 radio station, for whose disc jockeys we developed fierce attachments or dislikes. When the Canadian National Exhibition was on in the late summer, one of our great delights was to stand around an outdoor plaza watching the deejays spinning their discs in a glass booth.

More complicated by far were the sock hops occasionally attempted at school, dreary events at which many of the girls and very few of the boys were mad for dancing. Most of us boys plastered ourselves against the classroom walls and longed for the torment to end. Every once in a while there'd be a dance party at my friend Chuck Savoy's house, where, despite the best efforts of Chubby Checker and Little Eva, I'd squirm against the twin terrors of dancing and the proximity of flirting girls. The music was in my head, not my body.

For many months a banjo sat on display in the front window of that little music store on Jane Street. Banjos contributed little, if anything, to the music we were all crazy for, and yet I was strongly drawn to this instrument. I looked at it longingly, imagined myself playing it. The price was some outrageous sum well beyond my paper route life savings, and anyway it was inconceivable that I would spend so much on what might prove to be a short-lived whim. I didn't buy the banjo and eventually forgot about it. But over the years, every so often, I visualize that banjo again, wishing that I had bought it and mastered it, and wonder had I done so what curious avenues it might have led me down.

WANTING TO IMPRESS my friends and to be admired by pretty girls at school helped collapse the innocence of the early days and usher in a more complicated confusion of feelings. I had come to detest being poor, living in a poky house, and wearing cheap clothes. Going grocery shopping for my mum at the local A&P, where I'd often find bargains in the "reduced for quick sale" bin, no longer offered the excitement it once had. These frugalities didn't seem clever anymore; they were niggardly and shameful. To have owned a car, any car, back in England would have made us gentry, but here our family car was an embarrassment. We started off with an old Ford panel van, my parents sitting up front and us kids perched on crates in the back. Our eventual elevation to the relative luxury of a secondhand 1955 Chevrolet four-door sedan was permanently undermined when my dad hand-painted its exterior by brush. To make matters worse, he began periodically removing the rear bench seat in order to haul home buckets of sewage he picked up at a city treatment plant. His compost heap may have benefited, but the lingering stench never left the car—or, I think, us after riding in the car—and my mother finally put an end to his ingenious scheme for free fertilizer. Parking outside church on Sunday morning amid the gleaming new coupes and panel wagons of the parish, he'd make a great show of locking the car's doors, as though any self-respecting thief would lower himself to steal that crummy heap. I became embarrassed by my family and envied what looked like the cool, smooth sophistication of my classmates. Traitorously, I ignored the sacrifices my parents were making in order that we kids could have a better life and instead cringed at their idiosyncrasies of appearance and mannerism.

One occurrence typified that painful stage of distancing. Long after I'd outgrown my Wild West phase, I was given an unfortunate new set of clothes, claimed, I suspect, from Eaton's Annex, a sinkhole at the downtown Eaton's department store where merchandise returned by dissatisfied mail-order customers was disposed of at greatly reduced prices.

On this occasion the bargain in question was a matching pair of pants and shirt. The trousers were a vivid and thoroughly offensive green. They were several sizes too large for me ("You'll grow into them" was a guiding principle for our wearables), and to make them fit I had to hitch the waistband up around my rib cage like Stan Laurel. The shirt—also far too large—hung down like a horse collar around my neck. It introduced a Western motif: it was a depressing gray from waist to armpits; then there was a clever bit of Gene Autry–style cowboy silver piping with Western curlicues, above which the shoulders and sleeves exploded with the same reptilian green as the trousers. Thus attired I looked, and felt, like Howdy Doody.

To complete my humiliation I was compelled by family obligation to wear this preposterous getup to Sunday Mass. Entering the church, removing my winter coat in the vestibule, walking up the center aisle past the families of my schoolmates, assuming our pew, I could feel a warm gush of prickly shame rising through my body and blushing crimson across my face. I was certain that my heartthrob of the moment was somewhere in the congregation, observing me, pathetic and ludicrous. How awful it seemed to me that morning, how awful it is to feel poor. Yes, poor little me. Oddly, an old photo of myself wearing that ridiculous outfit, and looking sufficiently pleased with both myself and it, now leads me to wonder whether I haven't contrived a memory of emotional trauma about it for perverse revisionist reasons of my own.

MY FAITH NEVER wavered even as I entered the maelstrom of puberty, but now my prayers were frequently hijacked by the stirring of strange sensations in my body. Suddenly obsessed with the sweet mysteries of girls, but strictly forbidden to think "impure thoughts" about them, I took to praying for divine intervention toward arranging a successful love life. This attempt to cajole the divinities into giving me a hand represented a logical progression from all the times I'd fervently sought God's assistance, or the Blessed Virgin's intercession on my behalf, in getting top marks on a school exam or winning a race on field day. Ravished in my imagination by the charms of the Mouseketeer Annette Funicello, I prayed an entire novena—special prayers repeated in church on the afternoons of nine consecutive Fridays—to the Blessed Virgin Mary that she would contrive, however improbably, to have Annette and me meet, fall in love, and live happily ever after.

The novena apparently fell upon deaf ears, and shortly thereafter I lowered my sights from Annette to another lovely Italian girl named Mary, whose attainability was enhanced by the advantage of proximity: she lived in a large house on Jane Street, the very route we'd walk on our way to and from school. A year younger than me, with tawny skin and eyes that gazed from darkly wonderful depths, this exquisite creature moved like a dancer, with the ease of the truly beautiful. Far too shy to dare speak to her, I spoke instead to God about her. I sought His assistance in arranging things between Mary and myself. As with my Annette novena, this too proved an unsatisfactory courtship strategy, and I was left to encounter the beguiling creature in imagination alone.

The penalty one paid for sexual obsession, however sanctified it may have been behind transparent prayer, was exacted on Saturday afternoon in the darkened confines of the confessional. Never one to lie or steal, cheat or blaspheme, I began creating a smokescreen of imaginary sins behind which I could tuck in a quick mention of the "impure thoughts" that had been my only genuine transgression. "I disobeyed my parents three times," I'd exaggerate, "and I lost my temper twice and"—(quieter, almost a whisper)—"I had impure thoughts five times and"—(louder again)—"I was jealous of my brother once." There'd be an ominous pause from the other side of the screen. I'd see the darkened outline of the priest's head hover closer.

"What kind of thoughts?" he'd ask, and I knew I was sunk.

I mean, what did he expect me to say? That when I saw lovely Mary walking home from school ahead of me, her pert little bum swaying like lyric poetry, her gorgeous long brown legs, her dark hair cascading down her back in maddening ringlets, that I wanted to take her by the hand to some charmed and private place where we'd kiss and fondle one another until, until, until. . . Oh, God!

Of course not. Instead I fibbed and obfuscated as best I could and the priest pried and prodded as best he could. A confession of impure thoughts invariably aroused the priest's attention in a way that theft, dishonesty, or blasphemy seldom did. Perhaps even murder wouldn't. This didn't strike me as the least bit strange because I knew that the ejaculations that impure thoughts produced were mortal sins that, if left unconfessed, would doom me to Hell forever. I would never have imagined at the time that the priest might have been indulging his own prurient interest. Priests were holy men, the holiest and most admirable men we knew. Only years later, after the outrages of widespread priestly sexual predation were exposed, did the penny drop. Imagine living a life of lonely abstinence while having all these innocent young children whispering to you in the dark the most intimate details of their first confused experiences of sexual desire.

Released from the tortures of the confessional at last, you knelt to say your penance, then burst thankfully out of the church washed clean of all stain of sin and fired with a firm purpose never to sin again. But you did sin again. And again. Erotic dreams, infernal "nocturnal emissions," and that most catastrophic of all iniquities: to take upon your tongue the Body of Christ while the vile wickedness of impure thoughts and actions was still blackening your soul—oh, here was an abomination, a mortal sin of such magnitude that you would be condemned forever to Hell were you to die with it still on your conscience.

The God of Eucharist and confessional, of redemption and damnation, existed entirely within the fundamental virtue of faith. The spiritual apprehension of divine truths not available to intellect alone. *Credo*—I believe. Faith was a precious gift, vastly superior to any earthly wisdom. From the outset, we were pressed repeatedly by parents, priests, and nuns to guard our faith against transgression, to be constantly vigilant against its loss. This was why girls were to be avoided, lest a fascination with what was called "the flesh" erode and corrupt the fundament of faith. To lose your faith was to lose everything, a catastrophe worse than death.

THE UNRULY IMPULSES of "the flesh" were frequently described in incendiary terms, "the flames of lust." For me the hearthside flames of childhood had been comforting rather than ravenous, but I'd largely lost touch with fire after our great immigration to Canada. Our house in Weston had no fireplace, being centrally heated by an oil furnace in the basement. The only fire to be found—other than the pungent piles of leaves smoking throughout the neighborhood each autumn—was the fire of disaster. An old wooden church alongside the Saint John's schoolyard burned to the ground under mysterious circumstances. Even more spectacularly, a whole lumberyard in town shot massive flames into the sky one night. Arson was again suspected. The occasional wail of a fire engine's siren promised the excitement of fire as spectacle.

Though in the process of becoming engulfed by booming postwar Toronto, the town of Weston back in those days was still a relatively easy bike ride away from open countryside of fields, farms, and woodlands. Often in the summertime several pals and

I would plan an all-day bike hike out to the Credit River country or up to the Caledon Hills. I loved these long meanderings through the countryside, until the final one on which I received my baptism in the terrifying fury of fire.

After a hard morning's cycling, my pals and I had stopped to have our picnic lunch in a field through which a little brook meandered. Four boys sprawled languidly in golden grass, an idyllic summer scene. John, who was older than the rest of us by virtue of having failed a couple of grades but wise in our eyes with the wisdom of age, took out a box of wooden matches. He began striking matches and flipping them at each of us in turn. The instant it hit the dry grass, each match would ignite a small fire that one of us had to jump up and stamp out. We told John to quit it but he just laughed and flicked another burning match. Then another. After a bit I warned him that I wasn't going to stamp out any more fires. He laughed again and threw another match, perhaps thinking that whatever power was in play here lay somewhere between himself and me, rather than in the flame. As mistaken myself, I refused to stamp out the fire it ignited, and so did the other guys.

Within moments the fire crept out in a malignant circle and we all jumped up and began stamping frantically at it. But too late. The circle swept outward through the parched grass and within moments was beyond our control. Suddenly all was shouting and panic and swirling smoke. I dashed across the field and up the hill to where some cabins stood. I hammered desperately on the door of one, then another, then another. Nobody answered. The cabins were all unoccupied. I looked back down the hill and saw that the circle of fire had grown enormously, engulfing much of the field. The guys were running around frantically, trying to rescue our bikes and get away. I ran back down to them and we shouted incoherently at one another as to whether we should go get help or make our escape before we got caught.

By now the ring of fire was dancing field-wide and menacing some nearby woods. Before we could decide what to do, truckloads of people came roaring up the country road and charged into the field wielding brooms and shovels. They quickly formed a long line at the fire's advancing edge and methodically beat the flames out.

We had no hope of escaping the scene before being caught because our bike tires had melted in the fire, and we could hardly make a clean getaway on foot, pushing our disabled bikes along the road. A policeman appeared and asked us what had happened. John, as our elder, acted as spokesman and fibbed unconvincingly about how our little campfire had gotten away on us. The rest of us could have told the truth and sacrificed John to appease the authorities, but this would have been to break a solemn and unspoken code among grade 7 boys. The cop took our names and addresses—we hadn't the jam to lie—and told us we'd have to appear in court in a few weeks' time.

My God, that was a trail of tears we trod on the long journey home, pushing our pathetic bikes, sniping at one another over who was to blame for this calamity. Police, courts, fines, disgrace, the wrath of parents—unimaginable! Unbearable!

I told my mother the truth about what had happened and suffered no more than her chastisement that I'd be better off not associating with the fools I chose for friends. John's mother—an enormous and intimidating woman who always reminded me of an ill-humored hippopotamus—gave me a far worse tongue-lashing. She brought out John's precious Boston Bruins windbreaker, a gift from a cousin who played on the team. "Look at that!" she dangled the stupid jacket in front of my face. "Look at these burn holes. It's ruined." Only later did it occur to me that John, in total violation of the solemn and unspoken code sacred to grade 7 boys, might have told her that I was to blame for the fire. We were never contacted by the police and no more came of it, but even as a foolish lad I knew that far more than a field of grass had gone up in smoke that day. I had felt a first lick of the dragon's tongue and had lost whatever it is that dragons devour.

AMONG THE WORST of my days at Saint Bernard's school was the morning I brought our little brother Vincent for his first day at elementary school. Within a few minutes I was called from my classroom. The poor little guy was screaming and sobbing uncontrollably—he'd been suddenly plunged into a situation he'd found strange and terrifying. I walked him home and the school authorities advised my parents that his hearing was so badly impaired that he should be examined by an audiologist.

Tests determined that he had profound hearing loss in both ears. He was fitted with a hearing aid, a cumbersome device with a console hanging on his chest and twin wires leading up to large earplugs. From a world of silence, he felt himself involuntarily thrust into the world of sound, but it was a world he was condemned never to fully hear. "With the hearing aid," he later recalled, "I was able to hear very loud sounds, such as a plane flying low overhead. However, I could not hear softer sounds such as the chirping of a bird, the buzzing of a bee, or someone whispering softly. I was oblivious to those types of sounds." He was made to wear his hearing aid from the moment he woke up in the morning until he went to bed at night. But the technical limitations of the primitive analog hearing aids, which simply amplified all sounds indiscriminately, meant that he missed a lot of what was being said when having conversation with others. He had to lip-read when someone was talking. As he told me, "I required a good volume of voice to hear words properly; I required clarity of speech. My hearing aids didn't have the ability to filter out background sounds such as a normal person's ears would do in a noisy room." Nor was any sound directional—it came from a box on his chest, not from any particular point in a room.

Vincent was enrolled in a public school with a special class for training hearing-impaired students to listen to words and to speak properly as well as to learn the same things hearing students would be learning in grade 1. But the class of about twenty students had eight grade levels in it, and the teacher concentrated on teaching the upper three grades of students to prepare them for integration into mainstream classes at high school. "The students in the lower grades were left pretty much to play around by themselves," Vincent recalled. "Not much effort was put into teaching lip-reading, listening, talking, reading, and writing."

Feeling marginalized and left out, he learned very little during those two years. In grade 3, he was moved to another public school with a much smaller class of about ten students with three grade levels. Here he learned more quickly. The following year he moved to yet another class with about ten students ranging from grades 4 to 6. For the first time, in grade 4, he was put in regular class part-time. However, he was lost in that class because of poor acoustics in the room and his inability to follow what was being said. "Self-consciousness that I was somehow different from the others started with my integration in the hearing class," he told me. A year later more changes were made: He and a classmate who was also hearing-impaired were seated in the front of the class, close to the teachers, some of whom made a point of speaking slowly and clearly for their benefit. In grade 6 he spent half his time in regular classes but continued to have difficulty following what was said. He acquired a tape recorder into which he would speak, and then he'd listen to what he'd said. He used the tape recorder for a few years, trying to improve his pronunciation. He went on to attend regular classes full-time through grades 7 and 8, and, against all odds, he completed high school, then put himself through university.

Notwithstanding baby boomer nostalgia for the remembered simplicity and wholesomeness of the *Leave It to Beaver* era, this was a cruel time in which to be in any way different from the norm. Contempt and ridicule were heaped upon anyone whose language, skin color, or physical abilities differed however slightly from the one and only way everyone was supposed to be. Like other deaf people, Vincent was at times discounted as stupid by persons who had no idea what an agile mind and determined spirit he possessed.

ALL OF US kids were now attending school, my father continued working at a pace that would have exhausted most people, and my mother ran the household. She was responsible for all the cooking, cleaning, laundry, and shopping. Her meals remained steadfastly loyal to the tenets of British cuisine. Usually there'd be meat of some kind, perhaps sausages or bacon, chicken or an inexpensive cut of beef or pork. Potatoes almost always and at least one vege-table, typically boiled for far longer than necessary, then smeared with margarine and enlivened with salt. Rice was seldom if ever on the menu, nor was pasta. Herbs were kept on a very short leash, and exotica like yogurt or phyllo pastry remained beyond us. Amaz-ingly, with so productive a vegetable garden, we never ate salad. By and large, the vegetables my father grew—enormous volumes of onions, cauliflower, cabbage, brussels sprouts, broccoli, carrots, parsnips, rutabagas, tomatoes, and peas—were those we'd eaten in England. Questionable Americanisms like squash and sweet corn took a very long time to work themselves into the garden and thence into the kitchen. Also true to British tradition, we never ran short of sweets, as mother baked bread pudding, ginger cake, fruit pies, and scones. She made wonderful Irish soda bread, long slices of which served as platforms for a thin skim of margarine and dollops of homemade fruit jam. Both my parents had a tremendous capacity for drinking tea and eating toast with jam.

The closest we ever came to dining out was on Friday evenings, when the Catholic injunction against eating meat on Friday justified getting takeout from Ron's Fish & Chips. Located just a few blocks away on Jane Street in a small converted house, Ron's was the ultimate in fast-food cuisine. There were no franchise burger or chicken or pizza joints around in those days, so Ron's was where you went for takeout. Looking like the quintessential wiseguy with slicked-back black hair, wearing an apron of estimable vintage, Ron worked the vats in back, entirely free of concern about trans fats or cholesterol levels. Into the vats of simmering fat he plunged metal baskets of real fries cut from real potatoes and thick pieces of actual cod, oceans away from today's patties of reconstituted fish parts and God knows what else pressed and frozen in some sweatshop in Guangzhou. Ron's wife, whose name I never learned, wrapped each order in multiple sheets of newspaper, handed them over the counter, and took the money. I was hopelessly tongue-tied in my dealings with her; she seemed so like young Elizabeth Taylor with her mascara and vivid lipstick, her dark hair pinned up, and her tantalizingly bulging blouse unbuttoned to the point of revealing more than should have been revealed to innocents like myself. Occasionally fetching Friday dinner from Ron's was perhaps my favorite chore.

My mother was not an enthusiastic cook. She may have been so earlier on and then grown tired of producing from scratch three meals a day for six people, every day, year after year. Her solution was not to eat out but to devise cunning shortcuts. On Fridays when fish and chips from Ron's were not on order (damn!), pancakes were a meatless alternative. As a pancake flipper of not inconsiderable expertise myself, I can imagine how tedious it would become for anyone other than Aunt Jemima to be standing at a stove flipping sufficient pancakes to satisfy four ravenous boys. She decided that individual pancakes were an unnecessary complication and took to dumping the entire bowl of batter into a deep fry pan and cooking the whole works en masse. The resulting thick cake, served in stodgy blocks, was less than satisfactory, but we had been taught long before to be grateful for whatever food we were given and to never complain. Leaving even a morsel of uneaten food on the plate, however unpalatable, was not done.

Far more disheartening was her radical revamping of Christmas dinner. The nostalgia-inducing feast we'd so loved back in England was never quite the same in Canada, and my mother eventually decided that she had better things to do with her Christmas Day than spend the whole of it in the kitchen. Instead, she roasted the turkey the day before and for Christmas dinner served cold slices along with potato chips from a bag and cranberry sauce from a can. Only the Christmas cake and pudding survived in their former glory. I was horrified at the time, but in retrospect salute her independence of spirit, her refusal to continue being a perpetual domestic servant.

NOTWITHSTANDING MOTHER'S CULINARY shortcuts, in our familial value system the necessity of hard work was an absolute given. A life of abject misery in the parish poorhouse awaited those who did not put their shoulder to the wheel, their nose to the grindstone, and their heart into their work. We certainly didn't identify this ethos as the Protestant work ethic, but we wholeheartedly embraced its Calvinistic trinity of hard work, independence, and scrupulous saving. As already mentioned, I launched my working career with delivering newspapers, but nudging toward my midteens meant a ratcheting-up of employment, so I started supplementing that income with summer yard work in the neighborhood. One of the least successful entries in my employment dossier occurred at this time, when I was hired to feed and water several dozen ferrets kept in cages by one of our outdoorsy neighbors. He raised these fearsome creatures for hunting rabbits and showed me the mark where one of them had bitten right through his thumbnail. Left in charge one time while he was away, I must have failed to properly secure the latch on one of the cages, because a number of ferrets broke loose and took to terrorizing the neighborhood. A plump little lady who lived directly behind us dissolved into hysterical shrieking after opening her front door and encountering a snarling ferret on her porch. After this episode I eliminated zookeeper as a possible career choice.

Less dramatically, I mowed lawns for a pittance, pushing ancient and often ill-maintained reel mowers through sometimes impossibly long grass for hours on end, blistering my tender hands in the process. Then old Father Marshman, who tended to view our family as a ready source of indentured servants, hired me on as part-time janitor for the parish church. At least my lawn mowing improved, as I cut the extensive church and school lawns with a roaring rotary power mower. But most of the church work I was required to do was either boring or disgusting. Every week I had to wash, wax, and buff the church floor, which seemed about the size of a football field. While other kids were out playing baseball or idling away their summers at lakeside cottages in Muskoka country or making good money caddying at golf courses, I'd spend hours on my hands and knees rubbing with steel wool at black marks indelibly imprinted on the church's linoleum tile floor by cheap rubber pads on the kneelers. Cleaning ashtrays, toilets, and the kitchen of the parish hall after weddings or dances, revolting as it was, at least instilled in me an abiding empathy for people compelled to do such work for a living.

All of these formative experiences with "good, old-fashioned hard work" fell into the category of work as necessary evil, something one is compelled to do in order to survive. The money earned was the sole rationale for doing it. There was no question of job satisfaction, no delight in the nobility of honest labor, no sense of locking muscular arms in unity with the workers of the world. My father worked at jobs of not much better caliber all of his life, but I don't believe it would have occurred to him to complain that the work was boring, repetitive, or unfulfilling. He considered himself fortunate to have a secure job that allowed him to support his family and buy a house. Expecting nothing more, he made the best of it, taking pleasure in his gardens rather than the job that made them possible. For him garden work seemed more a hobby, a form of relaxation. I can remember him being out in the summer garden for hours in blazing hot sunshine, wearing no shirt or hat and returning to the house with blisters all over his back. But he didn't complain. I suspect he was happier in his garden than anywhere else. None of us kids took any interest in his gardens, nor did he encourage us to do so, likely because he loved the peace and quiet of working alone.

We did not socialize with, or indeed even know, any of his coworkers. He had nothing good to say about the union at the TTC, and apparently little sense of its having won for him the few privileges he enjoyed. I can remember him describing the popular socialist politician Tommy Douglas as "a dirty little Communist."

From very early on, I knew this life was not for me, but escape from the dungeon of unrewarding work was not as readily imaginable to the children of the British working class as it perhaps was to many North Americans, at least white ones. My brothers and I did not grow up with an expectation of attending university. My mother liked to emphasize that for people in our situation the two time-tested avenues for "getting ahead" were the military and the Church. For a brief time I did become infatuated with militarism—I suppose it was a logical progression from my gun-totin' cowboy phase—and began an avid study of warplanes and their armaments. I painstakingly glued together flimsy bits of balsa wood to create model fighters and bombers. The successful deployment of the first Soviet Sputnik during my grade 8 year ignited an interest in rocketry, and I took to making rockets propelled by metal cylinders packed with gunpowder extracted from fireworks. The air show at the Canadian National Exhibition came to rival the excitement of radio disc jockeys in their glass booths. Somehow it didn't occur to me that my terror of heights might be a wee bit of an impediment to a career as a fighter pilot.

I REACHED A great watershed at the end of grade 8. The choice I faced was either to attend the nearby public high school—a daunting place rife with vice and immorality—or try to get accepted by one of the three exclusive Catholic boys' high schools in the city. Paying the tuition fee was out of the question; my only hope was to win a scholarship. An immense anxiety gripped me as I journeyed alone by bus to these distant schools to sit for the scholarship exams. Then came nervous weeks of waiting, and finally the grand news—I'd won a scholarship to Michael Power High on the city's west side. I'm convinced that the only reason I succeeded was that dear Sister Rosalie had secretly provided me beforehand with copies of the examination papers used in the previous few years, in which many of the same questions recurred year after year. Quite how she justified this chicanery I never thought to ask.

As it turned out, this was a favor I could well have done without, for my grade 9 year at Michael Power was one of the most miserable of my life. The school had been founded only two years earlier by the Basilian Fathers and was a long commute from home, involving three different city buses. None of my pals from elementary school went to Michael Power, and I largely lost touch with them. Apart from a few scholarship kids like me, the student body came from wealthy Catholic families, the sons of doctors and lawyers and bankers. While some were thoughtful and intelligent, a disproportionate number were vulgar and arrogant bullies. Older ones would physically intimidate us younger kids and they in turn would be physically intimidated by a couple of the brawny Basilians. Some years later the school was amalgamated with a nearby Catholic girls' school, and today it boasts an active social justice program and a code of conduct that promotes "responsibility, respect, civility, and academic excellence in a safe learning and teaching environment." But that was scarcely the tone during my brief stay. I hated the bullies and I hated the place and, of course, soon came to hate myself as well. No longer able to deliver newspapers after school, I kept on with the dismal janitorial work at our church, but as for the charms of capitalism, the bloom was definitely off the rose.

After a year of high school hell, it didn't take much for me to convince myself that I had a vocation, called by God to the priesthood. I'd been more or less prepped for this all along. Our family's deep piety, our almost fanatical attendance at daily Mass and other religious observances, our diligence in work, plus the fact that I usually secured top marks in class, all conspired toward repeated suggestions from various priests and nuns that I think seriously about becoming a priest. As a final inducement, my brother Ger had gone off to the seminary the year before, returning home for the summer holidays with tales of the marvelous time he was having there. Detesting my home, my school, and my work, I decided to answer God's call.

4

DIVINITY AND
POETRY

You don't have to suffer to be a poet.
Adolescence is enough suffering for anyone.
JOHN CIARDI, *Simmons Review*, Fall 1962

A T THE TENDER AGE OF fifteen, bristling with anxiety and
excitement, I entered Holy Cross Seminary in Dunkirk,
New York, in the fall of 1960. Operated by a monastic
order known as the Passionist Fathers, the preparatory seminary
represented the initial stage of a long and demanding journey
toward becoming a monk and eventual ordination to the priesthood. "The Sem," as we called it, was a sprawling, four-story brick
building with crenellated roofline, set amid seventy acres of fields
and woods. Physically the place appealed to me immensely—the
venerable old building, the sense of religious depth that echoed
along its silent corridors, in its chapel and library, refectory and
study hall. Outdoors it was everything I loved, set in a rural area,
with mature trees, expansive fields, woodlands through which
a lazy stream meandered, and a long stretch of beach fronting on

Lake Erie. I was thrilled to be away from the confinements and neuroses of life at home but also apprehensive about finding my place among so many strangers. Things were eased for me considerably by having Ger, who was plainly liked and admired by his classmates, introduce me around, without ever showing even a hint of irritation over my having trailed after him there.

We were close to two hundred seminarians at the time, divided into six classes covering four years of high school and two years of junior college. "Fraternization" between the two levels was not allowed. An imposing Boston Irishman named Father Brendan Breen was our director of students, and two other priests served as his assistant directors. The entire community composed of priests, brothers, and seminarians was under the guidance of the rector, a dauntingly cerebral character named Augustine Paul Hennessey. It was widely whispered that he could think in Latin, which seemed to us the zenith of intellectual attainment. The seminary atmosphere was one of strict discipline, certainly, but not of oppression or meanness of spirit.

Two momentous events dominated all others in that autumn of 1960. The Pittsburgh Pirates were, against all odds, heading into the World Series against the mighty Yankees. A disproportionate number of our student body came from Pittsburgh, because of the Passionists' long and respected presence in that city. When the second baseman Bill Mazeroski hit his legendary home run in the bottom of the ninth inning of the seventh game to clinch the Pirates' Series victory, an unearthly jubilation erupted in the student body. Shortly afterward, Americans went to the polls to choose between John F. Kennedy and Richard Nixon for president. Seeking to become the first Catholic ever to hold the post, and familiar to some Passionists from their monastery in Boston, Kennedy was the house favorite. The evening before the election, we knelt in chapel while the rector bid us pray that the outcome of the vote would be whatever might best advance God's purposes for the nation. This we understood to be a nonpartisan suggestion that we implore divine intercession in having our good Catholic candidate give Nixon the thumping he deserved. Which of course he did, in large part due to the machinations of another good Catholic, Chicago's mayor, Richard J. Daley. Long before recognizing that mainstream politics and professional sport are cut from the same entertainment cloth, I sensed the symmetry of Mazeroski's homer and Kennedy's election.

The seminary was a sports-mad place. Here you had two hundred young men, deprived of any contact with females, spending most of their time in earnest study or prayer, but periodically released onto the sprawling seminary grounds that held two softball diamonds, a football field, handball and tennis courts, and a basketball gym. For many of us, sports provided a necessary diversion from the pressures of piety, purity, and silence. The three years I spent there marked the apotheosis of my sporting life. We'd have a track-and-field meet every spring at which I specialized in the one-hundred-yard dash, the long jump, and the one-mile run. On days when nothing else was happening, several of us would do a mile run around the grounds. I established myself as pitcher for our class softball team. But in autumn, as is true in high schools across America, football ruled. Back in Toronto I'd spent time tossing a football around with pals and had dutifully followed the exploits of my beloved Toronto Argonauts—the magnificent Dick Shatto, kooky Cookie Gilchrist, and all the rest—but I'd never really played the game.

At Dunkirk every student, whether willingly or not, was drafted into a team and regular games were scheduled. Although fully equipped with helmets and shoulder pads, we were confined to playing touch football in order to keep injuries to a minimum, but still we played with a bumptiousness not perhaps expected in divinity students. I took to the game like a maggot to rotting meat. Blessed with speed and size, I played wide receiver on offense, but playing defense was what I loved best, busting up opponents' plays by superior strategy. Every year we put together a school team to play against another nearby seminary. Disturbingly reminiscent of religious warfare, these games were bloodier than anything likely seen on the genteel fields of Eton. No game of the year was more important than the annual Mud Bowl played on Thanksgiving Day, in which the oldest students—first- and second-year college—did battle for overall school supremacy. It was an iconic event, with stories passed down through the years of particularly epic clashes, sometimes involving students who had become the priests now teaching us. Throughout this storied history there was an unquestioned belief that playing football, indeed all sports, was beneficial to both mind and body—*mens sana in corpore sano*—helping foster physical and mental toughness, a healthy competitiveness, and the cooperative skills required for community living. We suffered no delicate misgivings about football being a violent game of dominance and territorial conquest.

The best games of all occurred after a heavy snowfall. The southern shoreline of Lake Erie was occasionally buffeted by a winter storm that might dump two or three feet of snow, and if the snowfall coincided with a free afternoon, the most fanatical among us would bundle up and race out for a game of tackle football. This was brilliant, floundering through deep snow, piling into the mass of players, chasing the icy ball when it squirted loose from snow-caked mittens, not really caring who won or lost. We were playing a game in its purest sense, enjoying huge good fun and laughing companionship.

All this roaring around with sports eventually resulted in my first published writing. I was given a column in the school newspaper, a glossy little tabloid produced, I think, four times a year and distributed to parents and other friends of the seminary. My column was, rather unpromisingly, called "The Pogo Stick," the idea being that I should hop from topic to topic in a breezy and entertaining manner, like a sporty Walter Winchell. I suspect my offerings were quite dreadful, but they launched my career in print, and so I shan't disown them.

YOUNG AND ACTIVE, we were a ravenous lot and profoundly concerned with food. The big seminary kitchen was staffed by several brothers as well as a number of peculiar old gents whom we always referred to as "knights of the road," on the basis of their allegedly having come to us straight from the railway tracks that ran a short distance away. We sat in silence at long tables in the refectory and were served with bowls placed at the head of each table, it being a matter of fraternal charity that sufficient food be left in the bowl to satisfy everyone at table. This was inescapably institutional food, cooked in enormous pots, and leaning heavily toward rice, meat loaf, macaroni, winter squash, and anything else amenable to mass production. Presentation was not an issue. Instant mashed potatoes, allegedly acquired from army surplus supplies left over from the Korean War, appeared with dismaying frequency. I tasted zucchini for the first time and yams. Desserts were usually congealed rice pudding, tapioca, or something similarly insipid. Whenever there was a glut of local farm produce available—sweet corn, perhaps, or apples or squash—we ate it unremittingly (which served as something of a foretaste of our current cuisine on the island). The penitential seasons of Advent and Lent saw a further scaling back in variety; reconstituted powdered eggs became a tasteless mainstay. We devoured our food quickly, methodically, and without speaking, while one of the older students read aloud from an inspirational text.

The menial work I'd so chafed against at home was given a different spin here, being something done for love rather than for money. Tasks necessary to help maintain the place were called the "manual office" and, like everything else, were placed within a theological context. Joseph the carpenter was our exemplar here, and young Jesus trying his hand at carpentering too. Manual work was noble, a prayer, an offering to God. *Laborare est orare,* as the Benedictines put it: to work is to pray. Even unpleasant chores, such as cleaning shower stalls and toilets, were to be embraced for their intrinsic worth. Since the manual office occupied only about half an hour each day, plus three or four hours on Saturday afternoon, even the crummiest jobs were tolerable. My favorite by far was working outdoors with Brother Conrad, a tall, taciturn, and eminently practical character most frequently seen aboard a tractor or roaring around in his big army dump truck. Working for him— picking apples, heaving cut tree branches around, holding piglets while he castrated them—was engaging in a way that polishing candlesticks or waxing furniture never could be. But the yard work was seasonal, and for steady indoor employment I eventually specialized in the care and maintenance of venetian blinds, of which there were hundreds throughout the building, and all of which could, in the way of venetian blinds, be counted upon to malfunction on a regular basis. The work gave me access to the priests' wing, a sanctum normally out of bounds for students. Cornering the market on this skilled specialty also saved me from unsavory encounters with urinals and dirty laundry, sanctified work or not. In point of fact, for all their highfalutin talk about the nobility of labor, the good fathers generally avoided it like the plague, leaving the dirty work to us students or the brothers or the knights. Aside from a few obsessive walkers, most of the priests seemed not to exert themselves physically at all; the Congregation of the Passion of Jesus Christ was disproportionately composed of holy men as plump and puffy as Friar Tuck.

ONE OF THE elements I liked least about seminary life was its utter lack of privacy. We slept in bunk beds in large dormitories. Unheated, the dorms became frigid in winter, to the point where the holy water in fonts at the doorway, with which we blessed ourselves when entering or leaving, froze solid overnight. When the first bell of the morning tolled, we would rise, dress quickly in simple black cassocks, and proceed in silence to the washroom and then to chapel. Using the washrooms involved repeated indignity. A long row of sinks sat below mirrors against one wall with a facing row of toilet cubicles along the opposite wall, and a further row of urinals. With mobs of people constantly in and out, every aspect of one's toiletries was at best semipublic. Somewhat fastidious in these matters (as are the bulk of my fellow Virgos, I believe), I'd frequently squander precious minutes searching various washrooms for one that would afford at least a modicum of privacy. But solitude and silence, those elemental components of the monastic experience, were seldom to be had in the venue where they're most required.

Assembled in chapel, we'd chant the sacred hours of matins and lauds in Latin, followed by a period of meditation and then Mass, after which we proceeded to breakfast and then to our classrooms. At appointed times throughout the day the community bell would toll and we'd return to chapel to chant the various hours of the office, finishing with compline in the evening. The tiered stalls in which we stood ran lengthwise down the chapel sides with a wide expanse of mosaic floor in the center. Intoned by the cantor, the psalms were chanted antiphonally from one side then the other, back and forth, in a lilting and mesmerizing repetition. At its best, perhaps when spring sunlight illuminated the stained glass windows, our chanting rose and fell in a fluid, hypnotic harmony that lifted my spirit out of itself and set it for the moment free to fly. On feast days or other solemn occasions, and especially at the great liturgical pinnacle of Easter, we'd sing a High Mass of complex harmonies learned through arduous hours of choir practice.

I found the hours we spent in meditation arduous as well, largely because we were inadequately instructed in any techniques of meditation. The emphasis was more upon contemplation of what we understood to be divine truths, and most particularly on the passion and death of Jesus. "May the Passion of Jesus Christ be ever in our hearts" was the congregation's motto, and for me at least our times of contemplation too frequently degenerated into guilt and anxiety over my sinfulness and the suffering it had inflicted upon our Savior. This was a far cry from true calming of the spirit or lightening of the soul, such as I would experience years later in other forms of meditation.

Once a year, all normal activities would be suspended for a week-long silent retreat during which a retreat master would lead us through a course of meditative lessons aimed at refocusing our spiritual commitment. Time normally devoted to studies or recreation was instead taken up with additional spiritual reading, solitary walks, and contemplation. Invariably the retreat would succeed in convincing me that I must strive more diligently to throw off the habits and impurities of spirit that were preventing me from moving fully into the embrace of Christ's all-encompassing love.

Our classroom courses plodded through the standard dreary high school curriculum of history, math, science, etc., with a heavy dosage of Latin layered on top. By far my favorite was English literature, taught by a patrician young priest named Paul Joseph Fulham. Beneath his hauteur, he had a real gift for enticing us bumpkins into the elevated realms of great writing. Already predisposed to poetry through my ode to a trout, I soon became engrossed in the works of Emerson and Longfellow, Whittier and Bryant, Frost and Sandburg. Eventually I fell in with a half-dozen fellow seminarians as poetic as myself. We formed a literary cabal and took to holding clandestine poetry readings by candlelight in darkened corners of the old building. We sipped black coffee we'd pilfered from the kitchen. We discovered Walt Whitman and Robinson Jeffers, Ezra Pound and e.e. cummings. T.S. Eliot's "The Hollow Men" became our anthem. After each poem read aloud we'd snap our fingers in downbeat Beat appreciation. We brimmed with hip but unseemly cynicism.

A torrent of what I thought at the time was poetry poured out of me. I have these poems still, dozens of them, carefully hand-written in a small notebook. Every one is abysmally bad, a steamy conflation of adolescent angst, suppressed eroticism, and tortuous religious scruple. Christ is repeatedly encountered writhing on His cross and I writhing in my bed with a pillow so thoroughly drenched with tears it's a wonder I didn't drown in my sleep. Frequently I'm glimpsed groping through "a dark and barren tract of nothingness" or "walking down a corridor of despondency," not to mention "crashing into turbulent seas of emotion." Over and over again crucified Jesus is exalted as the only salvation from the earthly wretchedness in which I wallowed. I concluded one particularly grisly piece: "I am a worm, Christ / a dirty, writhing parasite / and You should step on me / save You would dirty your sandal / the strap of which I am unworthy to loose." (Actually I misspelled the final word as "lose" but the comic possibilities around my losing the Messiah's sandal strap were inconsistent with my melancholy theme.)

Even for a genre traditionally inclusive of misanthropes and tolerant of morbid self-regard, this was all a bit much. But not to me or my pals. In very short order we'd become literary legends in our own minds. Returning home to Toronto for summer break, I spent every free moment sequestered in the little Weston public library reading and taking notes on poets and their poetry: Lord Byron ("died in disillusionment of fever in small Greek town fighting for freedom") and Percy Bysshe Shelley ("poetry emphasizes joy of escape from earth to a freer element"). The "Depression of Wordsworth and Coleridge" seemed especially appealing to me: "Both were depressed at the decay of their youth, loss of fresh sensibility and the numbing of the poetic gift . . . They no longer held empathy with wild and naive life, no longer felt ecstatic pleasures of youth and novelty of experience." Layering religious anxiety on top of standard-issue teenage anguish, I became one with the Romantics in their melancholy disillusionment. The mournful grayness of Lake Erie in winter, the heartbreakingly lovely sunsets frequently seen at Dunkirk (unknown to me, a product less of nature's magnificence than of hydrocarbons spewed out by the heavy industries of the region), and the lonesome wail of overnight freight trains rumbling westward all fed into my pensive sensibility. Poetry had taken hold of me and, while it might never be productive of great verse, it would eventually provoke some major changes that I had no way of foreseeing at the time.

ANOTHER OBSESSION, WITH rock 'n' roll music, had accompanied some of us into the seminary, but here access was severely curtailed. After the evening meal, we seminarians would assemble in the large recreation room where one of us would take a turn at presenting the "sentiment for the day"—a brief reflection on some pious theme. The director of students would distribute the day's mail, calling out the recipient's name as he tossed each letter onto a table. For those of us who seldom got a letter this ritual contained a certain element of humiliation, but never mind, because it was followed by a thirty-minute recreation period during which we could chat or play pool or Ping-Pong. The dean of students, the one among us with seniority in the dean order, could on certain occasions ask the director for a special permission, one of which was "permission to listen to the radio, please, Your Reverence." Depending upon his mood, the director might or might not grant the permission. When granted, infrequently, this allowed about a dozen of us unrepentant rockers to huddle around an ancient console radio and listen through the static to freshly pressed classics like Skeeter Davis's "End of the World" or Dion's bluesy doo-wop "Runaround Sue." But this was thin gruel indeed, and we chafed to hear more of the music we loved.

Returning home for the summers freed us to catch up on the new tunes we'd been missing, but I soon outgrew CHUM Radio's punchless hits. By the early sixties the primitive energy of the fifties rockers was already spent, replaced with vapid balladeers—hell, even Elvis had become a vapid balladeer! Among the few bright spots, the great girl groups like the Shirelles and the Chantels wrapped their honey-sweet harmonies around a plaintive longing finely attuned to my newfound Romanticist sensibilities. Back home, I'd lie in bed at night in a stuffy little bedroom listening on my transistor radio to WUFO in Buffalo, the pioneering African-American station anchored by the famed DJ Eddie O'Jay, working in a rhythm-and-blues format—"race music," the racists called it— that was vastly more hip than anything on Dick Clark's *American Bandstand.*

In my final year at Dunkirk a progressive young priest who was assistant director of students acquired for us a set of vinyl records packaged as *The Folk Box,* a compilation of the folk music that was beginning to rise like a groundswell across America. That was my introduction to Pete Seeger, Hoyt Axton, and others, especially Odetta, whose husky renderings of "The Foggy Dew" and "Shenandoah" were a revelation to me. We got the early Bob Dylan albums too. Here was music fused with poetry and politics, resonant and real and light-years beyond the superficialities of commercial pop. Even to us huddled in our little seminary recreation room, it was unmistakable that there was an exhilarating sense of change blowing in the wind.

AN ESTABLISHED TRADITION decreed that on the final night of the school year at Holy Cross there would be an enormous bonfire on the beach. For weeks beforehand the senior class would be busy at work amassing driftwood logs. Elaborate arrangements were made for igniting the fire in new and ingenious ways. The last one I witnessed involved a wire being strung from the top of the log pile up the shoreline bluff to a tree above. At the designated moment, a roll of toilet paper soaked in oil was lit and sent hurtling down the wire where, upon striking the gas-soaked pinnacle of logs, it ignited a roaring blaze.

Notwithstanding the pyrotechnics, it was a melancholy night in many ways. We would all be dispersing the following morning, returning to our various homes across the eastern United States and Canada. It was never entirely certain who would be returning in September and who would not. Over the course of the summer some would decide monastic life was not for them; others would be told not to return—"shipped" was the term we used for being expelled. Sometimes this would involve good friends, fellows we'd played sports with and prayed with, studied and worked together with, perhaps read our hopeless poems together with long into the night. They would simply never reappear, and that would be that.

I intensely disliked returning home, for it involved losing for several months the pleasures of that place, the companionship, the solemnity of religious ritual, and the physical beauty of the lakeside property. Summers at home meant being crowded into a little house, returning to dreary jobs and to church services that were a tawdry imitation of the splendid liturgical rituals we knew at Holy Cross. And it meant being plunged back into mainstream culture, an environment that seemed even more crass and vulgar than it had before. One summer Ger and I spent dutifully trudging down to the local labor exchange, from which we'd be hired on for temporary laboring work, usually arduous and grossly underpaid, its singular virtue being that it was temporary. Another summer I worked in a dismal Chrysler parts factory out near what was then the Malton airport, fetching mufflers, manifolds, and miscellaneous gaskets to fill parts orders for far-flung dealerships. My coworkers were a rough-and-tumble bunch, united in a macho camaraderie that held their work, their bosses, and the place itself in unrelieved contempt. Near the end of my summer stint a group of them took me down to Hamilton to watch a football game between the Toronto Argos and the Hamilton Tiger Cats. Diehard Argos fans, my mates brought along several lengths of heavy chain stashed under the car seats in case unpleasantries erupted between us and any Ticats supporters. Less and less did I feel anywhere at home in this milieu.

ANOTHER CHANGE WAS in the wind. Vocations to the Passionists had grown so dramatically in the early sixties—part of the "generosity explosion" manifest in the Peace Corps and similar organizations—that Holy Cross was no longer able to accommodate the numbers. A decision had been made that the two years of junior college would be transferred to another monastery. So my third year at Holy Cross, grade 12, was my last. Assigned in English class to write a brief essay on the planned move, I struck upon the metaphor of transplanting, that as seedling plants are moved into a succession of increasingly larger containers, so too were we now being moved along for seasoning. I take this not entirely original concept as early evidence that gardening was, without my realizing it, surreptitiously insinuating itself into my consciousness.

 **5**

THE TAKING OF VOWS

Be patient towards all that is unsolved in your heart,
and try to love the questions themselves
like locked rooms and like books that are written in a very
foreign tongue. Do not now seek the answers,
which cannot be given you because you would not be able to
live them. And the point is, to live everything.
Live the questions now. Perhaps you will find them gradually,
without noticing it, and live along some
distant day into the answer.

RAINER MARIA RILKE, *Letters to a Young Poet*

I WAS STUDYING IN MY CELL one November afternoon when suddenly the community bell started tolling loudly at an unaccustomed time. My classmates and I peered out of our rooms to see what was going on and were urged to gather at a nearby small chapel. The shaken director of students stood before us and said, "President Kennedy has been shot in Dallas and taken to a nearby hospital." Stunned, scarcely able to comprehend such a thing, we knelt on the floor and prayed the Holy Rosary aloud, fervently beseeching the Blessed Virgin's intercession that the

Father, the Son, and the Holy Spirit would spare the life of the president. A short time later, still in a sort of stupor, we were informed that Kennedy was dead. Like the nation as a whole, the monastic community trembled in an altered consciousness of grief and incomprehension. The television set in our recreation room was left on much of the day so that we might follow the public rituals attending the president's death and burial, the wrenching scenes of his casket, his children's bravery, his grieving widow. What an abysmal descent from the reverie of Camelot it seemed to have Lyndon Johnson sworn in as his replacement. Then the pandemonium of Lee Harvey Oswald and Jack Ruby and wild rumors flying everywhere. I don't remember how long it took for us to assimilate all this and finally return to some semblance of normal life.

We were living then at Holy Family Monastery in West Hartford, Connecticut, where the seminary junior college had been relocated. We occupied a newly constructed wing attached to the existing monastery and retreat house, the whole of it forming a sizable complex sitting atop a hill surrounded by affluent and tastefully landscaped suburbs. The building was of soulless cinder block, the furniture plastic, and the lights fluorescent, every element spanking new and institutional enough to mortally wound the spirit of a melancholy poet. The place lacked any tradition and had no ghosts at all.

Granted, it did have certain advantages, not the least of which was that we each now had a private room—small and stark, yes, but blessedly private—and state-of-the-art washrooms that, although public, did not have the dilapidated showcase atmosphere I'd suffered through at Dunkirk. A large contingent of young brothers were in training in a different wing of the monastery, and on high feast days, and Thanksgiving Day especially, the banquets they prepared for us were more splendid than anything we'd dined on previously. There was also a class of about a dozen newly ordained priests who were studying "sacred eloquence" for a year in order to prepare for preaching. Their director, Father Norbert Dorsey, was a cultivated New Englander who took an interest in a couple of us would-be poets and inspired us with his grace and humor. I think he introduced me to Gerard Manley Hopkins and to Robert Lowell, and certainly he epitomized the kind of priest I longed to be, openhearted and sophisticated and beyond the creaking narrow-mindedness that afflicted too many of the others.

Again my favorite class was English composition, taught by an idiosyncratic geezer named Father Christopher Collins. Tall and gaunt, with a balding head of wispy gray hair, he'd had a formidable reputation among the older students back in Dunkirk, and we were all a bit terrified of him. Whenever someone provided a particularly inane response to a question, he'd make a little grunting noise followed by "Moron!" His assessment was usually spot-on. Some of the essays I produced for him were breathtakingly bad. I wrote a learned tract titled "Obscurity and Symbolism in Poetry" that came back with a tart comment in red ink: "Obscure in too many spots." Another assignment was to write three hundred words on the topic of friendship. This was a somewhat delicate subject, because "particular friendships" were frowned upon, presumably to keep any whiff of homoeroticism far from our sacred precincts. Hewing to the party line, I penned what may be my personal best run-on sentence of all time: "Thus a true friendship never becomes exclusive, for by excluding others, each member injures himself, his friend, and the friendship itself for neither party attains the opportunity for developing his personality or social inclations [*sic*] fully because they become habitually attuned to the select taste of his comrade, and eventually bickerings and quarrels arise between the two that are the result of un-diversified friendship ending in boredom, and thus the harmony, which is the cornerstone of the relationship is shattered and the elements of esteem and respect slowly crumble to disgust." Astonishingly, this drivel earned me top marks and a notation of "Very Good."

Completely outside the curriculum, this was the year I became an ardent devotee of the poetry of Dylan Thomas. Like many an undergraduate, I was enraptured by the wild Welshman's "feast of tear-stuffed time and thistles" and his fabulous verbal cascading down the "rivers of the windfall light."

The only other course that really caught my imagination was physics. The mathematics of it didn't interest me particularly, but the mysteries of theoretical physics were immensely intriguing—Max Planck grappling with the principle of elementary disorder on his way to formulating quantum theory; the Heisenberg uncertainty principle; Einstein's relativity theories with their gravitational time dilation and space-time curvature, and all the rest. Although we only scratched the surface of these matters in an elementary fashion, the scope and elegance of the material spoke to me in cadences similar to those of poets and mystics.

I SOON CAME to love the splendid countryside of New England in which we were living. Without a gym, a baseball diamond, or a proper football field, we took to taking long hikes instead of playing games. I reveled in the beauty of the hardwood forests, especially in autumn color, and of scenic small towns as yet unspoiled by freeways and strip malls. The traditional architecture, winding roads, and ubiquitous fieldstone walls touched an emotional chord in me, similar to what I would experience much later in life during visits to rural England and Ireland.

It's no surprise that in these surroundings I became infatuated with New England transcendentalism. I began avidly reading Thoreau and Emerson, and the more I read the more excited I became. As giddy as any college freshman, I gobbled down their insights about tolerance and optimism, the defiance of tradition, and the disregard for external authority. I felt one in spirit with other members of the Transcendental Club in turning away from Calvinist pessimism and rigid discipline, replacing them with a burning desire for freedom, release, and expansion. There seemed to me an intuitive rightness about the belief that each person's soul partakes in the soul of the world and contains all that the larger soul contains. I came to believe in the notion that Nature is the embodiment of spirit in the world and that through the beauty, truth, and goodness incarnate in the natural world, the individual becomes inseparable from the spirit and being of God.

Fired with this newfound sense of the indwelling of divinity in all creation, I co-created my first garden in an obscure corner of the monastery grounds. Since I had had nothing to do with my dad's gardens at home, other than occasionally being pressed into helping my mum harvest currants or other fruit, this sudden impulse toward garden making was a bit of an anomaly. Nevertheless, far from home, gardening now cast a preliminary grapple hook in my direction. Along with a pal, I hatched the idea of making a Zen garden in a small clearing in the woods. Some of my classmates and I were very much drawn to Eastern religious thought at the time, partly via the transcendentalists, partly from reading Thomas Merton, who was a student of Eastern mysticism, and partly because of the deliberations of the Second Vatican Council, which had opened in 1962 and was generating lots of interest in ecumenism and interfaith pluralism. Buddhism and Taoism particularly appealed, and thus the notion of our little garden came to be.

After receiving the necessary permissions, my friend Kenny and I set about building a perimeter wall to enclose the garden. An abundance of thin, flat stone lay all around, and we soon had a defining wall about two feet high. Within this we randomly placed several feature stones and raked the sandy and stony soil as best we could. We knew no more about Zen gardens than we did about Zen Buddhism, but we labored with purity of purpose and some vague sense of partaking in the embodiment of the divine.

BY THIS POINT, the folk revival was in full flush, a heady time during which the meaning of life was best discovered at a hootenanny, at which the assembled throng would sing along to "Kumbaya" or "Where Have All the Flowers Gone?" Nostalgia for an older and simpler time ran rampant across the campuses of the country. That was also the year the Beatles first appeared on *The Ed Sullivan Show*. There was a tremendous excitement around this performance, but not sufficient for our director to allow us to watch it on TV. Against the rules, several of us snuck up to the recreation room used by the young priests studying sacred eloquence. They were allowed to watch their TV far more liberally than we were, so we watched the four mop-tops in the company of the young priests. "Bunch of faggots," one of them said, dismissing the Liverpool lads with something less than sacred eloquence. I wasn't a candidate for Beatlemania either, imagining that a more hip and cerebral soundtrack better suited my poetical circumstances. This I discovered with Dave Brubeck, with Miles Davis and the Modern Jazz Quartet, with Gershwin and Copland and John Coltrane.

But hip only to a point. On the following summer vacation at home, Ger and I were summoned by old Father Marshman at Saint Bernard's parish church. He informed us that he was scheduled to celebrate a High Mass on a forthcoming weekday morning, but the woman who normally sang the choir's part for a High Mass other than on Sundays was unavailable. He asked us, on the strength of our several years' experience singing in choir at the seminary, to sing the choir parts. Knowing the folly involved, we resisted as best we could but were overruled. Aware that a debacle awaited, back home we practiced our "Kyrie Eleison," our "Gloria" and "Credo in Unum Deum," our "Sanctus" and our "Agnus Dei," but neither of us could hold a tune to save our lives, and the more we practiced the worse we sounded.

On the appointed morning we entered the church, checked in with the priest, and climbed to the choir loft high above the nave.

The church, whose floors I'd mopped so diligently for so long, was
an immense, high-vaulted barn of a place, entirely lacking in architectural interest or aesthetic appeal. Being as this was a weekday,
there were only a smattering of parishioners dispersed throughout
the acres of pews. The Mass began. On cue, my brother and I
launched into our "Kyrie" with as much gusto as we could muster,
but good God, we were dreadful. Our voices wobbled about
discordantly, a thin, plaintive, inharmonious wailing through the
vast and disapproving silence of the church. If one of us did, by
chance, get a few consecutive notes almost right, the other would
quickly lure him off course. The longer the Mass dragged on, the
worse we got. What was I doing here? A hipster devotee of MJQ
and WUFO engaged in this god-awful ecclesiastical caterwauling!
Happily, we were never again invited to sing.

BUT OUR CHORAL shortfall was a minor matter compared with
an unexpected turn of events that blindsided me that summer. The
priests gathered in chapter at Holy Family had voted that I should
skip my second year of junior college and head straightaway to
the novitiate. Such a step was unheard of and caught me entirely
off guard. I received an explanatory letter from the rector, Father
Gregory Flynn, whom I liked immensely and thought of as a
saintly Groucho Marx. He wrote in part: "Des, the big reason for
this step is that scholastically you can do the job. That is without
doubt. And as things were going, you were going along too
easily—not putting forth your full potential. That is not good. As
a matter of record you were not first in rank in your class. Another
outstripped you by a few percentage points. Yet, you are truthfully
at the head of the class. You could become very lazy! I know you
will have to exert yourself far more." This was a message that I'd
become accustomed to—the accusation that I was failing to match
up to the great potential of my gifts. I trace this theme directly back
to Sister Rosalie's manipulation of my scholarship examination,

whose artificially inflated results ever after weighed upon me as a burden of false expectation.

Father Gregory's letter went on to say that I could well have done with "another year of seasoning" toward emotional and spiritual maturity. "You must get the old 'ego' under control," he warned me, "and dissipate that lackadaisical air that you have. Not everyone can understand it and make allowance for it. Here is a challenge for you—and I think you will be a better man, a better religious, a better Passionist, because we have issued it to you." In a peculiar postscript, he mentioned, "I dug up the tulips this PM and I regret that you will not be here, come fall, to put them in the soil with your own green thumb!" I don't remember having planted tulips with the rector, but here again, hidden under the weighty considerations of my emotional and spiritual maturity, was another not-so-subtle nudge from the deities of gardening.

A second letter of similar tone arrived from Father Norbert Dorsey: "Your push-ahead is a just recognition of your God-given talent and, far from puffing you up, it should serve to remind you to traffic busily, yet humbly, with those talents in the years ahead ... Put on the mind of Christ, the charity of Christ, the compassion of Christ, His friendliness, patience, purity, willingness to work hard, loyalty, zeal for souls, obedience, humility, and so on ... Getting down to rock-bottom, the Novitiate year is when a man whole-heartedly gives himself over to the love of God, with all the fire, fun and fear that it implies."

Knocked out of kilter, feeling far more fear than fun, freighted with high expectations, I had to abandon whatever plans I had for the summer and soon set off with Ger to face the challenges of the novitiate.

THE MONASTERY OF Saint Paul of the Cross sat on a high hill overlooking the city of Pittsburgh. It was here that I would spend a spiritually rigorous year preparing to profess the sacred vows

that would make me a full member of the order. There would be
no academic curriculum as such—all our efforts would be devoted
to spiritual concerns. The expectation was that the unworthy or
unsuitable among the two dozen of us in the novitiate class would
be winnowed out during the course of the year. Straightaway our
heads were shaved almost bald. After a month of postulancy, we
participated in the ceremony of vestition, at which we were clothed
in the traditional black habit of the order, along with a cape for cold
weather and a pair of heavy leather sandals. Symbolic of putting
off the old man and putting on the new, we abandoned our former
names and were renamed, generally after a favorite saint. Still a
faithful devotee of Dylan Thomas, I elected to change my name to
Dylan and thereafter was known as Frater Dylan, C.P. (The C.P.
stood for "Congregation of the Passion.") Dylan was not at all a
common name back then, and I don't recall how I got permission
to be renamed after such a notorious boozer, womanizer, liar, and
petty thief.

Besides the habit, our worldly goods were reduced to a clerical
suit, some grubbies to wear for work and sports, and a few books.
Each novice lived in a small cell with bed, desk, chair, bookshelf,
and wardrobe. To curb any tendencies toward decoration or domes-
tication, we would periodically change cells, taking with us only the
bare essentials. The whole point was to abandon seeking the false
comforts of material things in order to find solace in the redeeming
love of the Savior.

Silence was at the core of monastic life. Passionists do not take a
vow of silence, as certain orders do, but we lived largely in silence.
The intent was to remove distraction and have the spirit be quieted
to accommodate contemplative experience. In silence there would
be the opportunity for the divine to be made known to us in our
hearts and minds. We would, it was hoped, achieve the simple intuition of that which is true, *simplex intuitus veritatis*. "When I am
liberated by silence," wrote Thomas Merton in *Thoughts in Solitude*,

"when I am no longer involved in the measurement of life, but in the living of it, I can discover a form of prayer in which there is effectively no distraction."

Even at those times when talking was permitted, during brief recreation periods, it was under controlled circumstances. Each novice was assigned a couple of "companions" with whom he could speak, but was to speak to no others. The companions were carefully selected so as to compel quite different personality types to get along.

Our novice master, the priest who served as spiritual director of our novitiate year, was Augustine Paul Hennessey, who had been rector back at Holy Cross. A Philadelphia Irishman with a bald head, protuberant ears, rimless spectacles, and a knowing smile, he was a true scholar, immensely intelligent, with a keen wit and robust enthusiasm for all he did. "A Christian career is a career in Christ," he told us. "A career in Christ is a career on the cross. A career on the cross is a career of sacrificial love." He spent a great part of the year explicating that apparently simple trilogy, and I still have my notebook recording these chapter sessions. "Sacrificial love," he maintained, "arises from inner tensions because of our social and hereditary failings, the demands of love within us in the presence of mystery and the necessity of loving our fellow men despite their unlovableness. The fear of being cheated in love is one of the greatest stumbling blocks to godliness." He could carry on like that for hours, speaking without notes, peppering his theology with curious asides and an occasional piping laugh. I admired him greatly, although at nineteen years old I was far too immature and self-consumed to adequately appreciate his teaching.

Some time later he published an editorial titled "A Personal Creed" in which he summed up much of what he explicated day by day in our novitiate chapters. "I believe that I live in a redeemed world," he wrote. "War, hunger, racial tensions, barbarous human cruelty, hatreds nurtured by man's own hellish inventiveness—all this horror is the unfinished business of redemption. I believe that the task of finishing this business has been entrusted to the minds and hearts of men ... Self-emptying love with its true dimensions always forms a cross. I believe all authentic love is crucifying."

On one occasion he brought into the chapter room an envelope containing fragments of dried brown material along with a letter he'd received from a disenchanted former student who'd left the order. Parodying the novice master's frequent use of the adjective "consecrated," the letter said the enclosed stuff was "consecrated horseshit," and Augustine Paul laughed with delight at the audacity of it.

Much of our study involved the vows of poverty, chastity, and obedience that we would profess at the conclusion of the novitiate year. Ever since entering the junior seminary I'd found myself looking at poverty in a different light, in contrast to the embarrassment I'd felt about my family's circumstances. Rather than a shameful condition to be despised, poverty was instead a virtuous frame of mind to be cultivated. We were taught that the essence of holy poverty was an emptying of self in order to liberate the spirit, thereby facilitating the ascent toward sanctity. This required not niggardliness or scrupulous penny-pinching but a detached contentedness with frugal comfort.

Saint Thomas Aquinas, the medieval theological giant upon whose teachings so much of Catholic doctrine is anchored, outlined the four functions of poverty as manifest in the life of Jesus. The preservative function prevents one from being consumed by the pursuit of wealth. The redemptive function is the self-emptying mystique of poverty—that as Christ suffered bodily death to give humankind life, so also did he sustain poverty in order to bestow spiritual riches. The unitive function of poverty aims to sustain a bond with the poor of the earth, so that it would be apparent to everyone that our apostolic work was done from zeal, not for monetary gain. Lastly, the sacramental function of poverty lets the power of God show forth. We were reminded that during His time on earth—and especially at His birth in the manger—Christ favored all things poor and lowly, seemingly despicable and wretched, in order that His poverty might cast a spotlight on the providence of God.

There is, of course, a world of difference between professed holy poverty and enforced abject poverty. G.B. Shaw maintained that modern poverty was not the poverty that was blessed in the Sermon on the Mount, but rather, as he wrote in the preface to *Major Barbara,* "the greatest of evils and the worst of crimes." Monastic poverty survives comfortably on three meals a day and a safe, warm place to lie down at night. It assists in freeing the spirit from worldly cares, not crippling the spirit as involuntary poverty does. For all our noble intentions about sustaining a bond with the poor, we monks had precious little in common with the poverty of entrapment or the evil of involuntary homelessness.

Chastity offered a different kind of challenge, but not necessarily in the way an outsider might presume. We were taught that while virginity is the simple avoidance of consummated sexual pleasure, chastity casts a far wider net. "There is great necessity for strong insight into the mystical significance of chastity," Augustine Paul told us at one chapter gathering. Acknowledging "the urgency of youthful passion," he maintained that everyone has a built-in need for love and goodness to be communicated to us by someone who reverences us as a person. Taking a vow of chastity meant that "we pledge ourselves to a lover whose voice we never hear, whose face we never see. We hardly ever outgrow the ability to love more someone we can see, feel, and hear than to love through faith an invisible lover. To struggle against the intangibility of the mystical love life is the day-to-day struggle of chastity."

We were warned against autoeroticism, listlessness, and religious frigidity, against internal impurity that can be a sacrilege against the vow. There was much talk of sublimation. "Healthy sublimation is to lift up primitive urges and conflicts to a higher plane and lead others up with us," said our novice master. "It is only on this higher plane that we can overcome and transcend the tensions of the flesh-spirit conflict" because "there is in this life an unending sense of psychological unfulfillment which can be borne only by the man with mystic insight."

Be that as it may, we were nevertheless introduced to one peculiar leftover from a more primitive approach to beating unruly impulses of the flesh into submission. This was the arcane practice of self-flagellation. Mortification of the flesh was to be achieved by, at certain appointed times, retreating each to his own cell and lashing oneself on the backside with a whip of braided cord while reciting appropriate prayers. Reputedly this had previously been a group activity carried on in the darkened chapel, until a clutch of lay retreatants had suddenly entered the chapel and come upon the spectacle. The resulting risk of scandal (from confused association with erotic spanking or other sadomasochistic acts) had forced the practice into darkened corners. I never quite took to it myself and, along with several others, substituted striking my old manual typewriter keys, which made a sound similar to the lashing of treacherous flesh.

Other relics of the past rattled around in that old house of prayers and penitence. The ghost of a former monk was believed to reside there and was perhaps semi-glimpsed down a darkened corridor by several of us. Also, one of the monks served as the diocesan exorcist, and during our stay at least one elaborate exorcism had taken place, the fantastic details of which were whispered in secrecy.

Although the challenges of chastity might seem paramount to an outsider, it was often said that the third vow, obedience, was in fact the most difficult of the three. Absolute and unquestioning obedience was at the very heart of monastic life. "Let their obedience be blind," decreed the Rule of the Passionists. "Let them obey promptly, simply, and gladly." We had come to the congregation not for self-expression nor for priestly posturing but to achieve the utter abnegation of self. That implied a willingness to become a model of meekness and docility. The command of a superior, even if it seems imprudent or absurd, must be taken as the will of God. The religious obeys unquestioningly, out of reverence for the superior as the mouthpiece of the Almighty. This is tough stuff, a theologically elaborated version of the ironfisted discipline at a marines' boot camp, and one of Augustine Paul's many catchy phrases was that he was prepared to be "as ruthless as a Nazi drillmaster" in dealing with any whiff of insubordination.

The vow of obedience formalized the surrender of self, the unqualified submission of one's own will to the mystique of a crucified God. Having left behind the vanities of the world, the religious desires to seek God alone and to this end performs acts of mortification and humiliation in order to become dead to one's self. Through an unrestrained offering of sacrificial love one would become a living image of the crucified Christ.

Taken together, the vows entailed accepting God's call to "walk in love" among members of a religious community, forgetting self and adapting to the needs of others within a brotherhood of supernatural friendship. It was a high calling and an exquisite ideal. The purposeful dedication to spiritual transformation that we members of the order shared bound us together, warts and all. We strove collectively toward abandonment of self for the greater good. Of course we fell short, repeatedly fell short, but then confessed our failing and renewed the effort. It was a community rooted in a venerable history and tradition: the founder of the order and several other members who'd been canonized as saints were exemplars whose lives we studied and sought to emulate. The monasteries in which we lived—with the chapels and libraries and refectories in which we spent silent hours together in prayer and study—held memories of the many who had gone before us. We dressed as they had dressed, chanted the psalms exactly as they had chanted them, celebrated the same high feast days, contemplated the same mysteries. The very bricks and timbers of those old buildings spoke of a devotion to holiness that stretched far back into a consecrated past.

THE EXPECTATION CLEARLY was that we'd devote ourselves to loftier matters than mere games, but the dwindling number of sports fanatics among us still found the occasional opportunity for a pickup game of softball or touch football. Our field of dreams was reduced to a run-down little bare-bones park located behind the monastery grounds. This was part of a working-class neighborhood formally known as Southside Slopes but familiarly called Billy Buck Hill. Beneath the hill's steep slope, on the Southside Flats along the Monongahela River, sprawled the massive steel mills whose smelters glowed eerily in the night and whose soot coated my cell's window ledge every morning. The mills themselves and the aging hillside houses where many of the mill workers and their families lived were an embodiment of the industrial rust belt in decline. There was a certain crumbling beauty about the place, and I felt far more at home there than I had in the swank environs of West Hartford. Our pickup games in the shabby park had none of the intensity or earnestness of earlier days, but they had the advantage of attracting people from the neighborhood, the regulars of Billy Buck Hill. They formed a peculiar cast of characters, working families like the Lawlors, the Gallaghers, and the Ceneys, a gentleman we called Mister Gray and another named Old Mike. There were eager ballplayers like Johnny Bosle and a funny beanpole named Russell whose response to almost anything was "Groovy, man!" And lovely girls like Kathy Gretzke and the Lawlor sisters, Jeannie and Georgie. Spending an occasional afternoon with them at the ballpark was a blessed relief from the relentless pieties of the cloister. I developed an apostolic solicitude toward them, and perhaps the slightest slackening in enthusiasm for the mystical significance of chastity. I began considering that the world from which I had fled was not quite so sordid a place as I had imagined. Sometimes of an evening I'd gaze out the window of my cell down to the valley below me where ribbons of moving light led away down the Ohio River to unknown places far beyond, and I felt the same melancholy longing that I'd felt when I heard the plaintive wail of overnight freight trains at Dunkirk.

But as the year wound down, I pushed these misgivings aside, telling my spiritual diary, "The longing for happiness is a silly sham. The heart must be beaten dead, stripped of the ego-search. How often I've mocked medieval sanctity as masochism. Yet, they're right. 'This world is half the devil's and my own' and I must abandon it if I would find the world of Christ." On August 15, 1965, my classmates and I knelt before the high altar at the Monastery of Saint Paul of the Cross and professed our holy vows. I think it was one of the proudest days of my parents' lives. Two sons now full members of a renowned religious order. The vows were temporary, to be made permanent in three years' time, but there was nothing provisional about them; I had made a personal resolve and public commitment "to spend my life seeking God and seeking Him both in and for His suffering servants."

6

EXILE

This world of intellectual, social, and cultural revolution has no
taste for the piety of the past. We cannot deal with this
world in the manner in which we dealt with the world of the past.

THOMAS BERRY, *"The Modern World:*
A Challenge to Christianity" (1966)

WITH A NEWFOUND APPRECIATION OF medieval
piety in mind, I could hardly have done better
than our next monastic stop on the journey, Saint Ann's
Monastery in Scranton, Pennsylvania. An exhausted coal-mining
town, Scranton was in economic freefall in the sixties. Huge slag
heaps smoldered ominously around the town. Periodically, a
section of roadway or other ground would suddenly disappear,
tumbling down into a collapsed mine shaft where supporting
pillars of coal were allegedly being removed by illegal mining.
The monastery building itself had enormous fracture lines angling
down its brick facade, also caused by underground subsidences,
which were believed to have been miraculously halted by the intercession of Saint Ann. An air of desolation and despair embraced
the landscape of abandoned strip mines and coal mining structures.

Or so I imagined; perhaps the greater desolation came from within, as I slumped into a period of religious doubt and deep depression.

The monastic community was a considerable downgrade from anything we'd experienced previously. The rector and vicar were both what might most charitably be called idiosyncratic. Many of the monks were older men, some suffering from illness or the pains of age, some obviously broken in spirit, a few quite mad in a harmless way. Our director of students was a dull little Italian straight out of the eighteenth century who made a point of forbidding almost everything. We were denied access to newspapers or magazines. On one occasion, when a small item of religious interest appeared in *Time* magazine, he pinned the relevant page on the bulletin board with a blank sheet of paper covering everything except the approved snippet. He insisted on authorizing any book we selected from the library, as though the shelves were stacked with works of satanic licentiousness. When I brought in for approval Samuel Butler's 1903 novel *The Way of All Flesh,* the poor little fossil sat there for what seemed like an hour peering suspiciously at various pages to determine whether there might not be too much flesh on display. Within weeks of my having professed it, the vow of obedience was beginning to look like a serious problem.

The monastery church served as a national shrine to Saint Ann, the patron saint of miners, and was particularly known for its annual novena. Held for nine days in the summer, the novena attracted many thousands of pilgrims, some of whom walked for miles to the shrine, the most zealous of them crawling on their knees for the last few hundred yards. Bishops, politicians, and other dignitaries were in attendance. The monks did brisk business in confessions and communions, and the spectacle was hailed as an inspiring example of the religious faith that was the inheritance of northeastern Pennsylvanians. But it seemed to me as much a relic of a bygone age as were the abandoned industries of the town.

How much relevance the piety of the past now had in our lives became for me a disturbing and dominant theme. The Passionists were in many ways a profoundly traditional group, some components of which I cherished while others I chafed against. The Congregation of the Passion of Jesus Christ had been founded in the eighteenth century by an Italian mystic and preacher named Paul Danei, who, following his death in 1775, was beatified as Saint Paul of the Cross. Saint Paul's ambition had been to combine contemplative life, as practiced by orders like the Trappists, with the more activist approach of orders such as the Jesuits. Periodically a team of two or three priests would leave the seclusion of the monastery and descend upon a particular parish to preach a week-long mission whose aim was to inspire all parishioners, and especially those of wobbly faith and attendance, to confess their sins and rededicate themselves to right Christian living. The apotheosis of this spiritual extravaganza was the Friday sermon, at which the preacher held a crucifix as tall as himself as a visual aid in recreating every painful detail of Christ's agony and death. The flogging, the crown of thorns, the dreadful march to Calvary, the nails driven through hands and feet, the sickening jolt of the cross raised high, the mockery of the crowd, the tears of the Blessed Mother, the cry "I thirst!" The sponge soaked in vinegar, the spear plunged into the side—on and on it went in an orgy of recrimination and blame. And it was to atone for my foul sins that Christ suffered such agony. My sins drove those cruel nails through his hands and feet, my sins pressed down that torturous crown of thorns. And if I continue to turn my back upon this bleeding man-god, I shall be forever condemned to the inferno of Hell. Although I was as moved as the next sinner at the time, this gradually came to seem like a superstitious regurgitation of the most morbid aspects of medievalism.

A man of ecstasies and visions, the founder talked of mystical union with God's love through the analogy of fire. "I want to set myself on fire with love," he declared in one of his sermons. "I want to be entirely on fire with love. More, more, I want to know how to sing in the fire of love ... I want to live in a continual agony of love for our divine lover ... I am crazy. Better if I were a butterfly burned and lost in divine love."

A far cry from the panic of my burning meadow, fire now symbolized the consummation of mystical union as well as the fire of lust, the cleansing fire of purification, and the eternal punishment of the damned. In a comic contribution to this litany of ecclesiastical fire, I myself almost put a chapelful of nuns to the flames when I accompanied one of the priests to a cloistered nunnery for the Holy Saturday midnight Mass. Part of the ceremony involved lighting the Easter Fire in the darkened chapel, a dramatic moment signifying the return of redeeming light into a darkened world. A brazier with charcoal briquettes stood beside the baptismal font. It fell to me as server to douse the briquettes with lighter fluid and at the appropriate moment to light the fire that would illuminate the darkness and proclaim that Christ, the Light of the World, was risen from the grave and had redeemed us from the stain of Adam's sin.

Lacking previous experience with lighter fluid, I splashed a generous amount over the briquettes. With the cloistered nuns sequestered piously behind their screen and the old priest muttering his Latin way through the service, on cue I struck a match and tossed it into the brazier. A sudden *bang* exploded through the chapel, and a column of fire leaped from the brazier almost to the vaulted ceiling. Luckily the whole place didn't ignite, as it might easily have done, but the old priest and I tottered through the remainder of the Mass in a sort of shell-shocked stupor.

THE FOOD AT Saint Ann's offered the best of times and the worst of times. The head cook was not a brother but a plump little Italian layman named Joe. He specialized in deep-fat frying, almost to the exclusion of all other methods of food preparation. He maintained an impressive row of deep-fat fryers and exhibited tremendous gusto plunging baskets of french fries or pieces of unidentifiable fish into his simmering oil. It was as though a demented reincarnation of Ron's Fish & Chips had returned from childhood to haunt me. In very short order, almost all of us came to loathe the sight of Joe's greasy cuisine.

Abstinence ruled in the refectory, limiting the desire for food and ensuring that it was taken as fuel, not a source of sensual pleasure or joy. Moderating the concupiscible appetites, we called it. Joe's handiwork certainly assisted in limiting the desire. But there was a singular exception at Scranton: Sunday breakfast. Weekday breakfasts were a blandness of porridge or boxed cereal, eaten standing up at a ledge along a wall, consumed quickly and in silence. But on Sunday mornings moderation met its match. The story was that when a handful of Passionist priests first came to North America in the 1850s to establish the order, they had been treated every Sunday morning to a feast of sweet rolls donated in gratitude by a local baker. Well, we were nothing if not sticklers for tradition, and so a suspension of strict abstinence on Sunday morning became enshrined in our otherwise limited cuisine. The mini-orgy varied somewhat from one monastery to another, but at its best—and it was absolutely at its best in Scranton—it was a thing of prodigious overindulgence: orange juice, bacon and eggs with hash browns and unlimited buttered toast, a bottomless cup of coffee, followed by tray upon tray of cinnamon rolls, croissants, and assorted marvelous sticky buns with slabs of real butter. It was cholesterol overkill of grotesque proportions. We still ate in silence, standing, alone with our reflections upon the evils of sensuous pleasure.

OTHER SUBTERRANEAN SHIFTINGS were at work that year. Again as a result of the Second Vatican Council, which concluded in 1965, the language of the Church liturgy was switched over from Latin to "the vernacular." The solemnity and mystery attached to old Latin prayers and hymns gave way to often hastily translated and woefully uninspired English. Eventually, the psalms of the office were also translated into English, but for me at least, and I'm sure for many of the older monks, something was lost in translation so that chanting the hours of the office never quite realized the sense of mystical transcendence sometimes achieved in the old Latin.

As well, the Passionist community entered into a period of intense and painful debate over how best to implement the directives of the council. The new emphasis on a church more actively involved in the affairs of the world put tremendous pressures on the contemplative monastic orders. The Passionists, like others, began the thorny process of trying to find and maintain a proper balance between seclusion from the world and active engagement in what they believed to be its salvation. Some argued for a wholesale restructuring and modernizing of monastic life; others spoke just as passionately about restoring and returning to the order's true monastic tradition. The very unity of the congregation seemed threatened. One senior monk described the congregation as "fragmented and somewhat convulsed by all that was happening."

IN THE MIDST of this turmoil and the sinking gloom of Scranton, I experienced what many a young poet dreams of: seeing one's poems appear in print. In 1966, I had two poems published in a national Catholic weekly magazine called *Ave Maria*. Here is one of them:

FALLINGS

If leaves should fall tonight
and I into a world
black-branched and wet should waken,
would much be greatly changed

from the sad and final flights
of every least octobering leaf
to which I've fixed
or only hoped to fix
my sand-castle life ago?

Or, graver yet, I know,
if midnight lights should,
on mountains which I've climbed,
most cruelly stop shining,
would my silly slips and pratfalls
be any less the fool's
or my peering through the darkness
be any less a terror
than my lonely vigils now?

This turning-time in life
when the dusts and dusks of summer
are apparent in their passings
is perhaps less cruel
only than the gibbet.
The terrors that it holds
are no less real than nails,
its future no less bright
than once seemed wise
the foolishness of death.

If worlds should crumble now
and all we know as good
should suddenly grow old
leaving not for us
one hope upon another
save juvenescent Christ

in a womb rock-hewn,
then worlds and lights and leaves
can die and so remain
while we in our tumblings down
(yes, even in our dyings)
are resurrection bound
and lunging God-like
toward the spring.

Let there be no doubt concerning the power of poetry, for the publishing of this earnest hybrid of Thomas Aquinas and Dylan Thomas marked a great divide in my life. Although I failed to realize it at the time, being a poet was beginning to become at least as important as being a priest. I considered the two not incompatible, nor need they be, as I savored the works of Gerard Manley Hopkins and the Dominican Brother Antoninus. But poetry had laid its claim and it would be at the eventual cost of priesthood.

The following summer the Passionists did something entirely new. In a nod to the spirit of social activism simmering within the Church, we "fraters" were being temporarily released from the cloister and sent out into what we called "the world"—an entity of which we were distinctly not a part—in order to study or do good works. On the strength of my two published poems (the Passionists, unlike the brainy Jesuits, were not widely published), I was assigned to live in a monastery in New Jersey and attend writing courses at Columbia University in Manhattan.

After being secluded for so long, I found simply taking the subway uptown to be a fantastic expedition. The swirl of traffic and the tremendous skyscrapers, the crush of people of every imaginable description—Hasidic Jews, buttoned-down businessmen, gorgeous black queens, miscellaneous crazies—yanked me out of the tiny, quiet niche I'd been occupying. I was required to wear my black clerical suit and a ridiculous black fedora, but within the city's extremes of attire my fusty outfit seemed no more outlandish than anybody else's.

Immense upheavals had bruised the school year just concluded at Columbia. Students for a Democratic Society had mobilized against the corporate/military/academic power structure under-pinning Lyndon Johnson's war in Vietnam. By summer of '66 the ruckus had largely subsided, at least on campus, but still there seemed to be an air of revolutionary fervor about the place. The course I had most eagerly anticipated taking was a workshop on poetry led by the New York poet David Ignatow. Acclaimed for his somewhat doleful urban imagist poems, he soon showed himself either unable or unwilling to conduct a productive workshop. Much of our time was devoted to a shoving match between him and a disgruntled student, an older lady who wrote maudlin rubbish but stood upon the dignity of being a distant relative of, I think, Edna St. Vincent Millay. However, a second workshop, English: Struc-ture and Style, with Thalia Selz as instructor, gave my writing the good boot up the backside it needed.

Thalia Selz was the first female teacher I'd encountered in six years. Moreover, she was an accomplished writer, which few of the priests who'd been attempting to teach us writing were. I'd grown accustomed to getting my essays back from them with top marks and only the occasional question mark, spelling correction, or "wrong word" noted. But many of the earnest essays I churned out that summer came back from Ms. Selz littered with observations—"glib, even if true," "archaic," "mixed metaphor," "stuffy," "now I'm lost." One careful essay she described as "virtually faultless," but then went on, "Sounds a bit like the encyclopedia...Where's your own idiom?" My own idiom was bloodstained Christ nailed to a cross for my sins, and I suspected that wasn't what she was looking for. She called my writing "stilted, unnecessarily abstract,

and trite." And she warned me against "a tendency to sentimen-
talize which betrays itself in trite expressions occasionally and a
kind of bookish way of inverting word order unnecessarily."

She was absolutely right—my writing was stilted, archaic, trite,
and stuffy, just as I was. What else might you expect from someone
who had spent his formative years within a mental enclosure essentially unchanged since the Middle Ages? Lord only knows what
she thought of me sitting in her class wearing my ridiculous suit
and hat, grinding out those musty compositions that she took the
time to so meticulously critique. Her forthright criticism, difficult
as it was to hear, cracked open a door for me into the real world of
writers and writing. I had no way of knowing at the time that this
was a doorway that would lead out of the cloister toward something else entirely.

AT SUMMER'S END, with my perspectives radically altered, I
rejoined my classmates for two years of studying philosophy at
Immaculate Conception Monastery in Queens, a borough of New
York City. As with West Hartford, this was a newer monastery in
an affluent neighborhood. I devoted myself to renewed piety and to
writing lengthy papers with titles such as "The Essence of Phenom-
enology" and "Immanence and Transcendence: Benedict Spinoza
and the Radical Theologians." But my heart was elsewhere.

At Columbia I'd connected with a well-regarded poet named
Joel Oppenheimer. A tall, grizzled character with the long hair and
beard of a prophet, he was one of the Black Mountain poets, a well-
known figure in the New York scene, a rabid Knicks fan, and a
regular at the Lion's Head Pub. At that time he was director of a
poetry project being run out of the renowned Saint Mark's Church
in the Bowery. He arranged to have one of the poetry workshops
occur on Thursday afternoons to accommodate me and several of
my classmates, Thursdays being a "free afternoon" when we could

leave the monastery for approved activities. Joel ran the workshops, sometimes attended by his fellow poets Joel Sloman and Anne Waldman. This was another world again, charged with the excitements of the Beat poets, radical politics, and the emerging cultural revolution of the sixties. We went to see Allen Ginsberg perform in Washington Square Park and Robert Creeley at Saint Mark's. I took to stashing a pair of blue jeans and an old shirt in a locker at Grand Central Station, so I could shed the black suit I was required to wear when leaving and returning to the monastery. I came to love the grit of the Lower East Side and Greenwich Village, the beauty of streets and alleys, the jostle of people from all over the planet.

A student of Charles Olson and admirer of William Carlos Williams, Joel Oppenheimer had very little use for my florid Dylan Thomas knockoffs, and I quickly jettisoned them. Now I was reading Kerouac and Ferlinghetti, Denise Levertov and Michael McClure, and writing poems like one that began:

> *love demands otherwise*
> *but I tell love*
> *to go fuck itself this time*
> *this last sad ride*
> *around the empty circus*

and included heretical metaphors such as:

> *the painted face of love explodes*
> *in the scientific shriek*
> *of an ambulance carrying god*

and ended badly, as:

> *even then, blinded on each other's*
> *lethal twist of love*
> *we might have made it*

and if we hadn't
started talking so professionally
just before the light began to fade
and the solid ethical blocks
of colors started decomposing
who knows?

Needless to say, this couldn't go on. And it didn't. Things came to a head when we organized Monastery Meets the Street, a series of poetic celebrations by monastery and secular poets. With all necessary permissions secured, the first event took place (without conscious irony) at Immaculate Conception on a February night in 1967. The room was packed, the poets passionate, and the evening a roaring success, hailed by the *Village Voice* as "Hip Scene in Queens: Poetry in a Monastery." But the authorities were not amused; after the first night the series was abruptly canceled by the rector, a troubled individual ill equipped for the office he held. One of the "secular" poets complained in the *Voice*: "The monastery higher-ups decided that a monastery is no place for poetry and that the monks had no business writing poetry (nobody tell this to Merton or Antoninus) the three monks that were attending the St. Mark's poetry workshop were told to stop and turn their eyes to God / what started out as a refreshing and surprising revelation of the modernity and creativity of the 20th Century Catholic Church had ended with the old clichés being proved almost true and the lid back on / harder than ever."

And that pretty much marked the end of my career as a monastic poet. I hung on to monastery life for another year, but the forces of change were massing at the gates. I could hear their siren songs in the evening air. At Pittsburgh and at Scranton we'd heard no secular music of any kind; it was all sacred music or silence. But at Jamaica things were a bit less tightly controlled, eventually allowing the sly Leonard Cohen to slip into the cloister, along with Dylan, Joni Mitchell, Phil Ochs, and many of the other poet troubadours whose music would in the end, for me at least, supplant the faded glory of "Per Omnia Secula Saeculorum," listlessly translated as "World without End." That world was ending even as we sang it.

Compared with the sizzling artistic and intellectual excitement of the world beyond our walls, our studies seemed increasingly dull and irrelevant. Our philosophy professors ranged from average to atrocious. One pedestrian crank insisted upon regularly inflicting on us a "surprise quickie quiz" as though we were grade 8s studying geography. When summoned to his room and held to account for not getting every answer correct, I told him, "I don't believe philosophy has anything to do with quickie quizzes." He fluffed himself up, outraged at my impertinence. "I'm teaching this course, not you," he spluttered, glowering at me, and I knew I'd made an enemy. I remembered old Gregory Flynn's warning about not everyone appreciating my attitude. But the thing was, I didn't care.

Two of the more enlightened teachers weren't priests but laymen. Paul Potter was a fey actor (specializing in soap operas, if rumor was to be credited) who was brought in to try to juice up our public speaking a bit. He'd wave his arms theatrically, exclaim "Excellent, Father!" at anything the least bit promising, and do whatever he could to inspire and provoke us into producing something more interesting than our standard pious niceties. He appeared to believe that we were all as mad as we knew he was, but his extravagance of character was a breath of fresh air in our typically claustrophobic classrooms. Professor William Osborne, who taught sociology at a nearby university, combined brilliance with a sense of mischievous fun in a way that few of our solemn teachers did. For a required sociological survey, my friend Ken Lijeski and I attempted to work up a statistical correlation between external appearance and responses received from priests and nuns on the streets of New York

City. Ken and I split up and individually approached nuns or priests in Manhattan, asking for emergency financial assistance. One of us would be well dressed and the other shabbily. This ran us into some difficulties with the resident panhandlers upon whose terrain we were encroaching and who largely failed to grasp the distinction between sociological research and old-fashioned panhandling, but Ken was a formidably muscled character with whom none of them chose to tangle. As pure sociology the whole thing was a bit of a farce, but Professor Osborne loved it and declined to give a final grade until we forked over half our earnings for his "consultation fee." Both these teachers had an appealing sense of spontaneity and irreverence that contributed further to the growing realization that our little ecclesiastical enclave was not quite the seat of all wisdom we had been led to believe.

ON THE FOLLOWING summer break from our studies, four of us were dispatched to Saint Gabriel's Monastery in Toronto. Our assignment for the summer was to conduct a census of a sprawling and almost moribund parish on the city's gritty east side. Working alone, each of us would tackle a block of apartments or a row of houses, tapping on every door to inquire whether there were any Catholics residing there and, if so, to update their names in the parish register. Well, you can just imagine the responses—violently slammed doors, snarls of "Fuck off!" and worse.

Two encounters particularly linger in memory. At one apartment I was greeted by a pair of saucy and scantily clad girls scarcely much older than myself. They were plainly accustomed to gentlemen callers attired somewhat differently than I was in my full clerical regalia. I muttered and stammered and fumbled for words, a full frontal flush blooming above my dog collar, finally blurting out, "Is your mother here?" at which the two of them burst into hysterical laughter. Humiliated, I retreated like the fool I was.

On a kinder afternoon, the front door of a little house on a tree-lined street was opened by a tiny older lady who greeted me effusively and welcomed me in as though I were the bishop himself come calling. We sat in her cluttered Victorian parlor where we discussed ecclesiastical matters for a good part of the afternoon, throughout which she plied me, as well as herself, with dainty glass after glass of sherry. As unaccustomed to alcohol as I was to saucy girls, I felt my theology beginning to wobble. When at last I withdrew in a merry haze to regroup with my companions, I was suffused with the honest satisfaction of having done a good day's work in the vineyards of the Lord.

But that summer's graphic demonstration of my utter unfitness, and unwillingness, to intrude upon other people's lives in order to instruct them upon how they might better conduct themselves added to the growing weight of evidence that I really wasn't cut out for the business of priesthood. I began dreading the prospect of ordination and thereafter sallying forth to proselytize and, if necessary, terrify sinners into penitence. I had far too acute an awareness of my own imperfection to presume that I could instruct others on how they might improve themselves.

Music made its move on me at the same time. I vividly remember one afternoon when I was driving back to the Toronto monastery after visiting my parents, at the wheel of a big blue Buick convertible, top down, sunshine streaming, the radio blaring Van Morrison's "Brown Eyed Girl." I felt an exhilaration of spirit that had less to do with the prospect of making love in the green grass than with the pure glory of the moment's freedom. Even more fatefully, one evening I somehow ended up escorting the comely sister of a fellow seminarian to a concert at the O'Keefe Centre featuring the Grateful Dead and Jefferson Airplane, who were just emerging from the San Francisco hippie scene. Whoa!!! Who were these crazy buggers? How could they look like that, play like that, be like that? The brilliance of Jerry Garcia picking his way through the galaxies, Grace Slick tripping out with the white rabbit. This was madness, this was reckless, crazy fucking freedom, and I was entirely mind-blown.

BACK I WENT to New York for a final, dismal year during which I had to decide my future. Perhaps I had already made a choice but was afraid to admit it to myself. Perhaps I was gathering evidence to support my case. I became attracted to the Catholic Worker movement founded by the charismatic Dorothy Day and Peter Maurin in 1933. Dedicated to a radical Christianity based upon prayer, voluntary poverty, and nonviolence, the group worked to provide shelter for the homeless and hungry at Saint Joseph's House of Hospitality in the city and operated a farm in Pennsylvania. A fiery combination of Christianity and socialist analysis, the *Catholic Worker* newspaper gave me the beginnings of a more substantive appreciation of the rights of working people and capitalism's systemic oppression of the poor. A saintly person herself, Dorothy Day was a merciless critic of pampered priests, accusing them of romanticizing the working classes and, in attempting to emphasize the dignity of the worker, of sanctifying forms of labor that are in reality degrading and dehumanizing slavery.

I'd gotten a different, but equally radical, perspective when two of my classmates and I received special permission to visit Father Thomas Berry, a member of our Order who at that time lived in a rambling old house at a beautiful spot along the Hudson River. Besides establishing the Riverdale Center of Religious Research at the site, Father Berry taught at Fordham University, where he was chair of the History of Religions Program. Within our congregation he had the reputation of being a maverick genius whose wild ideas were best kept well away from those of us diligently studying traditional Thomistic philosophy and theology.

This, naturally, was precisely his appeal to the three of us intent upon visiting him.

An affable, gentle man in his mid-fifties with a charming smile and easy manner, he was dressed casually and spoke with us candidly about his work and ideas. At that point he was a historian of world cultures and religions, though he would later be acclaimed as a historian of the earth and its evolutionary processes, a self-described "geologian." In 1989, *Newsweek* magazine would call him "the most provocative figure among the new breed of eco-theologians."

At the conclusion of our visit, he gave us a copy of a speech he'd recently presented, and reading it later I realized why the congregation held him at such arm's length: his critique of contemporary Christianity was scathing. He described how "the massive religious establishment of Catholicism" had been in retreat from change for centuries and had "developed an intense aversion not only to all basic change in the structure of being but even to slight modifications in established ways of thinking, speaking, acting, worshipping, educating." He described Catholics as "a marginal group of ineffectual survivors of a medieval culture that has disappeared forever." Then, relentlessly, "A rigorous examination would discover that we are neither as Christian nor as spiritual and not even as honest as we appear to be. Our piety is for the most part pathetic. Our learning is irrelevant both in the academic and practical spheres, our worship affected, our art devoid of aesthetic or religious value, our clerical and lay leadership terribly inadequate, our social sense dulled, our human abilities retarded, our general effectiveness as men, as citizens and as Christians at a low state."

This was precisely what I had been feeling for some time but had dared not say, had scarcely dared acknowledge to myself. The silence of the Church on the great moral issues of the day—the war in Vietnam, the struggle for equal rights, the deployment of nuclear weaponry, the vast disparity between obscene wealth and abject poverty—was undeniable. I'd become embarrassed at being a member of a church that sat largely silent while others ran the risks and suffered the penalties of challenging racism, inequality, and war. As I knelt for hours in chapel meditating upon the passion of Christ, it became unavoidably apparent that I was more concerned about unnecessary suffering and death in all of human-kind, more concerned about the destruction of the life processes of the planet, than I was about steering my wretched little soul safely toward the Kingdom of Heaven. My spirit craved something more expansive, a liberation of consciousness not weighed down with narcissistic guilt.

Amid this personal turmoil, during the spring of 1968, Martin Luther King Jr. was assassinated. Again, as with John Kennedy's death, I experienced that cataclysmic convergence of grief, anger, frustration, despair. A day or two afterward I participated in a march that wound through some of New Jersey's worst slums. The hundreds of us marching covered the spectrum of racial types, but the ghettos through which we walked were entirely black. The event was a strange and disturbing combination of memorial, peace march, and attempted demonstration of solidarity. The streets of run-down tenements were lined with crowds of black residents who stood silently and stared at us as we paraded past. Unable to read their blank stares—Was it anger we saw in them? Bitterness? Contempt?—I felt a potent, and impotent, surge of rage, guilt, and sadness at the obliteration of King's dream by a bullet and at the nightmare living conditions of the truly disenfranchised.

The psychological pressure to not abandon one's vocation was immense—the expectations of family, the fact that your whole life had been geared toward this and this alone, an inner predisposition toward guilt, an exaggerated fear of the world beyond the cloister. To "lose your vocation" was to squander a precious calling from

God Himself. It represented failure, a diminishment, an admission of unworthiness. I watched some of my classmates agonize their way into mental breakdown under the strain of indecision. Most of them had the additional consideration that draft boards were eagerly awaiting fresh fodder for Vietnam, and several of our former comrades were sent off to be killed in that hapless conflict.

For months I was tormented over whether I should leave. Then, harking back to my old dad's dustup with the mother superior at Knowle Park, I locked horns with the poet-busting rector. Fired with the spirit of rebellion and the questioning of authority that were leaping like brushfire across the youth culture of the sixties, I would not bend my knee to what I saw as ignorance. I declined in the end to continue believing that purification of self was to be found through obeisance to fools. Chafing against the arbitrariness of authority, just as my contemporaries were chafing on a larger stage against racism and imperialism, I was left with no alternative but departure. The rector more or less invited me to leave, but in a classic "You can't fire me, I quit!" maneuver, I cleared out before they could clear me out. For many years after that, even though life would open up for me in wondrous ways, I suffered from a recurring nightmare that I was still living in the monastery, still tormented with indecision over whether I should stay or leave.

But the decision was made, and it rocked my soul to its very foundations. All the momentum of my formative years shuddered to a halt; every conception of my future fled into darkness.

7

THE WEST

What care I here for all Earth's creeds outworn,
The dreams outlived, the hopes to ashes turned,
In that old East so dark with rain and doubt?
Here life swings glad and free and rude, and I
Shall drink it to the full, and go content.

ARTHUR STRINGER, *"Morning in the Northwest"* (1907)

UPON LEAVING THE SEMINARY IN the spring of 1968, I felt I had lost not just my vocation but also my place of being in the world. Who was I? What was I possibly going to do with myself? I went back to my parents' home in Toronto, knowing that it was no longer my home. My mum and dad gracefully showed no trace of the disappointment they must have been feeling over my abandonment of priesthood. The Church was in such turmoil, the solid rock upon which they'd faithfully based their lives was now so fractured with new ideas, a changed liturgy, priests and nuns abandoning their vows, that my own leaving was not the disgrace it might have been a decade earlier.

I had no real sense of attachment to anywhere, but placelessness sat more lightly on me in my twenties than it would today. My

fervent desire was to leave the places I'd known, and in that way
attempt to leave behind the person I'd been. I felt a strong instinct
to wander westward, toward prairie and desert, mountains and
woodlands. My brother Brendan was at the time living in a remote
corner of British Columbia, working for an Indian band, and his
letters had convinced me that the West Coast offered far more
appealing possibilities than Toronto. I decided to give Vancouver
a try and sent application inquiries to both universities there. Then
I hooked up with my friend Jim Conlon, a fellow poet and former
seminarian. Jim had been unceremoniously ejected from the seminary for famously presenting, to a high school class he'd been
teaching, his own poem that began, "Jesus / is a word like Fuck."
Although the complete poem was one of thoughtful reverence, the
opening lines raised a howl of parental outrage that chased Jim all
the way back to his home in New Jersey. As adrift as I was, he had
taken on the assignment of delivering his grandfather's car from
New Jersey to California, and I determined to join him. The open
road beckoned; I'd read Kerouac and Kesey and was primed for
whatever adventures awaited at all points west.

Jim and I connected at Pittsburgh, provisioned ourselves—as
any young and impoverished poets would—with crusty French
bread, apples, hard cheddar cheese, and cheap red wine, and
pointed the nose of our great boat of a Chrysler, enormous tail fins
and all, toward the Ohio state line. When we crossed the Missis-
sippi at Hannibal, Missouri, paying due homage to Mark Twain, I
felt the confinements and strictures of the past begin to shatter and
fall away. Here was freedom at last, damn it, the freedom of the
road running west and the great wide-open spaces of the future.

Short of cash, at night we parked in out-of-the-way places and
slept in the car without any real sense of danger. We were both
sporting beards by that point and attempting to look as disreputable as we could. I was smoking hand-rolled cigarettes. The car

had no radio, but we had a little transistor radio for picking up tunes and news whenever we got close to a town. Across the Great Plains of Kansas we streaked and into eastern Colorado, following the interstate through Burlington and Stratton, Flagler and Limon; and somewhere along that monotonous route, suddenly, like a vast apparition, the snowy Front Range of the Rocky Mountains rose majestically before us. Seen for the first time, approached from out of interminable flatness, this was like a vision of Valhalla.

After visiting friends on campus in Boulder (I swear the whole nation was swarming with ex-seminarians in those days) we trundled south through the Sangre de Cristo Mountains. Somewhere along that route we stopped on a Sunday morning to attend Mass at an ultramodern church. The back wall of the apse, behind the altar, was all clear glass, looking out across a mountain landscape. As the priest raised the Host in consecration, a golden eagle glided on thermal currents through blue sky behind him and there seemed to me at that moment a sense of the truly sacred here, a sacredness of wonderment and awe unlike any I'd known.

We pressed on down to Santa Fe, where we visited a rural commune we'd been told about. On a hardscrabble patch of dusty hillside we watched a morose and inhospitable back-to-the-lander scratching out planting holes with a sharpened stick and planting fruit-tree whips whose prospects of ever bearing fruit seemed impossibly remote. Then westward we went again, out of New Mexico into Arizona. Somewhere around Winslow on Interstate 40 we picked up a hitchhiker, a hulking farm boy out of Nebraska who was bound for the promised land of California to open a church and save the souls of sinners. He spoke of Jesus as though the two of them were bowling buddies. Just after we let him off at Flagstaff, because we were going to detour north to the Grand Canyon, we heard on the radio a warning from the police to avoid picking up hitchhikers because a disturbed and dangerous young male was on the loose, believed to be heading west. Praise the Lord! We went west again too, through the Providence Mountains and vast Mojave Desert, through desperate desert towns—Ludlow and Barstow and Oro Grande—and then down the spectacular decline into the labyrinthine sprawl of Los Angeles. We'd done it; we'd crossed the continent, shaken the dust of the past from our shoes.

Jim's uncle and his wife lived in a luxurious hillside home in Van Nuys. He worked as a casting director at Twentieth Century Fox, meaning he was a person whose good favor many were eager to curry. Evenings featured cocktails on the patio with guest appearances by innumerable "industry people." As naive young men fresh out of the seminary (Hollywood subtitles: *Virgins! Can you believe it?*) Jim and I were objects of considerable attention from certain aging bit-part actors already a facelift or two beyond credibility.

After a week or so of this, our virginity intact, we were ready for the open road again. Wanting to get to Vancouver, we contracted to drive a bonded car north from Los Angeles to Portland, Oregon. A deposit we paid in L.A. would be refunded in Portland upon safe delivery of the car. After stops at the requisite points of pilgrimage—Lawrence Ferlinghetti's City Lights bookstore in San Francisco, and Haight-Ashbury, already jaded so soon after its Summer of Love—we continued northward through the Redwood Empire at the furthest tip of which disaster finally knocked us flat on our smart young asses.

North of Eureka, where the coast highway wiggles its way between the vast Pacific and the rugged Klamath Mountains, we smacked our car broadside into a loaded logging truck and went tumbling into a roadside ditch. Shaken but unhurt, we had the wreckage towed to the little town of Orick, where it sat for several days while the dealership in Portland—not the least bit pleased—figured out what should be done. Disconsolate, Jim and I spent our nights in a local laundromat, the only warm place we could afford. We were instructed to get the absolute minimum amount of work done to make the car drivable and then get it up to Portland. An inventive mechanic at the garage pried the crumpled metal away from the wheels, replaced a few essential components (not including smashed windows or the fractured windshield), wired the crumpled hood closed, and sent us on our way. We limped north through Oregon in horrendous storms, the bitter wind and driving rain lashing at us through our absent windows. This was not the Merry Pranksters. This was not the Dharma Bums. This was bloody miserable beyond mention.

Somewhere along the freeway, a cop pulled us over, totally dumbfounded that we were daring to drive such a "broken-down piece of shit" on a public highway. We voiced complete agreement with his assessment and explained our circumstances in detail. He obviously concluded that dealing with us would involve far more hassle than not, so he waved us on, with a warning that "you won't get twenty miles in that wreck." Careful to avoid any more cops, we made it all the way up through Oregon and delivered the wreckage to the dealership in Portland, where a very pissed-off manager told us that the car was a total write-off and that we were definitely *not* getting our deposit refunded.

So we became true knights of the road: hitching rides north, dodging state troopers vigilant in enforcing the no-hitchhiking strictures on Interstate 5, and sleeping in derelict buildings. Cold, tired, dirty, and hungry, by the time we hit the Canadian border, we'd also hit rock bottom. Jim was denied access to Canada. Our deferrals from the Vietnam draft as "divinity students" (part of a draft board category that included the insane) were no longer valid, and I was grilled at length by border guards who were on heightened alert for draft evaders. We tried, and failed, to pick up some laboring work in the U.S. border town of Blaine. A local cop told us to get out of town. Our great adventure was done. Jim phoned home for money and flew back east. I caught a bus north to Vancouver.

I remember that forlorn bus ride into the city, alone, almost penniless, unsure of what to do and of my capacity to do anything. I telephoned the noted poet Robin Blaser, whose name I'd been given by Billy Little, one of my New York poet friends. Robin picked me up at the bus depot, fed me, and put me up for the night. Dazed and discouraged as I was, I must have been a singularly uninteresting tenderfoot, and in the morning he concocted an unlikely tale of family coming to visit and sent me on my way. I took off to find a room and settled on one in a dilapidated rooming house in the city's Kitsilano neighborhood for eight dollars and fifty cents a week. I think I had twenty dollars to my name at that point. All night I could hear behind thin walls my fellow lodgers coughing and wheezing. The shared bathroom at the end of the corridor was a facility I wanted to use no more than was absolutely necessary. For meals I ate the spoils from a nearby bakery. I spent day after day looking for work but was repeatedly rebuffed. During those dismal days and nights I experienced an intense and painful realization of what the loss of community and vocation really meant. While traveling with Jim I'd been sustained by the romance of the open road as well as by the belief that better things lay ahead of me than behind, but now all my thoughts were consumed with what I'd lost and how insufficiently I'd valued what I'd had at the time. Walking in downtown Vancouver one morning, I glimpsed a newspaper headline announcing that Robert Kennedy had been assassinated. First John Kennedy, then King, and now Bobby. Even amid the extraordinary beauty of Vancouver in springtime, these were dark days. I was experiencing a stripping down of the spirit altogether different from the cerebral relinquishment of self I'd been attempting to achieve within the supportive confines of monastic life.

THEN, JUST AS I was conceding that I'd have to admit defeat and retreat to the dreariness of Toronto, I was thrown a lifeline. I answered a newspaper advertisement for a high school teaching position and was summoned for an interview. It was already clear to me that teaching in the public school system was impossible without a teacher's certificate, but this was a Catholic school that was free to hire whomever it chose. I was interviewed by the principal, a wise and practical woman named Ruth Conlin, and against all expectation, a few days later I received notice that I'd been hired for the coming school year. Alleluia!!

Immediately the machinery of the parish kicked into gear to assist me. I was offered temporary lodging at the parish rectory, manned by a pair of affable Redemptorist Fathers. To get me through the summer they secured a temporary job for me through a prominent parishioner, laboring at an asbestos pipe supply yard, which was reminiscent of some of my more dreadful summer jobs of yore. Then I found room and board with another parishioner, a generous lady named Mary Clohosey, and her aging father, J.P. She was a social worker and her dad a grand old veteran of the First World War, who told wonderful tales of a bygone era. On occasion, we'd find him crouched at the side of his bed in the middle of the night, having dreamed of being back in the trenches of half a century before. I stayed with Mary and J.P. for two years and was treated royally throughout.

Having survived the asbestos pipe experience, I took up my teaching position in the fall. Our Lady of Perpetual Help was a small parochial school on the city's wealthy west side with a primary school and 165 high school students, most of them privileged, bright, and eager to learn. Lay teachers outnumbered nuns two-to-one on staff. The position offered a modest wage ($450 a month, no holiday pay or benefits) in return for a grotesque workload: teaching English to grades 9, 10, 11, and 12, plus two grades of religious studies and coaching the girls' basketball team. I spent most of the year frantically attempting to stay a day or two ahead of the kids in four unfamiliar curricula while simultaneously correcting mountains of essays and test papers. Perhaps it's a measure of what a glutton for punishment I was in those days that I decided to try to obtain a teaching degree. However, both Vancouver universities sniffed at my B.A. in philosophy from the seminary as though it were something contemptible. (The nugatory diploma hangs on the study wall behind me now. Ironically, as though to confirm its true worth, it is signed by my quickie-quiz philosophy professor and the poetry-bashing rector.) Sniffing back, I'd be damned if I was going to lower myself to slogging through dreary undergraduate courses for untold years. Plus a brouhaha erupted at the school that considerably chilled my enthusiasm for the educational system.

Ruth Conlin, the first principal in the school's history who was not a nun, was intent upon instituting some creative change in a badly hidebound system. Courses were realigned and rules relaxed in an attempt to foster a spirit of intellectual curiosity and discovery. "Basically I was attempting to distribute the children's education throughout the community, not just within the four walls of the school," she later explained in a *Vancouver Sun* interview. "I was trying to involve the kids in the community and vice-versa." For example, grade 12 students studying native issues took a week away from school and went up the coast to remote Indian reserves. They took along movie cameras and tape recorders, and when they returned, they produced a twenty-minute film. In my religion class, instead of just reading about Christian compassion, thirteen students spent part of their school days working with foster children, in daycare centers for children of working moms, in hospitals, and with parks and recreation programs. In economics, other students spent time at the Vancouver Stock Exchange as well as at businesses and factories. "We stopped treating children as part of the classroom furniture and started treating them as individuals with a sense of self-worth and service," the principal said in the *Sun* story.

Certain parents in the conservative, middle-class parish grew increasingly restive at what they took to be a breakdown of discipline. Tensions mounted and it soon became clear that a fracas was in the making. Eventually I and my fellow teacher Loren Miller— a young draft evader from the States—were summoned before a lawyer on the parish school board. Plainly we'd been fingered as the root cause of perceived problems. In an eerily quiet and dispassionate voice the lawyer read us the riot act. He demanded we sign a document of compliance with the board's pedagogical directives. We declined, standing our ground on the technicality that our contracts stipulated that we take our directives from the principal, which we were doing, not from the board. We were fired on the spot, forbidden to ever again approach the school, and were paid a portion of our monthly salary up to that day and not a penny more.

Loren and I took our leave and made an appointment to meet with Harry Rankin, the radical left-wing lawyer whose irascible defense of the downtrodden had made him a legendary and much-loved character in the city. After we'd explained the situation he agreed to champion our cause, muttering, "These Catholic bastards think they can get away with murder!"

Ruth Conlin resigned as principal, blaming interference from parents and the parish school board. In impeccable accord with the spirit of protest marches, sit-ins, and freedom rides of the sixties, the kids all walked out of school in protest and initiated a boycott, demanding our reinstatement. We secured the use of a nearby coffeehouse and set up an impromptu "free school" unfettered by any curriculum whatsoever. The unanticipated courage of the kids quickly brought the crisis to a rolling boil. A public meeting was convened at which the parish church was packed with concerned parents, teachers, and students. Speeches were made, tears were shed, and a compromise was hammered out whereby Ruth returned, Loren and I were reinstated, and all agreed to devote themselves to finishing the school year without further disruption. Shortly afterward the board announced that the high school would be permanently closed, in part because there were insufficient teaching nuns to staff the school and because lay teachers were unable to "inspire the proper religious attitude" in students.

Personally I thought the students' attitude was just fine, and a considerable improvement over the attitude of certain parents. Our hapless girls' basketball team was a classic case in point. I'd reluctantly agreed to take on coaching the team in the first place. The school hadn't had a girls' team previously, and I certainly hadn't coached previously, but on the strength of my knowing at least the rudiments of the game, I was handed the assignment of creating a team from nothing and preparing it to play against other schools with long-standing basketball programs. We really were dreadful. Visiting one powerhouse school, we were pasted 72–2. But, believe it, when we scored that lone basket, it was as though we'd won the game! The girls rejoiced together and finished out the game with a dignity and spirit that impressed me hugely. I was far prouder to be their coach than to be like the opposing coach, who shamelessly ran up the score. I don't remember rightly, but I think we may have even won one game that season. Either way, the experience was a triumph of sorts for us, in that the girls continued to play through adversity with spunk and good humor.

I enjoyed the intellectual challenge of teaching and the vivacity of the kids, but in hindsight I thought of myself as having not served my students adequately. I was too young, too inexperienced, in many ways still groping to find myself in the sudden psychic vacuum of abandoning priesthood. Some years later I chanced upon one of my former students, a spirited young woman who'd seemed to endure school more than enjoy it. "You were the only teacher I ever had who praised me for my work," she told me. "You always said that what I had done was excellent." In an ironic reversal of roles, her perspective offered a different, and welcome, version of my teaching self than the one I had been carrying. Nevertheless, after just one year, unmistakably my career as a teacher had peremptorily run its course.

8

REVELATIONS

Earth's the right place for love;
I don't know where it's likely to go better.

ROBERT FROST, *"Birches"*

ONCE THE SCHOOL YEAR DREW to a close, my land-lady, Mary, secured for me a job doing social work at the Catholic Family and Children's Services in the city. For almost two years I worked on a "transient youth" team, dealing with the growing hordes of young kids streaming into Vancouver from across the country. In those days the city was seen as a hippie haven, a magnet for the footloose and fanciful, and they drifted in by the thousands from all across the country. Again the workload was staggering—I'd frequently see about six hundred kids a month, encompassing everything from barely teenage girls fleeing sexual abuse at home to suburban kids out on a lark playing at being hippies. My job involved endless tacking back and forth among street people, police, social agencies, parents, and civic officials. We organized community meetings, festivals, and other events to try bridge chasms and create solutions. "Des knows the nomads," one *Vancouver Sun* column opined, quoting me as saying, "I want people to know these kids, to understand them, to know what has happened and what is happening to the young in the community, and to come out and help them."

The work was frenzied and ultimately frustrating, but I enjoyed the colleagues with whom I worked and there was a stimulating sense of being somewhere near the heart of the action. Vancouver was simmering with radical politics, rock music, and alternative lifestyles. I grew a beard and let my hair grow long. I smoked marijuana. I bought an old Volkswagen van, fixed up the interior for rough camping, and began exploring the wild country that lay almost at Vancouver's doorstep. I was given a large dog named Yuma, part malamute and part wolf, that proved a less-than-welcome addition to our quiet residential neighborhood. I never aspired to be a "far out, man," beads-and-feathers hippie, but I basked in the freedom and expansiveness of those heady times.

And then, unexpectedly, one afternoon, everything changed utterly.

Mary was laid up with an illness. At work she was supervisor of a department that assisted what in those days were called "unwed mothers." During her illness a small group of her workers came for a visit. They were all smart young women, none of whom I knew, as I worked in a different location in the city. One of them particularly caught my eye, as smart young women were wont to do. She was lovely, vivacious, and with something of the Gypsy about her, something "alternate," as we used to say. Unattached, entirely untutored in the arts of affection, I was instantly drawn to her.

Discreet inquiries were made. Sandy Lesyk was her name. We were the same age. She was the daughter of an English mother and a Ukrainian father. Born and raised on a farm near Edmonton. Graduate of Dalhousie University in Halifax. Master's degree in social work from the University of British Columbia. Unmarried. Living in a Kitsilano apartment not far from where I lived.

I began developing perfectly legitimate reasons for visiting the office where she worked. On one such occasion I found pinned to the staff bulletin board a letter Sandy had written from the Oregon shore, describing in exuberant detail the delights of a camping trip she was enjoying there with friends. If I had not been smitten already, which I was, I certainly would have been smitten by this glowing epistle from the great outdoors.

Decency prevents my detailing here the stratagems by which I insinuated myself into her awareness, or the various tentative steps, missteps, retreats, misunderstandings, rapprochements, and occasional triumphs of my clumsy courtship displays. Suffice it to say I worked my background material shamelessly, convincing her that I was both holy man and poet. Our mutual attraction quickly blossomed into tender romance, then passion. After an inconceivably protracted period of restraint (the strings of holy chastity proving not quite so easily untied as might be imagined) we at last made love. I was entirely besotted. With the soft, tender touch of her; the ways she moved and smiled and laughed; the scent of her; the essence of her. In her sweet embrace I was carried to a place I'd never been in my life before, to an exaltation of spirit that included, but surpassed, the most sublime of my spiritual flights of fancy.

We took to weekend camping trips almost straightaway, sometimes with friends from work or with Jim, who had returned to study in Seattle, along with his partner, Mary. Meanwhile my brother Ger had left monastic life the previous year and planned to marry in Ottawa in the summer. This seemed the perfect occasion for a cross-Canada camping trip, so off we went in my VW van, Sandy and I and the wolf-dog Yuma. We picked up my brother Brendan in the B.C. Interior, then headed eastward through the Rockies, across the Prairies, and into the endless woodland expanse of Northern Ontario. We pulled over for a break at some unknown point in the North. Sandy and I wandered off together through a wild meadow alight with blooming daisies and other wildflowers. In that hopelessly romantic setting, we talked of love and I ventured the question, "Do you think we should get married?" No decisions were made, but the wildflowers danced and rejoiced in the sunshine of the meadow that day.

When we finally arrived in Toronto, my mother was totally taken aback. My hirsute appearance and fashionably shabby clothes were bad enough, but "What's this girl doing here?" she whispered to me, pinched with consternation. How many times during my formative years had she warned against the subtle wiles of women, and now here I was gallivanting across the country with one—and her not even a Catholic! I dismissed her concern, too cavalierly I suppose, but by then I had well and truly separated myself from the creeping narrowness of that household. I still desired my parents' approval and affection, but their judgments about how things worked in the world now seemed quaintly ridiculous to me. As a child I'd been frightened of the Gypsies stealing me away, but the Church had stolen me away instead. Now here I was, in spirit more Gypsy than churchman. And Sandy soon charmed my old mum so completely that the moral delicacies of our situation were allowed to let lie.

My early visits to Sandy's parents in Victoria featured more tangible difficulties. For overnight stays I was assigned a small bedroom at the rear of the garage. I brought Yuma along one time and tethered him outside a door leading from my room to the back garden. Waking in the morning I saw to my horror that the dog had excavated an enormous crater in the flower bed where Sandy's mum grew her prized begonias, all of which were now uprooted and strewn about in the dirt. A formidable presence, and at least as magnificent a stoic as my own mum, Gladys barely mentioned the incident but the look on her face would have shattered glass. Another time, emerging from the shower, I was toweling myself so vigorously I dislodged from the bathroom wall two delicate ceramic planters from which grew long strands of miniature ivy. The whole works hit the floor with a crash, the planters shattering into numerous pieces. Sandy's dad, Bill, a thoughtful and generous man who'd retired early after selling his farm, came to my aid in these crises, but I was fully aware of the "bull in a china shop" references being made about me.

Sandy and I were married in the fall of 1970. We had a traditional Catholic wedding with the requisite contemporary touches. Sandy's long white peasant dress was adorned with dried leaves and she wore a traditional Ukrainian cap with trailing colored ribbons. I wore blue jeans and a leather vest with long, flowing fringes, perhaps an unconscious backward glance to my Davy Crockett days. Among our homemade pledges to one another, Sandy included the determination that we "grow old gracefully together," an ambition more lightly imagined in the youthful beauty of twenty-six than the sober judgment of sixty-four. We spent that night at a countrified motel south of the city where we made sweet love and laughed and laughed together. Then we drove down to the Oregon shore and camped on an expansive and deserted sand beach near Tillamook. We roughed together a little driftwood cabin on the beach and spent four or five days basking in late autumn sunshine and springtime young love. In the evenings we sat around a campfire, watching the stars and the long white combers breaking on the beach. When we finally, reluctantly packed up and climbed back over the sand dunes to where we'd left the van, a park ranger told us the beach we'd camped on was subject to rogue waves at that time of year and we were "darn lucky not to have been swept out to sea." I already knew we were darn lucky, or at least I was. Three short years before, Jim and I had been on our trail of failure through Oregon, and now here I was, freshly married to a lovely woman with all the world at our doorstep.

WE RENTED A tiny house on a large lot in Richmond, just south of Vancouver. The house was a squalid little affair, periodically visited by menacing Norwegian rats that thrived in the roadside ditches of the district. But we fixed the shack up as best we could and the following spring chopped away a section of heavy turf in the big backyard in order to grow a vegetable garden. The soil was rich black silt, part of the Fraser River delta, and our experimental vegetables burgeoned brilliantly. This new turn toward gardening was no whim, because from early on we'd set our hearts on getting out of the city and acquiring a piece of land of our own on which we'd grow our food and live in Arcadian bliss. I'm not sure where this shared impulse initially sprang from. Certainly there was a back-to-the-land movement afoot in those days, but we were not among its ardent disciples. We both found the social work we were doing interesting and rewarding as well as frequently discouraging, but whenever we'd go camping on a weekend, Sunday evening's return to the city and another week of work seemed increasingly insupportable. We hankered to spend more time in the wild places of nature and to simplify our lives. We wanted a change from rushing about, from commuting to work and back, from postponement of what our hearts desired.

Continuing with our social work jobs, we squirreled away every extra penny we could, and began spending weekends searching for the perfect piece of land on which to build our life together. We roamed up the Fraser Valley and the Sunshine Coast and over to Vancouver Island, exploring the possibilities of various clear-cuts, swamps, cliffs, and other inhospitable but afford-able spots. We placed advertisements in small-town newspapers, outlining the property we were looking for: minimum five acres, with a small cabin, fruit trees, and a creek, with an asking price in the $5,000 range. Unaccountably, nobody answered the ads. We became engaged with real estate agents, none more memorable

than an old duffer up the coast who proved to be an ardent prac-
titioner of "natural living," specializing in accommodating the
needs of young hippies with whom he could enjoy the delights of
communal nudism.

We were joined in this quest for land by our friends Bruce
and Daphne. Hailing from Québec, Bruce was another former
Passionist, though I'd barely known him back then. He showed
up in Vancouver and I got him a job at our transient youth unit,
because an increasing number of our kids were Québécois with
little or no English and Bruce was fluently bilingual. Daphne was
a lovely young Englishwoman visiting Vancouver. Eventually they
married in our Richmond backyard and decided to look for land
as well. We planned to either share one large property or buy two
adjacent lots.

We came upon Denman Island by chance, knowing nothing
about it, but we answered a newspaper advertisement of an acreage
for sale. A remarkable number of people who have settled on the
island over the years tell of first setting foot on the island and
knowing almost instantly that this was the place they wanted to call
home. That was certainly the case for us. The old farms and woodlands, rocky promontories and pebble beaches, the narrow roads
with almost no traffic, the abiding sense of peace and solitude—we
were altogether captivated. The advertised property we'd come to
inspect did not appeal, but the agent showed us another possibility:
two adjacent properties, eleven acres each, that would be coming
on the market shortly. Each had magnificent trees, and a small
creek threaded its way through the mossy woods. The lots fronted
on a small dirt road and were surrounded by dense woodlands.
Five minutes into the place, we all knew instinctively this was it.

If we were looking for land upon which to make a fresh start
today, I know we'd be far more rigorous in analyzing the advantages and disadvantages of any particular property. The quality of

soil, the patterning of sunlight, the availability of water, the zoning of the surrounding lands, and a host other factors would have to be carefully researched and considered. We didn't know back then, for example, that there was an air force base only a few miles away at which nuclear weapons were stored. We were blithely oblivious to the fact that no power lines came down the little road upon which we proposed to live. We didn't stop to consider that, being on the eastern side of a ridge, we'd lose the afternoon sun far earlier than one wants in springtime and autumn. No, the trees and the tranquillity of the place called to us, and their call was irresistible.

Each lot cost a grand total of $6,500—an outrageous amount by our reckoning, but we'd already saved more than that, and the deed was quickly done, paid up front in cash. That left a few thousand dollars of our hoarded savings with which to underwrite all that was to follow. Much to the consternation of colleagues, we announced that we would quit our jobs the following spring without having secured any prospect for employment on the island. We were considered something between foolhardy and mad, much as my parents had been in leaving the confined security of England. But monetary considerations seemed insignificant, bedazzled as we were by the chimera of self-sufficiency. We were young and healthy and blithesomely unconcerned with the finer points of finance. We would live close to the earth and close to the bone, considering ourselves wealthy in the freedom to do as we chose, beholden to none. With the bumptiousness of the young, we pitied our contemporaries enslaved by mortgages and career considerations. At that point in life we had little more than one another, our friends, and our precious bit of land, but we had no wish for more.

The vision we held at the time as to what we would do and how we would live was, in hindsight, a remarkable fusion of naive romanticism and instinctive genius. Much of it had to do with time, involving a personal reversal of history back to the perceived

simplicities and unities of the agrarian age. Like our distant forebears, we would devote the bulk of our time to provision of needs
as basic as food and shelter. We would cut out the middleman of
money and dispense with the expenses of sophisticated desires.
The arduousness of the heavy work that lay ahead didn't daunt
us, nor did our abandonment of a recognized profession and the
prestige that comes with it. We would no longer participate in a
culture that spends most of its time making preparations to live.
The work itself—the breaking of ground and planting of seeds,
the harvesting of healthy food, the raising of our own animals,
and the building of a home—would be its own reward. Success
and achievement would be registered on a scale unknown to the
financial pages. And, most alluring of all, we'd enjoy absolute
freedom to do what we wanted, when we wanted, and with whom
we wanted.

9

HOMESTEADING

I never had any other desire so strong, and so
like to covetousness, as that one which I have had always, that I
might be master at last of a small house and a large garden.
ABRAHAM COWLEY, *"The Garden"* (1666)

ON A BRIGHT APRIL MORNING in 1972 Sandy and I, having finally relinquished our jobs and packed up everything we owned, left Vancouver to begin life anew at our island home. My brother Brendan drove the cube van we'd rented to carry our stuff, though it was jammed less with personal possessions than with building materials—old windows and doors, used bricks and scraps of lumber we'd scrounged from a city busy tearing itself down in order to rebuild. We took the ferry from the Lower Mainland to Vancouver Island, then drove north for fifty miles past the woodlands, farms, and small towns along the big island's scenic eastern shore, and caught a tiny ferry to Denman. In fact, it wasn't even a real ferry, but rather an ancient tugboat with a barge lashed alongside by steel cables. The barge held six or seven vehicles, depending upon their size. To get aboard we drove down a concrete ramp on the beach, then carefully up twin narrow metal ramps onto the barge. The vessel was incapable of carrying motor homes, logging trucks, or stretch limousines, and the sheltered waters of Baynes Sound across which the little ferry shuttled seemed a sufficient moat to keep at bay the agents of progress that were busy cutting down and carving up the wild lands of the coast.

We were not journeying entirely into terra incognita because I'd spent two months of the previous summer working on our property. Brendan had come down to help, and Vincent had moved out from Toronto to lend a hand as well. Tom Verner, a friend from seminary days, and his partner, Laura Prince, had joined us, and miscellaneous others wandered in now and then. About two acres of the land had been logged shortly before we bought the place, so it wasn't as though we had to fell a lot of timber in order to fit in. But most of the felled trees, including one gigantic old-growth fir, hadn't even been hauled away. The clearing was a miasma of branches, logs, and stumps. We literally had to hack our way through the slash to be able to get off the road and onto the property. Thus I was introduced to the chainsaw, a roaring beast of terrifying energy. For weeks that summer we cut and chopped and burned in order to clear some ground. The loggers had left a scattering of spindly red alder trees standing forlornly in the slash. These were the first trees I ever felled, and in bringing them down, however amateurishly, I felt a tremendous exhilaration at what I had wrought. Suddenly I possessed an awesome power. But along with it came the thrill of terror when the tree would begin to topple menacingly and I'd dash away, chainsaw in hand, before the towering trunk could crash down on top of me.

We'd scarcely set to work on the clearing before an assortment of odd characters began dropping in. We'd assumed from the outset that the island community of about 250 residents was composed primarily of long-established families whom we'd gradually come to know at meetings of the Farmers' Institute and the

Women's Institute. But it turned out that there were also several dozen newcomers like ourselves who'd recently taken up residence. A few had homesteaded on government-owned Crown land parcels, some were living collectively on old farms, others in wee cabins in the woods, a few squatting along seldom-visited beaches. They, and we along with them, were a disreputable-looking bunch. Almost all us men were hirsute in the extreme, sporting bushy beards, with long flowing hair or Afros. Mostly sylphlike and lovely, the women inclined more to feathers and beads than to brassieres. Little kids ran around starkers.

Needless to say, a stir arose in the old community. Some of the grumbling old-timers were descendants of pioneers who'd homesteaded the island about a century before, displacing its aboriginal occupants in the process. Historically a number of Coast Salish groups, including the Pentlatch people, had occupied or seasonally visited the island, calling it Sla-dai-aich, "Inner Island." Besieged by white intruders, smallpox, and a changing world, the once-populous Pentlatch were harried into extinction. During its first century of white occupation the island had hummed with activity— logging of the enormous conifers, quarrying of sandstone, and small mixed farming. A smattering of retirees and others had drifted in after the Second World War, but prior to the arrival of us "new people" in the late sixties and early seventies the community had been slipping into torpor—the old farms and orchards that had once driven the island economy had largely fallen into disuse, many of the younger people who'd grown up on the island had left for other places with better opportunities, and the elementary school was on the brink of closure from lack of students. Then, suddenly, out of nowhere, the Age of Aquarius came wading ashore in all its barefoot, swaggering, draft-evading, dope-smoking glory.

Numbered among the invaders, during that first summer, we lived outdoors sitting at evening around a campfire, drinking cheap wine, smoking cigarettes and dope, and laughing with friends long into the night. Although we were working like mules all day trying to clear land almost by brute force alone, those nights around the campfire seemed a blessed disimprisonment after years of anxiety and discipline and crippling religious scruple. I couldn't quite believe that my life had now become what seemed like a lark, that we could live in a beautiful and essentially still-wild place, beholden to no one, accountable to no one but ourselves. I felt a giddy, almost unimaginable sense of emancipation. After a small patch of ground had been cleared of logging debris, we constructed a tiny shack using windfall logs. It was essentially an eight-foot-square bedroom with a summer kitchen attached, one side of which was entirely open to the elements. Though it squatted in the middle of a stump field strewn with logging slash, it might have been the Taj Mahal for the joy and pride we took in it. Then we returned to the city for another winter of work before the final exodus in spring.

Returning at last, we unloaded all our junk and Brendan departed with the cube van. We were here, ready to begin. Shortly after, Bruce and Daphne arrived to start work on their place, and Tom and Laura trekked out from New England to start building a house on the back end of our property. The six of us shared a vague, and largely unformulated, vision of creating an "intentional community" in which we would pool resources, share tools, and assist one another however we could. Before doing almost anything else, we cleared a patch of land for a vegetable garden, burning off logging slash, pulling out stumps using a hand-cranked come-along, and excavating scores of big boulders, some so large it would take hours of digging, prying, and levering to get the monsters lifted out of their holes and rolled away. Eventually we had a sizable patch of raw earth more or less cleared except for several old-growth stumps too formidable to be budged. We erected a temporary fence of upright posts split from cedar logs holding heavy fishnet to keep the deer out. A little greenhouse framed with poles and sheathed in plastic got us started with tray upon tray of vegetable seedlings.

With no other alternative, we continued to burn incessantly, firing huge heaps of stumps, branches, and slash. Sometimes we'd keep a fire burning for three or four days in order to scorch away a stubborn big stump. We'd often sit outdoors at night, under a cool starry sky, warmed by the radiant heat from an enormous heap of glowing embers, the remains of the burning day. My childhood fascination with fire could now wax to epic proportions and I could begin setting aside the figurative flames of lust, purgation, and damnation. Real fires had replaced metaphorical ones.

Sandy and I would lie abed in the morning, making love, listening to CBC Radio, and considering what work we might or might not accomplish that day. This was a somewhat more leisurely approach than what was called for, given the quite obvious requirement to complete a more weathertight building before winter set in.

THERE WAS NEVER a consideration that our vegetables and fruits would be anything but organic. Straightaway we went to a raised bed arrangement—I think it was formally referred to as the French Biodynamic System—with beds about four feet wide, running north and south, and narrow pathways between. To begin enriching the thin, stony soil we'd each take two five-gallon buckets on a footpath through the woods to a field where cattle grazed. We loaded our buckets with their fresh droppings and trundled them back to the compost heap. In a strictly legal sense this was larceny, but certainly pardonable under the extenuating circumstances. We drove to nearby beaches and loaded the pickup with buckets of seaweed that we dug into the soil or sometimes spread on the vegetable beds as mulch. We also brought home large sackfuls of starfish that had been removed from the beaches by local oyster growers. A starfish under each cabbage and tomato plant was the rule of thumb, but an insufferable stench arose if the starfish went unburied for too long. The compost heaps got a tremendous boost when we added animal husbandry to the undertaking. A flock of Rhode Island Red chickens, besides supplying eggs and an occasional rooster for the pot, contributed their nitrogen-rich droppings. So did several plump rabbits we kept in cages. Best of all, a pair of milking goats provided a constant supply of bedding straw rich with urine and feces.

For the first year or two I was fool enough to rent a rototiller from town with which I chopped up the whole vegetable garden, partly by way of digging in an overwintered cover crop of fall rye. I soon realized it was preferable to retain the raised beds where they were, so that all the compost and other soil amendments went into the permanent beds rather than onto pathways. Since then I've spaded the beds once or twice each year, removing any new stones that have grown and adding compost. But to begin with, the virgin forest soil was obviously rich in micronutrients while harboring none of the pathogens and pests that work their way into long-established gardens—clubroot, carrot rust fly, root maggot, gray mold, and all the rest. Nor at first were we plagued with any of the weeds—creeping buttercup, false dandelion, couch grass, and their cohorts—whose troublesome acquaintance we would later make.

Our principal challenge was watering. We were totally unprepared for how quickly and completely the island went dry in summer, especially in a clear-cut. After a few weeks of sunshine, the earth turned to a fine dust that coated every surface. Our little creek unexpectedly ran dry. Desperately we hauled barrels of water from a nearby pond while I hand-dug a succession of ultimately unproductive shallow wells. On one of these I installed a small pump attached to a bicycle, by which I planned to pump water uphill to the veggie patch. Although impeccably correct in principle long before its time, this scheme proved an abject failure. Eventually we had a backhoe excavate a deep hole in a low-lying area into which a slow but reliable pool of murky water seeped. From there we pumped it to the garden using a cantankerous gas-fired pump whose repeated malfunctions drove me close to madness. Such were our water woes that for several years I had recurring dreams of finding a splendid spring of fresh, clean water.

Oh, but the rewards were bountiful! Rows of robust spinach and lettuce. Enormous heads of broccoli and cauliflower, bulging cabbages, and even brussels sprouts and kohlrabi. Buckets of peas and beans. Brilliantly red beets and gleaming orange carrots. Sun-ripened tomatoes of a sensuousness in which there was no moderating the concupiscible appetite. The same with fresh strawberries and raspberries. Muscular sweet onions and sturdy parsnips, rutabagas, and potatoes for later on. This was a cornucopia beyond anything we'd imagined.

A vegetable patch on the island was not considered quite complete without a few *Cannabis sativa* plants discreetly tucked in. We grew our pot the old-fashioned way, from seed, and set them out so as not to be seen, especially from the air. Much heavy thinking went into whether they should be planted among the sweet corn or perhaps in the raspberry rows. It came to be taken as gospel that companion planting with Jerusalem artichokes was the preferred strategy, both because the plants were vaguely similar in size and appearance and because Jerusalem artichokes were reputed to foil the infrared cameras used by the cops to spot illicit crops from the air.

August on the island was like a scene from *Apocalypse Now* as an RCMP helicopter thundered over the treetops and came swooping across island gardens. Sometimes it would hover menacingly above a garden for a short time, then roar off someplace else. In the early days hardly anyone had a telephone, so advance notice of the cops' arrival would have to be brought by outriders speeding from place to place. As soon as the message was delivered you'd dash to the veggie patch, machete in hand, hack down your few plants—often they'd be six feet or more tall and quite bushy—and drag them under cover someplace. By the time the chopper roared onto the scene, all evidence was gone. Act II of this annual drama involved haughty public expressions of indignation and outrage at this unwarranted intrusion upon the privacy and dignity of upstanding citizens. Letters to editors fulminated against the trauma inflicted upon children, ponies, chickens, et al. by this militaristic invasion of our airspace. Why, we demanded to know, weren't scarce policing resources being deployed to track down and apprehend hardened criminals, rather than to harass peace-loving folk like ourselves. What did the venal politicians behind this idiocy have to say for themselves? Eventually the furor would subside, the cops would disappear for another year, and we'd be left in peace to puff our way through the dreary winter months ahead.

By today's standards our product was pretty harmless stuff, more leaf than bud, and more conducive to gentle meditation than to psychic blastoff, and for quite a few years, marijuana was a beneficial presence in my life. As much as anything it helped me find my way out of the labyrinth of guilt and self-accusation I'd lived in for far too long. It assisted in chipping away at hard places of righteousness and intolerance, creating more space for acceptance and joyfulness. *Lighten up!* it instructed me. Eventually the time arrived to bid the drug farewell. My body said, *Don't do this anymore*. It had served me well, but its time was done.

WITH SUMMER SLIPPING past, and the need for a winter-ready home becoming more urgent, we decided to build a small barn in which we would live temporarily until the dream home was completed. We mixed endless loads of cement for the footings and floor, sixteen by twenty feet. For structural members we used weathered posts we'd scavenged from nearby and long beams that I adzed from downed Douglas-fir logs on the property. Salvaged old barn boards made a stylishly funky exterior siding and we hand-split cedar shakes for the roof using a maul and froe—basically a large steel blade pounded down through a block of straight-grained cedar, then levered by its handle until each new shake pops off. But we paid a bitter price for having idled away so much of the summer, as heavy frosts and snow assailed us before the building was habitable.

Desperately cold, we took to heating bricks in the woodstove in our outdoor shack and placing the warm bricks in our freezing bed at night, a gorgeous comfort that soon caused our feet to erupt with painful chilblains, something I hadn't experienced since childhood when we kids would put our cold feet near the coal fire. The climax of this frigid ordeal came a few days before Christmas with the installation of a tall metal chimney. Sandy was inside the building struggling to hold up the wobbly column of pipe while I perched on the snow-covered roof fumbling with frozen hands, trying to secure the flashing and the Yukon chimney. Pressed to the brink of endurance like ill-equipped Arctic explorers, finally we got the wretched thing in place and were able to light a fire in the big airtight heater. Jubilation. Exultation. I don't know that it would have been possible to find anywhere on the planet a more self-satisfied, a more self-congratulatory pair of woodbutchers than we were at that moment. We snuggled by the blazing heater and gazed out through the warm glow of kerosene lamps upon a space as vast in its expansiveness as it was brilliant in its design.

The total cash outlay for this masterpiece was approximately $120. We lived for seven years in that simple structure, with rough kitchen cabinets, a wood cookstove, a dilapidated couch and armchair, and a sleeping loft at the far end accessible by a rough ladder of poles. With neither electricity nor running water, and certainly no television, telephone, or tele-anything, life was stripped down to essential elements. Finally losing patience with a cantankerous propane refrigerator, we took to storing milk, butter, and other perishables in the cool depths of a well I'd hand-dug nearby. An occasional bathing took place in a galvanized tub, placed indoors near the heater in winter, out in full sunshine in the summer, the water heated by fire or sunshine. A scattering of daffodils, planted before we even had a proper roof over our heads, bloomed jauntily among the stumps and slash in spring, followed by plantings of cosmos, snapdragons, and sunflowers.

Those were seven precious years of brilliant simplicity, and in hindsight I wouldn't trade them for any imaginable luxury. As Thoreau said in *Walden* of his hand-built cabin: "My dwelling is small, and I can hardly entertain an echo in it; but it seemed larger for being a single apartment and remote from neighbors. All the attractions of a house were concentrated in one room; it was kitchen, chamber, parlor, and keeping-room; and whatever satisfaction parent or child, master or servant, derive from living in a house, I enjoyed it all." And so did we.

Without electricity to run a freezer, setting food aside for winter entailed a lot of canning and drying, and many a blazing hot summer afternoon was made even hotter with a large canner simmering on the woodstove. Luckily, the benign coastal climate allows for many root crops to be left in the ground all winter. From the beaches we'd pick oysters, dig for clams, and (briefly) gather edible seaweed. As the long, wet winters dragged on and the jars of homemade tomato sauce and canned peas ran low, we were reduced to dinner after dinner of what we called "poor persons"— a large pot of boiled potatoes, rutabagas, and apples. A bit of grated cheese melted on top would be an occasional luxury. The current vogue for regional cuisine seems like transnational self-indulgence by comparison.

Had we been vegan or pure vegetarian at that point, things might have gotten quite grim, but our little band of animals helped stave off complete deprivation. The chickens began laying in early spring, and their fresh eggs were a godsend. "Free range" would have been too confining a term for these birds—they had a large fenced yard for roaming around, but its fishnet enclosure was only about eight feet high, and various of them would regularly sail over the top and away, in plain defiance of my attempts to clip their wings. Some would roost high in the cedar trees. Some would break into the vegetable garden and make a ruin of the seedlings. Some would lay their eggs in distant and obscure places, disappear, and eventually emerge with a brood of tiny chicks in tow.

The ducks and geese we didn't attempt to contain. They'd spend part of their time down on the creek that runs through our place, part of it pecking at the glass door in our cabin, begging for grains, and much of it waddling up and down the pathways defecating freely. Ducks were especially valued for eating slugs, of which we had an abundance. But the ducks developed a disturbing habit of gobbling slugs and then drinking water, which caused the slug mucus on their bills to form long beards of slimy slobber. A dozen or more of them pecking with slimy bills at the front door could put you right off your breakfast.

The goats had minds of their own as well. We never kept a billy, but even the does occasionally had to be wrestled to the ground and spoken to firmly so that they understood who exactly was in charge. For the first year or two we housed them in a little shed with a very small fenced yard. In winter I'd clip big baskets of salal, a native broadleaf evergreen shrub that's plentiful in woodlands, to augment their diet of alfalfa and grains. In summer we'd tether them out, but this was never satisfactory, as goats are not creatures with a temperament for tethering, and entanglements were commonplace. One tragic day, a young female we'd raised from birth was tethered slightly too close to a split-rail fence, and against all odds, she leaped over the fence and strangled to death hanging by her tether from the topmost rail. Spurred on by this tragedy, we got a proper little goat barn built and a fenced field in which they were free to roam and nibble, which is the goat way of doing things.

Breeding season was always a challenge. There was no billy on the island in those days, as the keeping of a billy requires a particular and rare sensibility, along with an impaired sense of smell and no nearby neighbors. At the right season we'd have to keep close watch for signs that a doe was coming into heat, something not as readily discernible in a doe as in an alley cat, often involving subtle tail flicking and uncharacteristic vocalizing. Once conditions seemed right, arrangements would be made with a breeder on Vancouver Island. We'd load the doe into the back of the pickup, never without a struggle, catch the ferry, and then drive to whatever nearby farm had a willing billy. Billies are always willing. We'd unload our poor little doe, she quivering with anxiety over the trauma of the truck ride and the arrival at this strange place, and then watch as a great snorting, smelly beast of a billy, all bobbling scrotum and bloodshot penis, went after her with a savage and slobbering lust. Here was the embodiment of the disgusting sexuality that Holy Mother Church had inveighed against, a revolting incarnation of the impure thoughts I'd had to confess. Here was why the Devil appeared with the cloven feet of a goat. The mounting would be fierce and brief and the billy quickly dragged back to his dungeon. As often as not, the terrified doe would abandon her heat at the sight of the monstrous billy and refuse to allow him to mount her, meaning either we'd have to leave her there or repeat the whole expedition once she was really ready.

The birthings, however, were events of great beauty and gladness. As her time drew near the doe would bulge to a rotund barrel with a swollen udder and a faraway look in her strange eyes. On the day itself she'd take to restless circling and pawing at the ground with a front hoof. We'd sit quietly by, not wanting to intrude, hoping fervently that she'd need no intervention, no reaching inside of her to disentangle an umbilical cord or turn a baby twisted the wrong way. Finally a tiny nose, then a face of glistening pink would appear. The doe would strain and circle, with the newborn hanging half inside her and half out. Then, just as the straining mother seemed to be losing strength, the baby would slide smoothly out and onto the bedding straw. We'd move quickly to wipe clear its nose and mouth so that it could breathe freely, and sever the umbilical cord. The mum would lick and nuzzle the little creature, sometimes while its twin was in the process of being born. We'd right away check to see if we'd been blessed with a baby doe or saddled with a billy.

Then the mother's milk flowed freely. Generally Sandy did the milking, but I pitched in on occasion. It was an exquisite experience to sit alongside the doe on her milking stand, leaning one's head against her ruminating rib cage while squeezing fresh warm milk from her bulging udder. The milk was a mainstay of our diet. We drank it fresh, and Sandy made wonderful cheese, yogurt, and butter from it, the kind of delicacies now much in demand in upscale shops. Besides these benefices, the goats were marvelous companions, both shrewd and affectionate, and time spent in their company—whether milking by lamplight on a bleak winter's night or sitting in the straw with them, awaiting a birth—had a quality of ancestral earthiness not easily duplicated.

Dealing with the young goats, especially the billies, was a challenge. They grew at an astonishing rate, rapidly mutating from adorably cute little long-legged beauties into bounding cannonballs of mischievous energy. Once a billy had achieved a certain size, it fell to me to kill and butcher it. I'd borrow a rifle for the execution, inexpertly attempting to put a single bullet through its brain. I'd suspend the carcass from a beam in the woodshed to disembowel it, strip it of its hide, and butcher it. The tough and stringy cuts of meat we softened in stews; choice pieces we roasted on skewers at the campfire, along with cubes of eggplant, onions, and cherry tomatoes. But after about a dozen years, killing the billies became something I no longer wanted to do. I balked at having to kill young roosters too, and the ducklings and goslings produced each year. Even with all its pleasures and rewards, the charm of animal husbandry began to fade. Around the same time I also gave up fishing, repulsed by the cruelty of the barbed hook, the fish with gaping mouth and bulging eyes fighting hopelessly against the pull of the line. Our big dog, Yuma, had stoutly guarded the barnyard for years, but following his death, mink began stealing in furtively at night from the nearby beaver pond. They slaughtered all our chickens. Twice. Bald eagles and ravens swooped in to snatch defenseless ducklings. Our little barnyard had become a killing field, and the time arrived for us to be done with the raising, killing, and eating of animals.

COMMUNITY LIFE THROUGHOUT this time was a peculiar mélange of strife and solidarity. Established island families could hardly help but have a sense of their familiar and comfortable enclave being overrun by brash intruders, just as their forebears had pushed the Pentlatch and other native groups off their ancestral lands a century earlier. A bitter divisiveness set in. The traditional Thanksgiving community dinner was permanently canceled once "the hippies" began attending. Fierce battles were fought over who would control the community hall and what activities would be permitted in it. Police were called in over unfounded accusations of theft. Nude swimming at Chickadee Lake became the flashpoint cause célèbre dividing the shameless new libertines from the righteous old-timers.

But the influx of "new people" continued unabated throughout the seventies. We were an eclectic bunch of dreamers and geniuses, charlatans and fools. We boasted more university degrees per capita than almost anywhere else in the country. Separations and romantic realignments occurred with dizzying frequency. More and more babies were born and birthdays celebrated. Work bees and housewarmings were regular occurrences and house parties were pandemic. Local musicians and poets and a theater troupe kept us entertained. The old community hall regularly hosted dances that were tribal celebrations at which you could fling yourself around in whatever combinations of number or gender struck your fancy. Groups of islanders, kids and all, would annually head off to fairs and music festivals, camping out with hordes of like-minded folks from other islands. Although people came and went from the island, there remained a core young community putting down roots and forging connections that would hold us in place for decades.

Throughout our early days on Denman, on Sunday afternoons in the summer many of us would gather at the community hall ball field for a softball game. These were leisurely affairs involving players of various ages, both male and female, and a goodly roster of bleacher bums seldom lacking for a pithy observation on the quality of play. The games provided one of the few venues in which old-family islanders and newcomers mixed freely. There was a quality of Norman Rockwell good-heartedness and rustic simplicity about the gatherings. Over time the better male players formed a team talented enough to compete with other teams from around the region, as the women also did a bit later. Although still good-natured, these games were considerably more intense, and I found that my old Vince Lombardi combativeness had not so much died away as lain in dormancy.

I was toiling as pitcher for the fastball team one fateful afternoon, locked in a tight game with a team from Vancouver Island. Late in the game, with the score still close, I banged a solid double into the outfield. The next batter flied out to the left fielder, and after the catch I tagged up at second and took off like hell on horseback for third, sliding awkwardly into the bag. There was a horrendous snapping sound, and frightful pain exploded in my foot and leg. I'd snapped my fibula in half and shattered my tibia with seventeen spiral fractures. That reckless foolhardiness put a definitive end to my playing days. The surgeon in attendance recommended that I have my ankle fused to control the pain, but I balked at the prospect of gimping along for the remainder of my days like Chester in the old *Gunsmoke* series. Thirty years later, my ankle still hurts after a heavy day's work or too long a hike. It renders me less mobile than I wish to be, and running is impossible.

War wounds notwithstanding, I look back fondly on those Sunday-afternoon softball games at the community hall ballpark. They were one in spirit with the summer evening games that had so excited me as a little Scouser freshly arrived in Weston back in the mid-fifties, and with the games we earnest young novices played with the denizens of Billy Buck Hill in Pittsburgh.

Christmas on the island had a hefty nostalgia content back in those days too. The elementary school Christmas concert was, as it still is, a highlight. The year 1975 had not been a happy one in the life of the community. The toxic antagonism between rednecks and hippies culminated in a bitter squabble over whether a preschool should be allowed to operate in the community hall. Appalled by the divisiveness, a gentle and much-loved islander named Dora Drinkwater decided that she and the little congregation of Saint Saviour's Anglican Church should help foster reconciliation. She came up with the idea of a Christmas Eve carol service at the church and recruited me as the closest thing we had to a clergyman. The church registry records that fifty-eight islanders wound their way through the dark that Christmas Eve to the impossibly picturesque little white wooden church at the top of the ferry hill. Inside they found a woodstove crackling against the cold of the candlelit church. A pungent smell arose from fresh-cut cedar boughs. Like the church itself, the service was clean and simple and somehow strangely moving—readings from the Scriptures and from poems, and robust singing of carols accompanied by the wheezing of an emphysemic old pedal organ. At the end, we clasped one another, wished many a hearty Merry Christmas, and slipped away into the darkness of the night, touched with light and gladness. The event became an instant tradition, one in which the imagery was real in a way that the plastic fakery of a credit card Christmas can never be. The darkness outdoors, the hushed expectancy of the children, the nip of cold in the air, the scent of cedar, polished wood, and candle wax, the exuberance of the carolers, the simplicity of the Nativity readings, the sense of fellowship freely shared—these were sweet sensations, harking back to memories of childhood, to visions of simpler and holier times.

THE WRITTEN WORD was scarcely part of our first year or two of life on the homestead. I seldom opened a book, other than manuals on carpentry or gardening, and wrote almost nothing. The immediacy of nature and brute physical labor and of a loving companion engulfed my consciousness. I had been sitting for too long, pondering too long, lost to my physical self. The swinging of an ax, the spading of earth represented glorious emancipation from the stenography of religious scruple. The old icons, the faithful metaphors, were well and truly smashed and only after some time did I begin to unearth their replacement.

The ragged coastline of British Columbia, its ancient forests and rocky headlands, the surge of surf, and the wild creatures that still roamed here became as central to my consciousness as the crucified Christ had formerly been. Gradually, now and then, something like a poem would come to me. Seeing a photograph of our group in the early bushwhacking days, I reflected on a similar "photograph of five boys" taken a decade earlier at Holy Cross Seminary, showing four of my classmates and myself. I pictured us as "young ruffians in the smoking holiness of youth" and pondered:

in that static windless second
no way of knowing
how the separate intervals
of each would lurch
and tumble towards today's
ironic reconstruction of the pose
why each one lashed
towards the camera's narrow angle
would break lose
like rogue logs
from the floating boom
to heave upon a separate
wayward course
upon what rugged coastline
where the bristling pines
shove down a wall of rocks
each would find a cove
or niche within the tumbled cliffs
in which to ram
his frenzied drift of days . . .

I had found a niche among the woodlands of the island. The potential for disillusionment, even disaster, inherent in the whole homesteading and house-building scheme never quite dawned on us. Wielding a big chainsaw in dense bush without previous experience, igniting huge bonfires, hand-digging a well deep into the earth—any one of these might have brought a sudden and bloody end to the enterprise. So might ill health or relationship instability. One or the other of us might have lost interest, begun hankering for city lights or other excitements. As it was, good fortune kept us company and all was well. The early toils of homesteading, unpaid and sometimes counterproductive as they may have been, were entirely engaging. We flung ourselves wholeheartedly into the tasks at hand. Sure, there were dirty days, frustrating times, curses, tears, and breakdowns. Every once in a while, when the work had been too damned hard for too damned long, we'd flee to some seedy motel where we'd lie in bed eating rubbish food and watching inane television shows, united in spirit with weary workers everywhere forced to compensate for time spent at monotonous and unrewarding work. But those were minor aberrations, infrequent and short-lived. Rejuvenated by the unlikely curative properties of munching fried chicken and french fries while watching *Happy Days*, we charged back to the worksite and began anew. Most of the time, life and work were one. What we were doing was inseparable from who we were. I had, in some way, at last come home.

10

HOUSE BUILDING

Shall we forever resign the pleasure
of construction to the carpenter? What does architecture
amount to in the experience of the mass of men?
I never in all my walks came across a man engaged in so simple
and natural an occupation as building his house.

H.D. THOREAU, *Walden*

THERE STILL REMAINED "THE HOUSE" to be built, but the relative comfort of what we called "the barn" was such that we felt no compulsion to get a house completed quickly. This was all to the good, as circumstances kept unexpectedly changing, and our house plans along with them.

There was nothing in my curriculum vitae, nor in Sandy's either, to suggest that we were in any way positioned to tackle the design and building of a house. My formal education, rich though it may have been in Latin and moral theology, offered scarcely a sliver of practical skill. I never attended a class in shop, in which to learn how an internal combustion engine functions or what one should do with a lathe. Once, in grade 8, we boy students had a short course in manual skills, during which I painstakingly hand-sawed bits of plywood into ornate shapes and glued them together to form a small hanging shelf thingy of which, once it was varnished, I was briefly, but inordinately, proud. On another occasion, back in Weston, I undertook the fashioning of a wooden lawn chair for my mother, but it was a rickety disaster, and when my mum made a sarcastic comment on its inadequacy, I flew into a violent rage and smashed the thing to pieces. This wasn't exactly the depth of preparation my old mentor Thoreau had in mind when he wrote in *Walden*: "However, if one designs to construct a dwelling-house, it behooves him to exercise a little Yankee shrewdness, lest after all he finds himself in a workhouse, a labyrinth without a clue, a museum, an almshouse, a prison, or a splendid mausoleum instead."

Nevertheless, it didn't occur to Sandy and me that, possessing neither expertise nor capital, it might be slightly beyond our reach to construct from nothing an attractive and comfortable dwelling. Prudence played no part here. Wisdom, which consists of comprehending what one does not know as thoroughly as what one does, was jostled aside by youthful enthusiasm and a loose affiliation with the do-it-yourself credo rife in *Mother Earth News*, the *Whole Earth Catalog*, and other necessary texts of the time. As Art Boericke put it in his 1973 classic, *Handmade Houses: A Guide to the Woodbutcher's Art*, "For, no mistaking it, building their own place had become the four-square gospel for scores of young rambunctious dudes."

Never exactly a young rambunctious dude myself, I sought to compensate for lack of practical training by becoming a devotee of Bradford Angier, an eccentric New Englander and fellow admirer of Thoreau who abandoned a career in advertising to go live in the wilderness of northern British Columbia with his wife, Vena. Ensconced in their log cabin, he churned out an astonishing plethora of books on wilderness living, with titles like *At Home in the Woods*, *Living off the Country*, and *Wilderness Neighbors*. While still living in Richmond and preparing for our own great exodus to the outback, we'd acquired a copy of Angier's *How to Build Your Home in the Woods* and studied it for the principles and procedures that would guide the building of our dream home. From the very get-go it was understood that we would, as advised, build a log house. There were, after all, hundreds of prime conifers on our property, and what could be simpler, sturdier, or more economical than using them for the house? I stress the term *house*, as the log building we envisaged was not to be some squalid little cabin no better than the rat-infested shack we were renting while these grand plans were being drawn. In the large backyard at Richmond we staked out with pegs and string an enormous floor plan encompassing three interconnected log structures, each twenty by thirty feet. Merely having the string pegged out like that had seemed to make the house already almost real.

During our early days on the island we spent a lot of time and energy stockpiling logs with which to build this mansion. Following Angier's advice, I meticulously selected tall, straight-stemmed conifers of appropriate size, about ten inches in diameter. I felled the trees, trimmed off the branches and cut the poles to length. Shortly after felling, each pole had to be debarked using a simple bladed tool called a drawknife. Astride the log, you'd draw the blade toward you with both hands, thereby peeling off the bark, just as you'd peel an apple. We then carried out the peeled logs and stacked them on racks to dry. We'd amassed a considerable pile of logs prepared in this way when a visiting old-timer asked, "What you planning to do with them logs?"

"Build a house," I said buoyantly.

"Nah, no good for that," he said. "They're hemlocks, most of them, rot out in a season." Oh. I laid blame for this miscalculation squarely on Bradford Angier and promptly abandoned both him and his crackbrained predilection for building with logs.

Undaunted, we acquired a copy of Ken Kern's *The Owner-Built Home* and promptly transferred our allegiance to him. Hailed as a grandfather of self-reliant building and living, Kern began back in the 1940s gathering information about inexpensive, natural, and simple building technologies. We were mesmerized by his critique of contemporary homes as badly sited, poorly built, unattractive to look at, and uncomfortable to live in. All the things you think but think you shouldn't think. He blamed conventional notions of style and oppressive building codes for the mediocrity of tract housing. Somewhat belatedly, we ascertained that there was no building code in force on our island—we were free to be as whimsical in our building as we wished.

A second twist of fate involved our friends Bruce and Daphne. By this time, Tom and Laura had left the island and returned to the eastern United States. Reduced from six to four, we needed a new plan. Rife as the times were with enthusiasm for communes and collectives, we had decided that, rather than building two homes, we'd jointly construct a large common area with two separate wings for private spaces. Site preparation and building commenced with this plan in mind. We chose a flat area covered in a stand of mature alder trees, maybe eighty feet high with trunks about two feet in diameter. The big sword ferns growing as ground cover were dug by hand and dragged into the woods, where we replanted them. But the standing alders posed a problem. We could easily fell the trees, but how to get rid of the stumps? Someone suggested blowing them out with dynamite, and this had an appealing ring to it. Off Bruce and I went to a little backwoods shack on Vancouver Island where an old codger kept a magazine stocked with enough explosives to give Homeland Security types a panic attack. We loaded the truck up with several sacks of explosive fertilizer, a box of dynamite sticks, and sufficient detonating caps and fuses. The old guy showed us how to crimp a cap onto the fuse and insert it into a dynamite stick. It seemed as simple as steeping a cup of tea. Driving home, we suffered mounting anxiety that if our vehicle were to hit a bad bump our explosive load could blow us halfway back to Vancouver. I don't think we bothered with the formality of mentioning to the ferry crew that we were transporting dangerous cargo. Back on site we set to work blowing out the trees, having cleverly calculated that if we dynamited the roots while the tree remained standing, its falling weight would lever out the entire root mass. Which was exactly what happened—there'd be a grand boom that would shake the earth and send the tree jumping into the air and then crashing to the ground, extracted roots and all. At least that's what happened when the charge actually detonated. Ignition failure required a furtive tiptoeing back to the tree and whipping out the malfunctioning fuse. How we managed not to kill or maim ourselves in this madness I still don't know.

As fuzzy-headed as the design phase may have been, we were rock solid in the matter of building materials. Along with several friends, we lucked into a salvage job involving the tearing down and removal of an old shingle mill on Vancouver Island. The building was an enormous skeleton, really, but what a skeleton! The frame was made of large-dimension old-growth Douglas-fir beams lag-bolted together. The long rafters were true two-by-tens of the same material, and so was the three-by-ten plank flooring. The four of us pulled and pried and hacked at that old place for weeks and came home with truckloads of prime lumber—far superior to most anything you'd see in a lumberyard today—that would form the backbone of the house.

Bruce and Daphne wanted their part of the building to be an octagon, and that's what we started building, but before we'd gotten very far our friends' situation changed and they decided to leave the island. At that point we had in place the footings, floor joists, and subfloor for an octagon twenty-four feet in diameter.

Rather than tear it out and start over with a new plan, Sandy and I decided to proceed with the octagon and add a wing to one side of it. Just how the wing would be attached we'd figure out as we went along. You might call it a "wing and a prayer" approach to house design, but never mind, it was all incontestably organic in its unfolding.

A hand-hewn house in its purest form is fashioned with hand tools; this was an orthodoxy to which we could relate, as we had no electricity on site. The chainsaw was indispensable for dealing with logs and big timbers, and we did eventually bow to the necessity of buying a small generator to operate a Skilsaw, angle grinder, drill, and belt sander, but a large part of the work was accomplished with handsaw, hammer, plane, and adze.

Wherever possible we were determined to use local, hand-hewn, or recycled materials. In hindsight one could pretend that this approach was a conscientious attempt to minimize our footprint on the planet, but in reality penury was the principal motivation. Having enjoyed relative success with the post-and-beam style in the barn, we were encouraged to go the same route with the house, my theory being that if you construct it with hefty enough pieces, it's less apt to fall down. Our woodlands provided tons of stuff—again all the cedar shakes for roofing we split from old-growth cedar logs lying on the forest floor. We acquired an Alaska sawmill, a problematic device that bolted onto the blade of an enormous chainsaw and guided the horizontal saw down the length of a log. This arduous, noisy, backbreaking work provided all the one-by-twelve cedar boards for siding the house as well as gorgeous two-inch-thick slabs for countertops and shelving. The half-dozen long beams needed to span the octagon ceiling I cut from stout Douglas-fir trees, squaring them using an adze.

Salvage gave us our doors and windows. In those days people were tearing out wooden-framed single-pane windows and replacing them with double glazing. The old windows hadn't yet acquired the patina of "antique" they enjoy today and were often free for the taking. As was a great stack of oak flooring that we frantically tore from an apartment building in Victoria scheduled for imminent demolition. Sandy and I worked all night levering up the flooring with pry bars and hauling it out to our truck parked beside bulldozers that sat menacingly in the dark, awaiting the morning's demolition. In one exhausting night's work we got enough tongue-and-groove oak to floor a good portion of the house. For foundation posts we secured pieces of fir logs, pressure-treated with creosote, that were discarded on the beach after construction of a new ferry wharf. The horrors of creosote were unknown to us then, though the blisters we got on any exposed skin that touched these brutes should have given a hint.

Our methodology became to amass as much material as could be had for little or no money and then ponder what configuration the stuff might lend itself to. During this process two design principles arose, one practical, the other aesthetic. On a practical level, and most critical from my perspective, was the need to have no roof so high that I would be reluctant to climb it. I am not a heights person and the prospect of regularly scaling a high and steep roof in order to clean the chimney held no appeal at all. A second, more conceptual, consideration was that the building's overall configuration should be in the service of whimsy rather than common sense. The barn, during whose construction we had honed our skills, was a box, and an efficient box at that. For the house we would tolerate nothing remotely boxlike. Already committed to the awkward octagon, we elected to incorporate as many peculiar additional angles as possible. The roof would have multiple peaks, and dormers would poke out wherever permitted. Who cared if each new gangly angle increased the complexity and slowed the progress of construction? This wasn't just a building we were about, this was a *statement,* a bold cry of defiance against the tyranny of architectural conformity. This little house was *us!*

WE WERE BUSY at work on construction one sunny afternoon when Danny Lucas, new co-owner of the general store, unexpectedly showed up. A man of few words, Danny mumbled to me that he'd just gotten a phone call. "Your mum's in a bad way," he said. I dropped everything and called home from the pay phone at the ferry landing. My dad told me that my mum had been hospitalized and was not expected to live much longer. I caught the first available flight to Toronto and met up with my dad and brothers at the little house in the Rexdale neighborhood to which my parents had moved a few years earlier. My mum had been ailing for quite some time but, typically, refusing to let anyone be told of her condition, not wanting to be "a bother." She'd never had any use for doctors or hospitals and had adamantly refused to seek medical help. Eventually suffering unbearable pain, she'd been taken by ambulance to the hospital where she'd slipped into a coma. I went to visit her, alone, as soon as I could. I found her lying in a hospital bed, unconscious, restless, and moaning. I couldn't tell if she was suffering physical pain or mental torment, or both, or neither. I sat with her for several hours, holding her hand and attempting to convey my love to her. I was strangely composed in this, largely, I think, because Sandy and I had just days before completed a two-week silent retreat in Vipassana meditation, an exercise focused upon healing human suffering through enhanced self-awareness and transformation. I could not have been better prepared for the dreadful experience of watching my mother dying slowly and painfully. She passed away that night, and I was grateful that I'd had the chance to see her at least, to be with her, although I greatly regretted that I hadn't been able to say thank you and goodbye while she was still conscious. Perhaps she had been subliminally aware of the love I was communicating to her, perhaps not.

"Well, there'll never be another like her," my dad said later, and that was certainly true. She was a most peculiar character. I have no memory of her ever telling me "I love you," and yet I was entirely certain of her love. During that dreadful grade 9 year I'd spent at Michael Power High, when I arrived home from a long day at school, she'd be waiting with a pot of tea and a plate of cakes. We'd sit and chat, and I imagine in hindsight that she was providing what comfort she could, knowing how miserable I was. We were not a family given to hugging, but in her later years I made a point of embracing her with a big, warm hug whenever I saw her, which wasn't often. She gave no indication whether she liked, or merely tolerated, this breach of emotional protocol, but after her death my dad told me that she'd loved how fondly I'd hugged her.

I remember one time she and I were batting a shuttlecock back and forth on our driveway in Weston; I was probably ten or eleven. The shuttlecock got caught in the twigs of a tree, out of reach. I picked up some pebbles and threw them, one at a time, hoping to hit the shuttlecock and dislodge it. As this was going on, a car sped down the road, then screeched to a halt just past our place. The enraged driver leaped from the car and ran toward us shouting that I'd deliberately thrown a stone at his son in the car. Seeing him bearing down on us, I fled to the backyard, but my mother remained standing where she was. Towering over her the fellow roared incoherently, but she stood there calmly, small but unmoved, and kept gently but firmly repeating that I'd had no intention of throwing the pebble at his car. When the man had left, I slunk back out. My mother, apparently not the least bit perturbed, said to me, "Never run away."

It was because of her that there was always an abundance of books in our childhood home, and that each of us kids grew up with a love of reading.

She had very little patience for self-pity; "moaning Minnies" was what she called people who complained about their circumstances. Of course she was one herself, in an understated way;

she didn't at all mind insinuating that life had, by and large, been a disappointment to her. Although she'd written from England to my dad that "we'll lose no time in getting out of this place," she never really did adapt to life in Canada. She made no real friends and became increasingly reclusive over the years. Her grandchildren, Ger's first two children, Christine and Greg, were among the few delights of her declining years. It's ironic that I was in the midst of house building at the time of her passing, because she'd occasionally mentioned to me how much she regretted that she'd never had "a proper house" of her own, their final home in Rexdale being a magnificent garden on a large lot with a poky little shack in the middle. One of her favorite pastimes had been to take a Sunday drive with my dad to look at new houses being constructed in the district. Once, when I'd showed her some rough sketches of the house we planned to build, she looked at them in her deadpan way and said, "Not my idea of a house."

I RETURNED FROM Toronto with the radically altered perspectives that are among the gifts of death. I was relieved that my mum's suffering was at an end, and happy to have the absorptions of gardening and house building with which to occupy myself.

In hindsight, a functional box might indeed have been a wiser choice than our romantic cottage with its dormers and gables. Certainly straight walls and rooflines more readily accommodate subsequent additions. A single long wall on the south side would have offered better opportunity for a glass house to be incorporated into the main structure, just as an extensive south-facing roof would have been preferable for holding solar panels and for rainwater catchment, neither of which was in our minds back then. A sod roof, such as the one we later installed on our woodshed, I now see as highly desirable for aesthetic and heat retention reasons.

Still, we weren't entirely impractical in our design. Three large, south-facing windows in the octagon—which became an open-space kitchen/dining/living room—proved quite efficient at admitting winter sunshine while largely excluding the high sun of summer. The centrally located wood heater sits on a floor of flat sandstone that acts as a heat sink, as does the freestanding brick chimney, a thing of beauty and efficiency that Sandy constructed single-handed from piles of old bricks picked up for free in the city. The heater encloses a water coil that leads to a nearby copper tank that in turn feeds the preheated water into an electric hot water tank. The tanks are located midway between, and close to, both the kitchen and the bathroom, so far less energy is wasted from having heated water turning cool through a long run of pipe. And the heater's close beside the back door, so firewood doesn't have to be trundled through the house, dropping bits of bark and adventitious spiders en route. A covered walkway connects the back porch to the woodshed and to the compost privy, so we don't have to really brave the elements when visiting either. On the north side of the building a pantry, set off from the kitchen and containing a large freezer as well as food storage shelves, is insulated from the rest of the house, with a small window to the outdoors, and so remains cool throughout the year. All in all, we ended up with a peculiar combination of impractical whimsy and intelligent design.

Remaining true to the spirit of Thoreau, we kept the total construction cost to about $4,500. The only paid labor was an electrician who put in the wiring. A boomlet of young owner-builders on the island offered the great advantage that we each lent a hand with other people's projects. Tools were shared around, resources pooled. At our place we had work bees for raising the big timbers and for shaking the roof. Our new neighbor Kel pitched in to fashion the kitchen counters and cabinets. Another friend, Robbie, did all the plumbing. Our handy brother-in-law, Richard, cut and installed glass for odd-shaped windows. An island drywaller volunteered to do the plastering because he wanted to experiment with the techniques of applying authentic lime-putty plaster.

In return I did some stonework for him. All this help from the community, and more, compounded the affection we felt for the finished product and culminated in a series of rip-roaring house-warming parties.

NOTWITHSTANDING THE SHORTSIGHTEDNESS and haphazard that attended our siting and design considerations, we somehow ended up in an appropriate spot and facing in the correct direction. The house nestles in a little valley through which the seasonal creek chatters and splashes merrily in the winter months. The hillside rising to our west both removes us from the road, about eighty yards away, and provides us with the perfect site for a terraced garden. The design principles we unearthed while constructing the house (sometimes only after the fact) proved invaluable in the subsequent design of the garden and in understanding the relationship of each to the other. From the outset it was important to us to have the buildings blend into the woodlands and gardens of which they are a part. Having so much of the house fashioned from the bones of the forest helps immensely in this effort. Composed largely of local materials and possessing a scale that acknowledges nature as the primary player here, our little house, I like to think, embodies an awareness that the higher role of humans is not to flaunt the dominance of ego, as manifest in "monster homes," but rather to fit into nature's schemes as unobtrusively as possible.

In this regard we were somewhat at odds with the great Carl Jung, who likened his own experience of building a stone tower retreat at Lake Zurich to making "a confession of faith in stone." Writing in *Memories, Dreams, Reflections*, he tells how he set out to build not a standard house but a primitive one-story dwelling in the spirit of a single-room African hut. But following the propensity for midcourse improvisation that characterizes many owner-builders, he came to see that two stories were required for "a suitable dwelling tower." Several years later, again like many an owner-builder, he added an annex. Within a few more years he'd appended a second tower to serve as a place of solitude and meditation. Still not finished, in the fullness of time he recognized that the little annex connecting the two towers not only was too low and crouching, but also was a representation of himself. Straightaway, he wrote, he added an upper story that "represents myself as my ego-personality. Earlier I would not have been able to do this; I would have regarded it as presumptuous self-emphasis. Now it signified an extension of consciousness achieved in old age. With that the building was complete."

But here's an astonishing footnote, psychologically speaking. Not long ago I unearthed from a storage trunk a set of long-forgotten sketches of our house I'd made while we were still in the planning stage, an improvement on those I'd shown my unimpressed mother. The primitive sketches are almost exactly identical to those of Jung's two towers and connecting annex, which I'd certainly never seen at the time. I have no idea what role coincidence played here, or presumptuous self-emphasis on my part, but I was thrilled to bits to find that our little confession of faith was a virtual mirror image of Jung's extension of consciousness.

For Jung the building was a manifestation of his inner self, embodying profound messages from his unconscious, and I imagine the same might be said of other owner-builders, ourselves included. This is not an entirely sanguine consideration. We might, for example, ponder whether our own house is so squat merely from the alleged discomfort with heights, or whether it might not indicate chronic low self-esteem. Does having a spacious octagon on one side and crowded rectangular compartments on the other have anything to do with extreme unconscious dichotomies? Moreover, having two people conceive and create a living space additionally requires that two sets of conscious and unconscious selves somehow achieve an alignment of purpose. Which is perhaps one reason why building a house together consistently rates as one of the severest causes of relationship stress and marital breakdown. If my unconscious yearns toward a particular type of dwelling as a manifestation of deep-seated psychic processes, and my partner's unconscious hankers for something very different, serious trouble is bound to follow and the resulting building either will be a dog's breakfast of unreconciled elements or will sit unfinished while our respective divorce lawyers discuss things over lunch.

Balances of power are every bit as important as balancing on beams. As Clare Cooper Marcus writes in *House as a Mirror of Self,* "Many 'house conflicts' come down to the issue of who has the power to make decisions, who is considered the primary home-maker, and what each individual feels about this." In our own case, conflicting points of view—and, presumably, conflicting uncon-scious desires—were very rare. In part I think that's because we were both endowed with a lack of expertise. Had one or the other of us been an accomplished builder or designer, there'd have been more opportunity for power struggles. As well, not being pressed by a deadline helped enormously—we could, and did, take the time to talk things over, stop and reconsider, occasionally tear down what we had only just put up, and look at alternatives. And there was a certain serendipity that derived from complementarity of instincts: Sandy's keen sense of space, proportion, and design dovetailed with my intuitions about the possibilities and limita-tions of materials. The result is a very long way from brilliant, and closer in spirit to the African hut than to the suburban split-level my mother might have preferred, but it is, in every sense of the term, home. A place of comfort, safety, and freedom.

NEITHER OF MY old building mentors, Bradford Angier and Ken Kern, for all their merits, gave adequate forewarning as to the inordinate attachment an amateur owner-builder can develop toward the marvel she or he has wrought. The whole idea at the outset was to escape the egoism of the trophy home, the unseeemly chest-thumping of "My home is bigger and better than yours." We rambunctious dudes were striving for simplicity, practicality, individual expression, and escape from the clammy materialism that rates land and home as an "asset." And I imagine that I still retained lingering bits of my monastic training, in which we were discouraged from developing any personal attachment to place.

But all of that noble detachment went up in smoke the night our home was attacked by fire a few years ago. This occurred while we were refinishing the hardwood floor in our kitchen. We'd lightly sanded the surface and put down a fresh coat of urethane. But the product proved to be defective because by the following morning the whole floor surface was blistered with bubbles. We had to let it dry completely, then sand the whole works off and start over. We spent a tiresome day on hands and knees with a whining belt sander getting down to clean wood. Exhausted and coated in wood dust, we packed it in around seven o'clock, showered, ate a quick supper, and collapsed into bed.

The next thing I remember was being jolted awake in the middle of the night by Sandy's cry of "Fire!" Leaping out of bed I dashed to the kitchen, where a ring of fire in the center of the room was throwing flames as high as the ceiling. While Sandy called 911 I grabbed a bath mat from the bathroom, soaked it in water, and ran to the fire. I hit the burning floor with the bath mat, but the fire snarled and leaped at me, throwing burning bits of wood all over the floor. I was naked and barefoot and gagging on the swirling black smoke. Urged by the 911 operator to get out of the building immediately, Sandy was shouting at me to leave. But something in me wouldn't abandon our home to the flames. There was too much of ourselves in it. I was roaring with an adrenaline frenzy that matched the frenzy of the fire. I ran to the bathroom, fetched a bucket of water from the bathtub, and poured the water on one bit of the fire. The circle of flames was by this time about five feet wide and intensely hot from burning oak, Styrofoam insulation, and the hemlock subflooring. The swirling smoke was choking. Sandy filled another bucket and back and forth we went, each bucket-load dousing another portion of the fire, and eventually we had it knocked down to a smoldering stench.

At about this time the local fire brigade arrived with trucks and lights and hoses. Helmeted and booted, the firefighters tore at the still-smoldering floor, ripping a large circle away to be sure the fire would not restart. Amazingly for a volunteer crew in a rural area at two in the morning, they'd gotten to the house exactly eleven minutes after our 911 call.

When the firefighters departed we were left with a house stinking of smoke and a huge hole in the floor. My feet were severely burned from the embers and we were in a state of nightmare-like shock. We tumbled back into bed but couldn't sleep at all as every creak and rustle in the night warned of the fire's return. As I had in that summertime meadow long ago, we had met the dragon of Bad Fire in the dark of the night and would never forget its menace.

OUR FIERCE RESISTANCE to the fire underscored how much a part of us this place had become. It's a young people's place, really—built by and for young people—lacking the single-level conveniences of your average rancher. Unremitting work is involved in its maintenance. It serves high principle more faithfully than it accommodates the creature comforts whose allure increases with age. Still, while I don't particularly admire our wobbly crafts-manship, especially when compared with the finesse of skilled owner-builders hereabouts creating cob houses and off-the-grid homes powered by solar and wind, I do delight in the building's textures: old red bricks, stout fir posts and beams, the gorgeous surfaces of cedar slabs, the smooth sculpting of waves caught in beach sandstone on the bathroom walls. I rejoice in its eccentricity, in its saucy refusal to conform, and at how it snuggles comfortably into the garden and woodlands. I like how every piece, every detail of the place has a story attached—where this old window came from, how we struggled to get that big beam pegged into place. This isn't so much a building as a structural memory bank, a repository in wood, stone, glass, and plaster of thirty years' experiences, of affection for its creation and the sharing of it over the years with a loving partner.

We're now at the point where buildings, gardens, woodlands, and self compose a unity that only extreme circumstances could justify being broken. I like to think of the house slowly decomposing back into the earth from which it arose, the forest reclaiming her timbers, perhaps leaving the chimney and garden stonework still in place long years from now, giving silent testimony that people sheltered here once, in simplicity and pleasure.

11

THE FATE OF THE EARTH

The earth we abuse and the living things we kill will,
in the end, take their revenge; for in exploiting their presence
we are diminishing our future.

MARYA MANNES, *More in Anger* (1958)

IN THE SPRING OF 1974 I received a message from my brother Brendan asking if I'd come up to the native reserve where he was working and lend a hand with a dispute that had erupted over planned logging on traditional native lands. Setting house building aside and leaving Sandy to run the homestead alone, I headed north. The first time Sandy and I had visited Nazko Village in the Cariboo country of central British Columbia, its gaily painted houses formed a tiny outpost at the end of a narrow gravel road that wound for seventy miles through jack pine forest and meadows. The people living in this remote corner were the Nazko (Nazkohwhoten) and Kluskus (Lhusquzwhoten), members of the Southern Carrier people who historically occupied a huge swath of what is now central British Columbia. Prior to the arrival of Europeans, the Carrier lived by a pattern of seasonal migration, moving in spring and early summer to catch trout and whitefish in lakes and streams. In late summer they'd move to traditional fishing stations along the major rivers to catch salmon, and in fall they'd travel back into the higher hills and meadows to hunt caribou and, in later years, moose.

With the arrival of Europeans, this seminomadic way of life began to disappear as the Carrier were systematically pushed off their ancient campsites and fishing stations. Small reserves were established in places not of the natives' choosing. As was the case in most of what became British Columbia, no treaty was signed, no compensation given for expropriated lands and resources. The Carrier lands far to the west were spared the worst of this usurpation, and although the residents were squeezed onto small reserves, they retained the ability to hunt, fish, trap, and travel through vast tracts of largely undisturbed forest. But the spectacular growth of the Cariboo timber and pulp industry after the Second World War eventually threatened even this western haven, and by the time I made my way out to Nazko Village in the summer of '74, the recently widened road sliced through a landscape of vast clear-cuts. The provincial forest service had advertised timber sales in the watershed from which Nazko Village drew its domestic water. The band was neither informed nor consulted. Native trappers operating traplines in the area weren't contacted either. A residential subdivision to accommodate up to a hundred logging families was planned to be located within a mile of Nazko Village, again without a word being said to the Indians.

After a year and a half of polite but futile insistence that their rights be considered, the natives had as a last resort put up a barricade, preventing a bulldozer from starting construction of a logging road right beside Nazko Village. Gaining a three-month reprieve, the bands hired a small study team, of which I was a

member, under the leadership of Walt Taylor, a veteran peace
and native-rights advocate of gentle disposition and unshakable
conviction. Brendan, who worked as a community development
officer for the bands, oversaw the whole undertaking. We spent the
summer talking with band members, mapping their traditional and
current uses of the territory, and working with them to develop a
strategy whereby they would have some voice in what occurred on
the lands of their ancestors and derive some benefits from it.

Cathy Patrick, the dynamic young chief of the Nazko band
(population 148), wrote a powerful account of her frustrations:

> Now Whiteman's world is much too fast for our Indian
> people's way of life. If we want to say something, we wonder
> what or how we should say it, but by the time we've thought
> of the right words to say, they're already on the next topic.
> Whiteman can talk all day, all night because words come
> automatically to their educated minds. It is *their* language ...
> We can't keep up so we are left behind.

Contributing to our study report, Cathy's husband, Dennis
Patrick, wrote,

> The native people have been trampled by development since
> the arrival of the foreigners. Now is the time that we have
> to find new approaches to development, even if it has to be
> non-development for an indefinite period of time. We have to
> inform the people first and prepare them for a change that is
> accepted by them. The most benefit should go to the affected
> community. The community should cause the effect, not an
> external force.

The Kluskus people dwelled farther to the west, in small
reserves scattered along the Blackwater River, up which their
ancestors had guided Alexander Mackenzie and his North West

Company crew on their historic 1793 trek to the Pacific. Kluskus chief Stanley Boyd, a soft-spoken and thoughtful young man, contributed an intriguing challenge to the report:

> If you want to come and make a road through our land ... If you want to come into our land and strip it so nothing can live there any more—then I don't think you should come in ... So the only way I think we'll solve this problem is by letting you live here with us and understand our culture, our way of life, our thoughts, our feelings, our land.

Had any of the decision makers accepted Stanley's invitation, they would have found, as I did, within the log homes and other village houses a remnant outpost of a remarkable indigenous culture. They would have found people wise in the ways of their environment, possessed of an intimate knowledge of how fish, birds, and mammals were adapted to that challenging place, along with practical skills for sustainable harvesting of plants and animals. They would have found people conversant in the Southern Carrier dialect, possessors of a living language threatened with extinction. They would have found remnants of a traditional world view and mythology and a traditional understanding of illness and methods of healing. The decision makers would have experienced a people still attached to traditional kinship patterns and child-rearing practices. Despite the indignities of the residential school system to which many had been subjected, despite systemic racism on the part of white neighbors and townsfolk and the ravages of poverty and alcoholism, here lived a remarkable community that deserved, and was by any measure of justice entitled to, far better treatment than what it was accorded.

But the decision makers did not accept the invitation. The position of government at that time was that all aboriginal rights to land and resources had been effectively extinguished; that a native claim existed only in the imaginations of ambitious Indian leaders and their idealistic nonnative assistants. The election of an extreme right-wing provincial government put an end to the discussion, and in August of 1976 the bulldozers were back at Nazko. There were no blockades this time, but there was no victory either for the perpetrators of what at best could be thought of as criminal negligence on the part of government and industry. And for what? Logging trucks loaded with spindly pine logs thundering down eighty miles of gravel road, leaving behind huge clear-cuts on topsoil so marginal any real regeneration will take lifetimes. In the intervening years, a mountain pine beetle infestation has laid waste to many of the Interior's pine forests that were not already decimated by logging.

I returned to Nazko for several winters, sometimes with Sandy, continuing to work for the bands on their land claims. We lived in a little log cabin overlooking a small lake. We'd go out on the ice and chop a hole with an ax in order to draw up a bucket of cold water for the kitchen. As I walked into the village each morning to work at the band office, I'd be assailed by a pack of mongrel dogs, all barking and snarling, but strategically just out of range of a good boot in the bum. I remember attending movies at the community hall and dances there too, with four or five young guys flailing away on guitars and drums. I remember walking with Sandy on a cold, clear, starlit night to the little wooden church in the village for Christmas Eve Mass. Approaching visitors from the back country fired their rifles in celebration from the nearby hills before descending into the valley on horseback or in horse-drawn sleighs with tinkling bells. We all squeezed into the little church for Mass celebrated Carrier-style that was in its own chaotic way every bit as splendid as the most solemn High Mass of my past. The following morning we were roused from our bed and urged to hasten to Cathy and Dennis's house for a Christmas feast of grand food and continuous laughter.

Laughing, joking, and teasing were staples of social interaction. Almost any circumstance could elicit a story about something ridiculous that had happened elsewhere in similar circumstances. Pantomimes and gentle ridicule were commonplace. The little kids of the village were forever teasing and tumbling over top of one another.

Of course there were tough times too, often associated with abuse of alcohol. Bootleggers appeared at times, preying on the vulnerable. Vicious fights would sometimes erupt at dances or parties, with serious injuries inflicted. Accidental death, particularly among the young, occurred with dismaying regularity. Several times during my stay the whole community assembled at the little graveyard above the village to bury a young person, one killed in a traffic accident, another from suicide. The mood of collective grief surrounding these events seemed deep and ancient and inevitable.

I greatly appreciate having spent at least a little time among those remarkable people. As is frequently the case in such situations, I'm sure I learned and benefited far more from the experience than they did in having me there. Among other things, I came to know a little about patterns of silence markedly different from the relentless talk of what we consider normal social interactions. Oftentimes in conversation there'd be long pauses between comments, something it took a while getting accustomed to. Had I just said something offensive? Was I prying inappropriately? We are conditioned to consider silence among people awkward, a breakdown of communication. More than five seconds of silence around the dinner party table hints at social disaster. The notion that everyone may have been pondering what was previously said and taking the time to formulate a considered response—which is what I eventually recognized my native hosts were doing—does not occur to us. But as my native friends seemed to appreciate, words gather resonance when surrounded by silence. They become the notes, clear and articulate, between the musical rests without which we get the verbal equivalent of white noise—relentless, monotonous, meaningless.

I HAD ONE memorable winter journey up to Kluskus. Scattered along the Blackwater Valley, the community was then accessible only by horseback in summer or snowmobile in winter. I had business to attend to there, so a plan was hatched that several of the young guys and I would go up by snowmobile. I'd never been on one of these contraptions in my life and viewed them with considerable contempt. But the boys assured me there was nothing difficult about driving one. After a course of instruction that may have extended to five or ten minutes, including any number of jokes and asides, I fired the beast up and roared off recklessly down the hill and out onto the frozen lake. On the flat lake ice, with no impediments, I was able to scream along at breakneck speed, feeling the thrill of the machine's noisy rush. Then we set off for Kluskus. Whooshing along narrow trails through the jack pine was arduous work, relieved occasionally when we broke out onto a frozen lake where there were neither trees nor slopes to worry about.

After a few days in Kluskus it was time to return to Nazko, but the boys were in no hurry. We idled over coffee as the pale winter sun advanced across the low horizon. Finally we bid our goodbyes and set off at a great roaring pace. The boys raced far ahead of me, and I struggled between not wanting to be lost in this snowy wilderness and not wanting to smash headfirst into a tree or tumble down a bluff. Twilight descended and still we roared forward. I could barely pick out the lights of the others far ahead on the twisting trail. Then darkness came down, the impenetrable gloom of a dense pine forest at dusk. We continued for what seemed like hours more. I was bouncing recklessly through a dark, cold world alone. Then, marvelously, a distant light glowed through the trees.

I raced for it and gratefully entered the cozy home of a family who lived not far from Nazko Village. Everyone had a great time teasing me for my tardiness, and then we departed for the final, less traumatic few miles to home. It was an apt and interesting instruction I received during those torturous hours on the trail, about how it feels to fall behind when racing through unknown country at a pace that is too fast.

BACK HOME ON the island we were faced with development pressures of a different kind. During the sixties land speculation and development had been roaring out of control on many of the Gulf Islands between Vancouver Island and the mainland, especially the southern islands close to Vancouver and Victoria. Massive small-lot subdivisions threatened to wreak havoc on communities and the environment, and public outcry had eventually prompted the provincial government to impose a ten-acre minimum lot size until adequate planning could be developed. This temporary freeze is what had allowed people like ourselves, who were interested in low-impact rural living, to acquire sizable properties for relatively little money.

The development community was most interested in small waterfront and view lots, where the real money was to be made, and planners set about providing what the developers wanted. The local regional government planned on zoning all of Denman Island into parcels of one, two, or five acres, with a projected build-out in the vicinity of eighty thousand people. There was no consideration of where domestic water would come from, nor of sewage disposal, ferry capacity, or much of anything else. Denman is almost identical in size and shape to Manhattan, but not all of us were keen to have it chewed up like a Little Apple.

And thus the battle was joined, a struggle to protect this special place, this community, this way of life, against what would become a decades-long parade of politicians, bureaucrats, and developers intent upon maximizing opportunities and profits with scant regard for what might be lost in the process.

But serendipity played her part here as well. Right around the time I was first working at Nazko, the recently elected New Democratic Party provincial government enacted two pieces of progressive legislation that were of immediate consequence to our island. The first established an Agricultural Land Reserve that severely curtailed development options on land with agricultural capability, including a sizable chunk of Denman. The second, the Islands Trust Act, created a distinctive form of local government for the Gulf Islands with a mandate "to preserve and protect the unique amenities and environment of the islands." These special places were, the government had concluded, "too important to the people of Canada to be left open to exploitation by real estate developers and speculators." Seldom has any government statement matched my own sentiments so precisely.

Under the new Islands Trust regulations, each island was to elect two local trustees who, along with a third trustee from off-island, would be the principal decision makers on local land use matters. Although in the midst of building our house and working at Nazko, I decided in the full bloom of youthful impetuosity to toss my hat into the electoral ring. Running against a clutch of old geezers, I fell short by a half-dozen votes, and in hindsight I recognize that the judgment of the electorate may well have proved sounder than my own.

Creation of the trust has helped spare the smaller islands of the Salish Sea—between the mainland and Vancouver Island—the worst of the rural sprawl that continues to engulf much of Vancouver Island's eastern shoreline and has all but obliterated the Coastal Douglas-fir Zone, one of the smallest and most threatened ecosystems in the country. But the trust was never granted all the powers it was intended to have, as other ministries of government fiercely defended their turf. Subdivision approval still rests,

incongruously, with the Ministry of Transportation and High-
ways. Control of logging—or, rather, lack of control—remains
the purview of the Ministry of Forests. Several years ago a logging
outfit butchered several thousand acres of our island forests in the
most brutal and thoughtless manner imaginable. Despite its best
efforts, the trust was powerless to prevent or in any way control
the logging. But it has succeeded in limiting development to
some degree, and in securing certain natural areas for conservation purposes. Moreover, merely having a local government with
a specific mandate "to preserve and protect" (ought not every
government be similarly tasked?) aids immensely in the effort to
make at least one tiny portion of a better world.

Many islanders share a passionate attachment to their home
place, although not necessarily the same vision, hence the well-
worn maxim that an island is a difference of opinion surrounded by
water. But volunteerism, the lifeblood of all small communities, is a
way of life for many islanders. Committees and work crews abound.
Precious little time elapses between one fundraising event and the
next. One week it'll be a fashion show featuring outfits salvaged
from the reusables store, all proceeds going to the community hall,
perhaps followed quickly by an illustrated lecture of somebody's
trip to Thailand, with money raised donated to an orphanage there,
or maybe a dance at the hall to raise funds for the food bank, then
the volunteer fire department's pancake breakfast—and on and
on it goes in a peculiar and endearing blend of social activism and
community celebration.

The gang with which we associated specialized in environmental activism, and we became adept at activities like organizing
marches on the legislature in Victoria. One time we held a mock
funeral for our bylaws after a developer received approval for an
illegal subdivision. It was brilliant to see busloads of islanders of
all descriptions defiantly marching in unison in front of the legislature. After much public relations and legal wrangling, we were

successful in having that decision overturned. Another time we joined with delegations from the other islands to protest an attempt by the legislature to dismantle the Islands Trust. Again the ferocity of opposition forced the government to withdraw the offending legislation.

My personal favorite example of guerrilla theater took place during a two-year struggle we were engaged in to prevent an enormous log sorting and booming ground being established at Buckley Bay, the tiny outpost on Vancouver Island from which the ferry sails to Denman. The proposal would have entailed massive industrial intrusion, including dredging and foreshore excavation, in an area that produces sixty percent of the province's oysters and provides important habitat for migratory and overwintering wild-fowl. The approval process had been flawed, and a small group of us islanders, never shy when the opportunity for a good dustup presented itself, threw ourselves into the battle for Buckley Bay. By chance, the provincial government cabinet was touring the province at the time and had scheduled a session at Courtenay, a few miles up Vancouver Island from us. Briefs could be presented to the cabinet, but they had to be submitted for approval beforehand. We dashed off a polite and undemanding brief on our issue and were granted ten minutes to make our case before the cabinet. On the appointed day, about a dozen of us trundled into the hotel meeting room where the cabinet members were arrayed formidably along one side of the room. But instead of dutifully reading the approved brief, we broke into a theater piece of song and dance lampooning the Buckley Bay bungling of certain cabinet ministers. Bill Bennett, the tough-guy premier of the day, glowered at us menacingly but did nothing to interrupt our saucy performance. In the end, thanks to the intervention of the provincial ombudsman, the Buckley Bay proposal was withdrawn and never again resurfaced.

One of the enduring aspects of environmental activism is that you never run short of projects, and our group of island zealots soon found ourselves engaged in a whole panoply of issues around the region. When the nearby towns of Comox and Courtenay decided to pump raw sewage into the Strait of Georgia, just off Denman's northern shore, we leaped into the sewage fray and—notwithstanding the pricy testimony of a slick California consultant who had it on the best authority that marine ecosystems are actually improved by generous applications of human excrement—succeeded in getting the would-be polluters to install enhanced secondary treatment with sludge removal. We opposed the spraying of herbicides along a rail line that crossed innumerable fish-bearing streams on Vancouver Island. We protested the presence of nuclear weapons at Canadian Forces Base Comox and the nearby naval base at Nanoose. We chartered buses to participate in massive annual peace walks in Vancouver. Through all of these actions we became part of the wider environmental/peace community, forming alliances and lasting friendships with a widespread coalition of dreamers and seekers of a better world.

AFTER A FEW minor skirmishes with logging outfits on our home island, I got my first real taste of the War in the Woods in the early eighties on Meares Island, the 21,000-acre ancestral homeland of the Ahousaht and Clayoquot bands of the Nuu-chah-nulth people. A short boat ride from Tofino on the west coast of Vancouver Island, Meares is a mountainous island, renamed for a shady Victorian gentleman adventurer, that's densely forested in giant spruce and hemlock trees and some of the largest western red cedars on earth. Although included in the Nuu-chah-nulth land claim, most of the island was designated "Tree Farm Licence" and available for logging. When MacMillan Bloedel—at that time a $2-billion-per-year forestry giant controlled by Noranda and, ultimately, by the multibillion-dollar Bronfman international business dynasty—began moving in on the island, all hell broke lose.

Along with the Nuu-chah-nulth, the Friends of Clayoquot Sound—a group of feisty freethinkers who included artists, fisherfolk, and oyster growers—mounted a stout resistance. Defiant speeches were made. Corkscrew spikes were hammered into tree trunks and survey tapes torn down from branches. Cops with dynamite-sniffing dogs were called out. Helicopters buzzed about. Court injunctions were sought. The standoff became a media cause célèbre, attracting celebrity supporters. I was invited over by folks I knew who were at the heart of the struggle, and I helped out with some national magazine writing on the issue. Eventually the B.C. Court of Appeal made an unprecedented decision: It granted an injunction against logging Meares until the native land claim could be heard in a full trial. "Justice to the Indians in these unusual circumstances," wrote Mr. Justice Alan MacFarlane, "means giving a decision on the merits of their claim before destroying the forests involved in that claim." (This was exactly the argument we had made at Nazko a decade earlier, to no avail.) The provincial government, adamant in its refusal to acknowledge that a native land claim had any legal validity, announced it would continue resisting the claims of aboriginal title because to do otherwise would "cost taxpayers hundreds of millions of dollars." But in the end the government was proven wrong and the protesters right. The necessity for recognition of aboriginal title is now a political reality and the great trees of Meares Island are still standing.

Two years after the Meares campaign, another battle began brewing even closer to home. The provincial cabinet had passed an order-in-council, without benefit of parliamentary or public discussion, dramatically altering six of British Columbia's biggest wilderness parks and threatening the future of the province's park system. Thousands of acres of wilderness was deleted entirely from parks, and thousands more acres was reclassified to "recreation area" status, a euphemism meaning that mineral exploration and other resource developments would be permitted. Any area designated for a future park would have a minimum (and renewable) ten-year resource exploration and extraction period. The concept of a park was to change fundamentally from an area left in its natural state to one from which everything of financial value has first been removed.

Strathcona, the oldest park in the system, whose 500,000 acres straddles the mountainous spine of Vancouver Island, contains alpine meadows, glacial lakes, waterfalls, and valleys of ancient timber. An existing mine inside the park had for years been a source of contention and contamination. Now the plan was to lop thousands of acres off the park entirely and to allow further mining inside the park, with all the clear-cutting, valley flooding, strip mining, and mine tailings pollution involved.

For over a year the Friends of Strathcona Park—an eclectic group of naturalists, mountaineers, peace activists, and general hell-raisers—had lobbied and petitioned Victoria to rescind the troublesome order-in-council, but to no avail. The group notified the government that any new mineral exploration in the park would be met with civil disobedience, but in the early days of 1988, a mining company began moving drilling equipment into the park. Within hours, the Friends blockaded the remote access road, and for a week protesters, police, and miners uneasily faced one another across the barricade. Eventually, armed with an injunction and a determination to break the blockade, the RCMP issued an ultimatum: clear the road or be arrested. After lengthy discussion—we dutifully maintained the discipline of the talking stick whereby all listened to whoever held the stick—we opted to have three people arrested that morning and initiate a tactic of intermittent blockades geared to attract increasing participation and public attention. Over the following six weeks we organized a series of rallies, attracting several hundred people to the park each weekend. Each rally ended with a small group of people risking arrest by invading the drill site and forcing the drilling crew to shut down its rig. In total sixty-four people—half of them, including Sandy, from Denman Island—were arrested in a dozen different incidents. Some ended up spending a week or more in jail.

Throughout this time I was acting as vice-president of the Friends and one of the coordinators of the park blockade. After weeks of blockades and arrests, Strathcona Park was on the front pages of Vancouver newspapers and the lead item on regional TV newscasts. The high-profile environmental campaigner and television personality Dr. David Suzuki lent considerable support to the campaign, including addressing rallies in the park. Membership in Friends of Strathcona Park ballooned to about three thousand, making this the biggest single-issue environmental case in B.C. history. The First Nations people of northern Vancouver Island added their voices to the campaign, never more movingly than at a gathering in the park when one of the elders called out the traditional names of the mountains and waters around us with words whose strength and sibilance seemed to echo the sounds of this wild place we'd come to know, the evening cry of wolves, the splashing of glacier-fed creeks, the soughing of wind combing through ancient conifers. Eventually the mining company fled with its drill rig under cover of darkness, and the provincial government abandoned its ill-considered plans for this and the other parks. By standing our ground we'd won a huge victory, albeit temporary, as most environmental victories are.

ONCE ONE'S LOCKED into a full-bore, all-out political campaign like this, a kind of manic energy takes over. The phone rings incessantly, emails (added later) zip back and forth through the ether, meetings extend long into the night, strategies are hammered out, politicians harassed, supporters rallied, funds sought, speeches made, bold ultimatums thrown down. In full flight, a good rip-snortin' environmental campaign pumps as much adrenaline and testosterone into the system as any commodity trader or celebrity lawyer could cope with. (The pay, of course, is not commensurate; in fact, it is nonexistent.) I consider such jolts to the system of immense value, but best administered only on occasion and always with discrimination.

Incongruously, while we were delivering what blows we could against the empire of exploitation in Strathcona, Sandy and I were simultaneously assembling the landscape elements of our new garden. While the Strathcona blockade was building to a crisis, I was dividing my time between it and the laying up of drystone walls. I'd spend three or four days camped out in the mountains, organizing civil disobedience actions and negotiating with cops, security guards, and miners, and then dash back to the island and heave stone blocks into place for several days, work the phones on park business, then return to the blockade. It was a time of absolute focus and frenzied energy, and it's a marvel that the park got saved and the walls got built without my collapsing from severe nervous disorders.

Around the same time, the simmering conflict in Clayoquot Sound was heating up again. The Friends of Clayoquot Sound—some of whom had stood with us in Strathcona—and the Nuu-chah-nulth people became locked in a tense standoff over a logging road being blasted into the scarred hillsides of Sulphur Passage, north of Tofino. Taking up positions in the bush, protesters were preventing the road construction crews from blasting. Dozens were arrested and charged; two were jailed for repeatedly ignoring a court order restraining them from interfering with road construction. One of the arrestees, Ahousaht hereditary chief Earl George, described his ravaged ancestral homeland as "bald mountains, just like the face of the moon."

By 1990 it had become apparent that the woodlands and wild places of Denman could suffer similar trashing. Most of the forestland on the island was privately owned, and there was nothing to prevent its being clear-cut and subdivided. Rezoning those forestlands into far larger lot sizes was part of the answer; another part was establishing a community land trust for the purpose of acquiring and preserving areas of ecological significance. I put in about a dozen years working with other community members to obtain a number of tracts of forestland and wetlands, and I take great satisfaction in seeing those wild areas now set aside primarily for other creatures and plants. However, this work frequently involved many months, sometimes years, of hard bargaining with politicians, bureaucrats, loggers, and land speculators. Prolonged exposure to these elements may temper the spirit but not necessarily feed it. In the tempest of activity, even for the noblest of causes, a host of unruly emotions may run riot, like looters in the pleasure grounds of an overthrown despot. For me the hardest lesson in all of this was learning to engage in this necessary work while retaining tranquillity of spirit. It was that old familiar tension between the active life and the contemplative life, come back to bedevil me in a new disguise.

IN 1993, FUELED by a growing public awareness of the consequences of global deforestation, resistance to continued clear-cutting of Clayoquot's ancient temperate rain forest ignited a full summer of confrontation and mass civil disobedience. A peace camp, established in a nearby clear-cut nicknamed the Black Hole, accommodated thousands of visitors through the summer months. Young volunteers took the lead in staffing a camp kitchen that fed hundreds every day and in orchestrating the highly disciplined blockades that were carried out each morning. Celebrities, politicians, and musicians like the Australian rockers Midnight Oil came in to support the camp. News coverage spread to the lofty heights of the *New York Times* and the *New Yorker*. I visited the camp several times through the summer, giving speeches and helping with civil disobedience training, and finally got myself arrested in

September, along with Sandy and her sister Barbara and several dozen fellow islanders. In total 859 people were arrested, ranging from teenagers to octogenarians, making this one of the largest mass arrests in Canadian history. Each of us was marched through a ridiculous charade of being hauled off to a filthy jail cell, eventually released, and later being forced to attend one of many long and immensely tedious mass trials. In the end, our particular group was sentenced to three weeks of house arrest, each of us wearing an electronic anklet whereby our movements could be monitored. Since it was springtime by then, with the new garden needing to be planted, we took the liberty of including the garden as part of our electronic prison. To be confined for three weeks to the spring garden, forbidden to go elsewhere, was pure bliss. Nor did we consider an evening glass of wine on the patio after the day's labor to be too egregious a violation of the stricture against consuming alcohol.

I greatly value the experience of having stood at various of these blockades and risking arrest. The act of stepping forth from the comfort and security of the everyday in response to the demands of conscience is an illuminating thing. There's a remarkable freedom to be found in voluntarily risking incarceration—a freedom from habitual cowardice, from fear of the judgments of others, from preoccupation with less significant matters. For myself, the act of civil disobedience also put a definitive exclamation point upon my tattered old vow that had instructed, "Let their obedience be blind." Most gratifying of all, the Clayoquot summer of arrests, along with the Meares Island campaign and the battle for Strathcona Park, marked a turning point in the War in the Woods. The assumption by government and industry that they could continue pillaging publicly owned forests and parkland without anybody else knowing or caring, and without reference to native title, had finally been shaken down to its roots.

12

DREAM GARDENS

Gardening is not a rational act.
MARGARET ATWOOD, *Bluebeard's Egg*

ALMOST TWENTY YEARS ELAPSED BETWEEN our first
arriving on the island and our full immersion into ornamental gardening. Clearing land, house building,
growing fruits and vegetables, along with political activism and
scraping a few dollars together now and then left little spare time
for ornamentation. But a grand tour of Europe, taken as a reward
after completing the house, ignited a passion for landscaping that
was destined to change our lives entirely.

Setting out from home in late autumn, with parsimony as our
guiding star, we each bought a bus ticket for seventy-five dollars
that allowed you to continue traveling forward across North
America as far as you wanted, with stopovers permitted. Thus we
would travel from Vancouver to Toronto, visit my dad, continue
on to Ottawa to visit Ger, then finish up at New York City, where
we'd catch one of Sir Freddie Laker's no-frills flights to London
for ninety-nine dollars. The price was right and the experience
proved invaluable. Pulling into squalid bus depots in godforsaken

locations at all hours of the day and night, observing and chatting with the cast of characters who came and went from town to town, munching on fruit and foods we'd prepared at home, smoking smelly hand-rolled cigarettes all the way, we made almost a reverse version of the epic trek Jim Conlon and I had made a decade earlier.

After visiting my dad, who was by then reasonably well adjusted to living alone, we carried on up to Ottawa, and here there was much sadness because a few months earlier Ger's wife, Linda, had died shortly after giving birth to their third child. Now he had a new baby on his hands as well as the other two kids, who'd suffered the awful trauma of losing their mum. This was a magnitude of pain and loss I'd never known, and I still marvel at the courage and fundamental goodness of how my brother dealt with it.

In late November Sir Freddie deposited us in London with our battered rucksacks stuffed with camping gear, and from there we began an extended ramble through Europe in an old Volkswagen station wagon. Innocents abroad, we wandered for five months, camping out, with all the excitements and astonishments such trips provide.

Greece particularly was a great revelation, the farthest east I'd been to that point, and thrillingly soaked in an antiquity I'd thus far known only through reading. All the deadening hours I'd spent translating portions of the *Iliad* and the *Odyssey* back at school now seemed like time entirely well spent. We toured the Acropolis of Athens, the brilliant symmetry of the Parthenon's columns putting our primitive woodbutchery back at home into proper perspective. Returning to the Acropolis in the evening, when the place was deserted, we walked for hours around it while a full moon rose and bathed its ancient marble structures in unearthly silver light. Another evening I sat for hours drinking ouzo with a boldly mustached character straight out of *Zorba the Greek* who spoke no English but managed to convey volumes concerning the perfidy of the Turks, the rise of Iran under the Ayatollah Khomeini, and the imminent collapse of the American empire. "U.S.A. kaput!" my companion would shout with an incisive slash of his hand across his own throat. By the time anemones and other spring wildflowers began blooming in extravagant swaths of gay colors, we were wholly entranced with the place. And we left with a particularly worthwhile landscaping insight gained while camping amid the terraced olive groves of Corfu. The island's rock terracing inspired the realization that what we absolutely *must* do was terrace the rough hill beside our house with stone walls.

Before getting to the great gardens of England in April, we executed a classic case of becoming lost in the mountains, without which no extended ramble seems quite complete. Heading northward out of Greece, we entered Yugoslavia, which was in the final days of Marshal Tito's rule. Barely across the border, heading for Skopje, we took a wrong turn that sent us climbing along a narrow road that reached higher and higher into the rugged mountains of Macedonia, hard against the forbidden border of Albania. Snow was mounded up well above the car on either side of the road, and we passed no buildings of any kind for mile after mountainous mile. Stopping at a clear spot, we looked out over a vast landscape of snow-covered mountains in which there was no sign of human habitation. We had absolutely no idea where we were, what lay ahead, whether we had enough gas to get out of these forbidding mountains. I believe on principle that being lost in this way is a beneficial thing every once in a while, providing a definitive release from one's carefully constructed and maintained versions of reality. However, at the time I think we were experiencing more apprehension over our predicament than delight in its mind-opening possibilities. We spent the night sleeping in the back of the car parked in a small gravel pit. By morning, everything in the car, including several hard-boiled eggs, was frozen solid. Eventually, mercifully, the road began descending and finally deposited us in the middle of a long parade of horse-drawn carts loaded with produce, animals, and brilliantly costumed people all heading to town for Saturday market.

Finally in England, we poked around Devon and Cornwall, then up through the Cotswolds and into rural Wales, gradually making our way toward Merseyside, where we visited my childhood haunts in Woolton. We found the old family home on Church Road, now bearing a plaque on its front wall designating it a heritage building. A sleek sedan glided through the Romanesque archway, and we followed it in. The courtyard where the barnyard fowl of my childhood had wandered about was now a parking lot. The old stone buildings had been renovated into chic little residences, each with a small front garden replete with white picket fence and tasteful statuary. The open fields I'd roamed as a child still stretched up the hill behind. The convent house, slightly less imposing than I remembered it, sat in a garden of big deciduous trees and carefully tended flower beds, just as when my father had worked there. I was glad to see it all again, essentially unchanged, this place where so much of me had been formed.

But, however unconscious we may have been of it at the time, our English ramble had as many implications for the future as it had evocations of the past, because it included a fateful exposure to several of the great gardens of Britain. While in Devon we visited Knightshayes Court, where a perfectly absurd Victorian Gothic house overlooked fifty acres of splendid gardens blending into woodlands. There was not a single other visitor on the whole estate, but drifts of spring bulbs were blooming everywhere. Enormous rhododendrons and camellias were swathed in blossoms. We wandered in pale sunshine into an enclosure of meticulously clipped yew where a circular pool reflected a nearby white statue and a silver weeping pear. Even the ridiculous topiary fox and hounds seemed marvelous, and meandering through the celebrated "garden in the wood" of rare trees and shrubs was utterly enchanting.

The formal gardens of Hampton Court Palace, its famous maze and two-hundred-year-old grapevine planted by Capability Brown, were entirely different in spirit but equally astonishing. Most of the estate's 200,000 flowering bulbs seemed to be blooming precisely on time for our arrival. And, just to ensure that the stake of fine gardening was well and truly driven into our hearts, we finished up at Wisley Gardens, the lovely flagship property of the Royal Horticultural Society. Somewhere in this process, as our spirits simultaneously leaped in response to the great beauty of these places, the desire to begin seriously gardening at home was surely born.

FOR THE NEXT half-dozen years we were busy with other affairs. For one thing, our little Pickles Road neighborhood had undergone a renaissance of sorts with the arrival of two young families. Kel and Leyah Kelly, with their little son, Shad, had bought Bruce and Daphne's acreage next door and set about building a house there. Meanwhile, Vic Shulman and Willa Cannon, with a delightful little daughter named Cedar, moved into the barn once we'd vacated it. There was much coming and going among the households, as we shared meals and worked together on building or other projects. Celebrations at winter and summer solstice or Thanksgiving were joyful collective gatherings. Leyah gave birth to a second child, Melina, and the coming of these three children into our lives was a wonderful thing. The kids were free to wander from place to place as they chose and, as the possessors of the only television in the vicinity, Sandy and I often had them around. Football and Frisbee games regularly broke out on the lawn. Whenever their parents were away for whatever reason, the kids would stay with us and think nothing of it. We had never been especially driven to have children of our own and had adopted a laissez-faire approach of "if it happens, fine; if not, that's fine too." And it hadn't happened. But having these three little tykes cavorting around the place throughout their formative years was a considerable blessing.

Group camping trips, involving them and other kids, usually included an annual junket across Vancouver Island to the great sand beaches of Pacific Rim National Park Reserve, just down from Tofino and Clayoquot Sound. Back in those days we used to hike through half a mile of rain forest, then along the shoreline to Schooner Cove, where we'd set up tents and a kitchen of driftwood logs. A series of sweeping beaches are dotted there with small islands of rock, on some of which ancient Sitka spruce lean against the wind. It's a transformative place of roaring surf, breaching whales, glistening sea mists, mesmerizing tide pools, and heart-breakingly lovely sunsets.

STILL, WE CONTINUED to nurse the inspiration of the great gardens we'd visited in Britain, and by 1987 the impetus to put in a large ornamental garden, to surround the house with beautiful plantings, would tolerate no further postponement. Our cabin in a clearing would become a garden in the wood. The decision was an instinctive thing, a call of the heart, undertaken without any thoroughgoing analysis of what future implications it might entail. Only long afterward did we realize that this was as consequential a decision as our intuitive move to the land had been two decades earlier.

We blithely laid out a garden space around the front and side of the house, encompassing an area somewhat larger than two people could reasonably be expected to maintain. We split dozens of stout rails from cedar logs in the woods to enclose the space and exclude ravenous deer. Some of the rails were used to create a rose arbor along one side, others to form a snake fence above the hill.

Still harboring the vision of stone-walled terraces on the hillsides of Corfu, we dug out dozens of huge sword ferns from our hillside and dragged them to the woods for replanting. Then we excavated the stony hillside by hand into three level terraces, held in place by Corfu-esque curving walls of local sandstone. Once under way, the stonework became a mania of its own, calling for stone pathways, alcoves, and steps, and a stone-rimmed pool and cascade. Altogether we unearthed by hand an estimated seventy pickup truck-loads of sandstone with which to form these stony features. No part of garden making would in the end prove more pleasing, durable, or worthwhile.

With all the garden hardscape—the sandstone features, the cedar arbors and trellises—hewn from the land itself, the only cost involved was that of endless heavy lifting and cartage. We weren't so much imposing stuff upon the landscape as rearranging, reformatting what was already here. It was essential to us that the garden be knitted into its environment, rather than imposed upon it, and this was greatly facilitated by the use of local stone and cedar, as well as by retaining several enormous cedar stumps whose fluted silver bases became colonized with mosses, lichens, and liverworts, with native huckleberries growing from their tops. For the same reason, we incorporated plenty of native species in the garden—leathery-leaved salal, native bleeding hearts and columbines, fireweed and mahonias.

Our initial planting choices involved acquiring several dozen antique roses, which were just becoming all the rage back in the eighties, and half a dozen ornamental crabapples, both white-flowering and rosybloom. Clematis, herbaceous peonies and Pacific Giant delphiniums were accorded pride of place. Beyond these, a great tumble of annuals, biennials, and perennials. Being larger than reasonable, the new garden required considerably more plants than we first anticipated, and so we welcomed in any number of wildlings like oxeye daisies, mallows, and Queen Anne's lace that have subsequently been banned as too unruly. Other self-seeders, like foxgloves, hollyhocks, California poppies, and Arabian thistles, we continue to entertain.

On our infrequent sorties to town we'd keep a sharp eye out for plant sales of the deep discount variety. In late autumn we'd undertake a grand tour of nurseries, some offering substantial discounts for trees and shrubs the nursery people didn't want to hold over winter. Back in those days there were any number of adventuresome small nurseries popping up, their owners willing to bring in exciting plants that were out of the ordinary. Unfortunately, adventuresome nursery owners were perhaps more sophisticated than the general public in their tastes, so that by the end of the season there would frequently be unusual and choice specimens available at prices we could afford. Sometimes the clearance tables at larger nurseries would offer plants so wizened and close to death that only a fatally flawed optimist would take a chance on them. That would be us.

Many of the plants with which we got started were raised from seeds or cuttings. Others were gifts from friends, part of the vast underground economy in which gardeners avidly participate. Some of these gifts have special memories attached, like the laburnum given to us by Sandy's mum. A beautiful white-flowering Mongolian ash came from a cutting provided by the eminent ecologist Dr. Chris Pielou. An equally lovely *Styrax japonica,* the Japanese snowbell, was passed on to us by a much-loved Surrey gardener named Francisca Darts. A half-dozen juvenile sugar and silver maples, slim beauties now forty feet tall, were sent to us as whips by my father from my parents' second, and last, Toronto garden. Sandy's sister Barbara and Barbara's husband, Richard, for a time ran a native plants nursery from which we were the beneficiaries of numerous choice plants.

Drought tolerance was one of our guiding principles, although it took a little while to get the hang of it. With its winter-wet/ summer-dry climatic regime, the island can become intensely parched by late summer, and because our place is largely stony ground from which moisture rapidly drains, it's of prime importance that most of our plants be able to survive without repeated soakings that would soon drain the well. Introductions that showed themselves unstable unless repeatedly watered didn't last long. But there are dozens and dozens of trees, shrubs, grasses, succulents, perennials, and bulbs that have settled in, put down deep roots, and acclimatized themselves to the alternating damp of winter and drought of summer.

Two other guiding principles informed our planting choices. First, we wanted a range of species that would attract wildlife through much of the year. By wildlife I decidedly don't mean the lovely but destructive deer with which we share this place, nor the occasional black bear that has rambled through, but rather creatures both useful and beautiful in a garden setting. There must be birds, of course—rufous hummingbirds buzzing through the sunlit garden, sipping nectar from red-flowering currants in early spring all the way through to fuchsias in late summer; clans of violet-green swallows swooping and gliding; brilliant tanagers and crossbills, chickadees and rufous-sided towhees pecking at seeds; and dozens of others. Provision was made for accommodating bats, frogs, snakes, and salamanders. Butterfly-friendly plantings got top priority, bringing the reward of dozens of big swallowtail butterflies drifting like airborne petals among the delphiniums and dianthus. We planted as well to attract the less glamorous but essential beneficial insects: aphid midges, tachinid flies and syrphid flies, lacewings and parasitic wasps. Bees and beetles, dragonflies and damselflies, pirate bugs and spiders: all of them were made welcome to feast upon pest insects. Our ambition was to have a garden that resembled as closely as possible the splendid diversity and richness of the ecosystem within which it exists.

A second principle, which dovetailed nicely with the first, was to plant for scent as well as sight. This was a main consideration for bringing in so many antique roses, and they didn't disappoint, for their combined scents in the height of midsummer provide a spirit-lifting ambience. The sensuous fragrances of dianthus and philadelphus, trumpet lilies, honeysuckle and dame's rocket, catnip and valerian, together create an ethereal presence within which the purest rapture is both permissible and possible.

Gradually, by way of seeds, cuttings, layerings, and root divisions, we were able to expand our collections to fill a garden space far beyond what flimsy finances would alone allow. Stepping into our garden now, a visitor might be forgiven for concluding that we were a pair of shameless moneybags able to buy all these lovely plants, which at today's giddy prices would bankrupt a billionaire.

THE GARDEN CONTINUES to evolve over time, some of the changes motivated by ease of maintenance, others by the desire for all-season performers, still others by the enforced rigors of climate change. For example, we've introduced far more drought-tolerant ornamental grasses, sedums, and conifers. The textures and forms of foliage have become more prominent, and so have big-boned perennials, like *Romneya coulteri* and *Macleaya cordata*. Along with smoke bushes, Korean dogwoods, and other small trees, we put in a half-dozen slender Skyline gleditsias that now cast a dappled shade across the areas closest to the house.

Additionally, in recent years I've had the good fortune to lead small-group garden tours to many of the finest public and private gardens in Ireland, New Zealand, China, and Great Britain, mostly organized by our friend the travel consultant, Julia Guest. There is much to be learned on expeditions of this sort, as well as great inspiration to be drawn. There's also an impulse to scuttle home and attempt to duplicate in one's own garden a particularly stunning feature encountered elsewhere. After several weeks touring exquisite classical gardens in China, I was throbbing with readiness to get home in order to begin constructing moon gates and leak windows around the homestead. The gardens of Ireland convinced us we needed a tumbling stone ruin on the rose hill if our place was ever to amount to anything. New Zealand gardens inspired in me an urge to uproot everything and replace it with expanses of tussock grasses and slender sedges that might dance gracefully in the breezes of all seasons. These enthusiasms are mercifully tempered by the time one gets home, before too much damage can be done.

The classical gardens of China I found particularly instructive, in part because they embody a worldview and an aesthetic sensibility vastly different from what underlies Western gardening. I was repeatedly impressed by how, whenever we stepped inside one of these great walled gardens, even when located in the heart of as uproarious a place as Shanghai, the commotion of the outer world subsided and was left behind. Quietude gradually calmed the spirit, settled the inner and outer noise, and disposed the visitor to a state of calm receptiveness. These gardens are masterworks specifically designed to accommodate a lifetime's tranquil meditation, emphasizing the connection between inner and outer realities, between spirit and nature.

There is considerable deep thinking nowadays concerning the integration of house and garden, and in this the classical Chinese garden truly excels; its buildings and gardens are so profoundly intertwined that neither element could properly exist without the other. Each of these gardens seeks to create within a relatively small walled space a miniaturized version of the natural landscape—mountains and valleys, ancient trees, lakes and islands—located within a complex of parlors, chambers, pavilions, kiosks, and pagodas from which different aspects of the garden can be appreciated at various seasons and times of the day. Stone, water, plants, and buildings are the garden's fundamental elements. Trees are essential, but flowering plants are used sparingly and always with symbolic or literary associations.

Within these masterpieces there occurs a sense of revelation as one is led from room to room, area to area, encountering aspects or configurations that are different from what went before and yet also echo it. Division is a fundamental design concept, with each area assigned its own name: the Pavilion for the Advent of the Moon and Wind, for example, and the Wafting Fragrance Hall. Windows and doorways, especially the exquisite moon gates, are used to frame a particular view or object so as to intensify one's perception of it. Leak windows, with elaborately decorated lattice designs, provide the passing viewer with partial glimpses into courtyards or other enclosed spaces. Connections between various features—by way of corridors, pathways, and bridges—tend to wind and zigzag, encouraging the visitor to move slowly and pause frequently to savor each view and the mood it induces.

It would be ludicrous to try to insinuate that our own rustic gimcrackery is in any way comparable to these masterworks, and yet I flatter myself that our garden's sensibility is not entirely at odds with theirs. In many ways our own buildings and gardens are also of a piece. Because our house hunkers down within the garden, the surrounding landscape seems almost to cascade indoors through every window. Each view offers a distinct perspective. One kitchen window opens onto the sod roof behind the house where multiple crocuses bloom in early spring, and while working at the kitchen sink or counter it is as though you were gazing uphill at a mountain wildflower meadow. Another window looks upward toward the sandstone walls and steps of a hillside that might be a slice of rural Ireland. Yet another view leads the eye down the garden's central pathway massed with perennials. Access from house to garden is immediate through French doors on two sides. One set opens onto a glass-roofed patio that literally presses itself out into the garden to where a small cascade trickles down the hillside into a pool set within the patio. The other doors take us into a sunken Mediterranean garden outside the front door.

As with the Chinese pavilions, there is an easy flow between indoors and out, so that the walls between the two seem almost permeable. From April through October most of our living is done outdoors—we sleep in the summerhouse at the far end of the garden, eat on the patio or at the campfire ring close by, and spend leisure hours either reading, chatting, or pondering at one of the garden's several viewing spots. From each of these the house is seen to be an integral part of the garden, an essential element of the overall composition. But where the Chinese master garden designers achieved brilliant contrasts between the formal regularity of buildings and the purposeful irregularity of rocks, pools, and trees, our intent is far more one of harmony, attempting to have the buildings blend into the woodlands and gardens of which they are a part.

MOST RECENTLY, SANDY and I enjoyed an extended summer ramble among the gardens and landscapes of southern England and Wales, a more intensive version of that seminal visit twenty-eight years previously. We spent two months exploring the great gardens of Kent and Surrey—marvelous places like Great Dixter and Sissinghurst—and walking the Shropshire Hills, the Dorset coast, and other equally lovely landscapes. The closest we came to Liverpool this time was Powys Castle in Wales. We'd gone there to see the estate, now a National Trust property, and especially its famed yew hedges. They didn't disappoint, cascading down the hillside below the mighty castle like enormous living green clouds. Extravagant topiary was one of the repeated glories of the trip as we visited garden after garden in which boxwood, beech, yew, lime, and hornbeam had been clipped and sheared and sculpted into astonishing shapes.

Thus it was that we returned from topiaried Britain with a determination to further extend our evergreen plantings, something we've been doing in recent years, gradually replacing leggy and labor-intensive perennials with structured plantings that serve less demandingly throughout the year. Scarcely were we home when Sandy came by chance upon a clearance sale of Green Mountain boxwood plants in five-gallon pots at a price she couldn't resist. So I spent the better part of a week moving out some underperforming roses from the hillside to make room for the boxwoods.

I dug a series of large holes in the fractured sandstone of the hillside, carrying heavy buckets of stone down to the wheelbarrow, then barrowing it away for fill in the driveway. Over the years we've spent untold hours excavating planting holes in this stony hillside, sifting out sandy soil with a wire-mesh screen, then lugging the screened gravel away and in return carrying up buckets of compost and fir bark to refurbish the planting holes. To those who do not garden, this would seem the height of madness, carrying the hillside away bucket by bucket, as futile as Sisyphus with his stone. But in a bizarre way it's strangely gratifying, involving as it does real earth and stones, honest labor.

I set the burly boxwood roots in at the proper depth, filled around them with compost and soil, and soaked them thoroughly. I muttered a requisite few words of encouragement to the effect that up here on the hillside is a perfect spot for them to eventually form a clipped installation in the spirit of Powys. From the hilltop I looked down across the garden and felt a sudden rush of exhilaration. The winds and rains of autumn had stripped it down to its underwear, revealing something every bit as lovely as in the full dress of summer. The big grasses—the *Miscanthus* and blue oat grass, the *Stipa* and Karl Foerster—were at their finest, waving their full, wild heads of hair as though set free by the winds of fall. So were the heavenly bamboos and the green and golden and variegated boxwoods. Japanese maples flared in crimson flames against the somber forest. A familiar little buck and his sidekick, a motherless fawn who looked too small to survive the oncoming winter, tiptoed into the woods and were gone.

This is my home, I reflected, a stony place where my roots run as deep as four decades allow. It has taken me that, and longer, to apprehend the simple truth that the creation of sanctuary, like the attainment of solitude, occurs within the heart as much as through one's surroundings. To establish an equilibrium of peace and beauty and harmony requires, as the gardens of China illustrated, a looking both inward and outward. But as we sat out that evening to watch the full moon rise, the blood moon of October, the garden shimmering with earthly beauty, wild deer watching from the forest's edge, I was reminded of the gifted Canadian travel writer Paul William Roberts writing in *Empire of the Soul*: "Although God is omnipresent, there are places, as well as people, through which it is *easier* to look upon the Eternal." For me at least, and certainly for Sandy, this garden of dreams and memories, which partakes in its own way in the sacred, is one of those places.

13

WORDS

Writing, like dreams, confronts, pushes you up
against the evasions, self-deceptions, investments in opinions
and interpretations, the clutter that blinds, that disguises
that underlying, all-encompassing design.

TONI CADE BAMBARA, *"Salvation Is the Issue"*

THE GARDEN, ONCE CREATED, SOON grew into an axis around which larger and larger chunks of our lives began to rotate. My writing, for example. I had never remotely imagined any likelihood of my becoming a gardening writer. I'd tried my hand at poetry. Next came a stint as a self-taught journalist. After living on the island for about two years, Sandy and I and several friends decided to start publishing a monthly magazine for the community. Packed with gossip, local politics, poetry, recipes, and outlandish manifestos, the *Denman Rag & Bone* was typed onto wax stencils using an electric typewriter and printed on an ancient Gestetner whose rolling drum in hindsight seems closer to Johannes Gutenberg's movable metal type than to the laser printer on my desk today. Timidity was never a feature of the *Rag & Bone*'s editorial stance, and we managed to get ourselves into all manner of roiling community dustups. Whenever I went on a particular tear, I adopted the nom de plume Desmond the Red and mounted the rhetorical barricades with both fists bared. After so many years of monastic self-restraint, I'd lost the art of temperance entirely. The one thing you experience immediately from no-holds-barred journalism in a small community—we were fewer than five hundred residents in those days—is reader feedback. I gained unequivocal and invaluable insight into how best to please or antagonize a readership.

While staying in Athens during our grand tour of 1979, we'd received a large bundle of mail forwarded from home, including a copy of *Harrowsmith* magazine that contained a feature article I'd written about owner-built homes on Denman. Sitting in a cold *kafenion* and feeling just a touch of homesickness, we'd gazed with excessive excitement at photos of our house, and I felt the special thrill of seeing my first-ever "big ticket" writing in print. After several years of freelance writing for local newspapers and magazines, this *Harrowsmith* piece marked a quantum leap in exposure and income. I became a regular contributor to that estimable publication and soon did the same with *Nature Canada* and *Canadian Geographic*. I wrote mostly feature pieces on natural history, environmental issues, and rural living. Some would require painstaking research, possibly travel, and often extensive interviewing. In the process I got to meet some fascinating people and explore places I otherwise wouldn't have. For a piece on the Fraser River estuary I hired a fishing boat and poked around hidden spots with a wise old fisherman who knew the history of the river and its people as thoroughly as its currents. A story on selection logging had me journey down to the Willamette Valley in Oregon to interview a forester practicing intensive forestry using an individual tree-selection system. I flew up the B.C. coast to remote Bella Coola to write about a tile-maker who'd built a marvelous Victorian house in that unlikely setting. A piece on the reintroduction of sea otters to the west coast of Vancouver Island found me bobbing around in a skiff with five young female biologists, which was great fun until that delicate moment when I was required to relieve myself over the side of the boat while maintaining what dignity I could. Another assignment sent me off to the wilds of Haida Gwaii (the Queen Charlotte Islands) to tag along with the bryologist Wilf Schofield, an internationally renowned expert in mosses and liverworts, in whose company I learned far more than I could have imagined about these fascinating plant forms. By choosing the stories I wanted to write, I was getting a first-rate education in the people, places, and creatures of the coast. And in the process I was learning how to write, attempting to mold words into something more than dull reportage, to find my own voice, as Thalia Selz had urged.

In the mid-eighties a half-dozen of us islanders formed the Red Heart Theatre Collective and set about producing original material on social animation themes. Our guiding light was the Brazilian director Augusto Boal, who'd developed his "theater of the oppressed" in the 1970s and later developed "forum theater," in which issues of oppression were explored by having audience members intervene in the action and reconstruct scenes in a way that defused oppressive elements. Although we were fervently collective in our working—including regular group "check-ins" during which "held feelings," "appreciations," "paranoid fantasies," and other scraps of psychic debris were examined and dealt with—we looked largely to our friend Juan Barker for direction, as the only one among us with formal training in theater. Thanks to the "generous assistance" of the Canada Council, we mounted two productions: *Power Play,* dealing with issues of domestic abuse, and *Islands,* which tackled connections between individual isolation and exploitation of the planet. We toured both productions around the coast, dragging our set, costumes, and props with us, frequently sleeping on church basement floors or in community halls. Much of the material was collaborative, developed through workshopping, but I did get a chance to explore writing for performance, which was not something I'd done before. The lessons learned became invaluable in subsequent social action work, and for several years theater became almost as much an obsession as poetry had been.

In 1990 a feature piece I'd written about slugs for *Nature Canada* caught the eye of the Vancouver publisher Colleen MacMillan. She invited me to do a book about animals and plants that people tend to loathe. Jubilantly, I signed a contract to deliver a manuscript within six months. I spent several dreary weeks in the bowels of the old Vancouver Public Library reading and researching everything I could on rats, maggots, dandelions, and the like. The writing life before Google was even less of a lark. But the tediousness of research was rewarded with wonderful promotional possibilities. Although I didn't realize it at the time, the nineties were a golden age of publicity for Canadian authors, particularly at CBC Radio. In very short order, I found myself chatting on air with the star hosts Peter Gzowski, Vicki Gabereau, and Arthur Black. Television bits, newspaper reviews, magazine feature profiles—there seemed no end of opportunity for publicizing one's book.

After the modest success of that first book, called *Living Things We Love to Hate,* engendered by the torrent of publicity, I received another call from Colleen MacMillan. "How about trying your hand at a gardening book?" she said. For me to write a gardening book seemed the essence of temerity, what with the legions of horticulturalists, master gardeners, botanists, taxonomists, and their ilk all grinding out learned tomes on every conceivable aspect of gardening. "Does the world really need another gardening book?" I asked in the opening sentence of my book, unhappily titled *Crazy about Gardening,* and by way of answer I quoted Eleanor Perenyi, who wrote in *Green Thoughts* that "a writer who gardens *is* sooner or later going to write a book about the subject."

Fair enough—write a book on the subject and get it out of your system. Except that writing about gardening is rather like an intestinal worm, far easier to get into your system than out. Shortly after the book's publication, an editor at the *Globe and Mail* approached me and invited me to write a gardening column for the paper. She said the column would be rotated each week among Marjorie Harris in Toronto, Lois Hole in Edmonton, and me. These were women of immense talent and reputation, and I would be the worst sort of arriviste charlatan to try to clamber onto their pedestal. Plus I thought of the *Globe* as a bastion of deep thinkers and aesthetic heavy lifters among whom I should soon be exposed as a grubby poseur. I declined the invitation. The editor persisted. She offered me a fee about quadruple the per-word rate I'd been getting as a freelancer. This is the point at which any writer of integrity looks to his principles rather than to his bank balance. Instead I accepted the offer. For a good chunk of the nineties I produced a gardening column every third week, this being as close as I've come to steady employment for most of my working career. I came to enjoy the conciseness of the 750-word limit, packing into a small space the information intended to be both useful and at least moderately entertaining. Writing so steadily about the garden compelled me to pay attention to its seasonal nuances, so that the gardening and the writing became ever more intimately intertwined.

Gardening had yet another trick up its sleeve: around the same time that the *Globe* came calling, so did the Canadian Broadcasting Corporation. (This symbiotic relationship between the *Globe* and the CBC is, I came to understand, a very Toronto thing and not to be wondered at.) I signed on to contribute a weekly monologue to the national CBC TV program *Midday*. A crew from Vancouver would come up to our place every five or six weeks and we'd spend a day shooting a half-dozen separate segments, often in the garden, sometimes at a beach or in the woods, each of which would run about two or three minutes. Here was another whole set of lessons to be learned in the craft of concinnity. My producer, Robin Barber, preferred to shoot each piece without interruption or subsequent editing, so I'd just launch in and rattle away with as much vivacity and affability as I could muster. Then we'd do it again. And again. Mostly we'd nail it within two or three tries. Sometimes there'd be brilliant little snippets of serendipity, as on the occasion when we did a piece on dragonflies. I had netted a beautiful big specimen the evening before and placed it in the refrigerator overnight. Next morning I perched the numb creature on the tip of my index finger, where the camera could peer right into its bulging eyes and examine its gossamer wings as I rattled on about "Here be dragons." Just as the final words fell from my lips, the dragonfly, now sufficiently warmed, with perfect precision flitted from my finger into the blue summer sky.

Even while gardening was tightening its grip upon my writing, I continued producing material on other causes and issues I felt passionate about. After years of attending peace walks, wilderness gatherings, and assorted protest rallies, I'd begun developing an allergic response to long-winded speeches by well-intentioned but florid orators, myself included. Surely, I thought, we can dream up cleverer ways of conveying information, attitudes, and feelings. Words, not music, being my métier, I set sail into the relatively uncharted waters of eco-satire (this was long before the age of an eco-everything around every eco-corner.) The performance pieces I created were a hybrid of stand-up comedy and storytelling. Seldom suffering from a surfeit of good taste, these offerings were sufficiently topical and passionate that I ended up presenting them at all sorts of events, oftentimes sharing the bill with musicians. At Greenpeace's twentieth-anniversary party at Vancouver's venerable Orpheum Theatre, I was billed with Billy Bragg, alongside Garnet Rogers and Ferron. At a wilderness gathering in Clayoquot Sound I did a satire on civil disobedience as a warm-up act to the very young and rapidly rising Sarah McLachlan. For a couple of years I toured around with the talented musicians of the Holly Arntzen Band, who provided musical accompaniment to my rants. Here at last was partial redemption for my boyhood pusillanimity with the banjo and the humiliation of Ger's and my discordant kyries.

I WAS, FOR a while there in the nineties, very full of myself, as my old mum would have put it. I enjoyed the dreamed-of ideal for the freelance writer: being able to market related material through books, feature articles for magazines, a gardening magazine column, and a newspaper column, along with TV work and giving speeches at gardening events across the country. Our income shot up to the point where it threatened to leap over the national poverty line. Most of this was due to gardening, and to the fact that a gardening mania had engulfed North America. But then, almost overnight, the financial bubble burst. By the end of the millennium, the gardening mania that had served me so well was already showing signs of having peaked. The *Globe and Mail* abruptly canceled its gardening column. The CBC, ever faithful to the symbiotic relationship, pulled the plug on its *Midday* program. My gardening magazine column was dropped when the editor had a hissy fit over my satirical excesses. Within the space of a few months we plunged from boom to bust.

It was definitely time to diversify the portfolio. I hooked up with the independent film producers David Springbett and Heather MacAndrew to work on a documentary adaptation of my first book, *Living Things We Love to Hate*. Straight off we recognized that we were birds of a feather and, while arrangements for the film were going forward, we leaped into another project, a TV series rather ambitiously titled *Reinventing the World*. This involved five one-hour documentaries, each segment dealing with a topic of importance involving work, food, time, and economics. I worked with Heather and David distilling hours of filmed material down to a compact form and writing the narrative, then served as on-camera host for the series. A second series, titled *Finding the Future*, had me interviewing a bevy of brainy and progressive people, including the likes of the ethnobotanist Wade Davis, the social affairs critic Linda McQuaig, the radical theologian Matthew Fox, the writer Michael Pollan, and the feminist Sunera Thobani. This was bracing work to be engaged in, exploring ideas with such insightful characters and working in close collaboration with David and Heather and their film crew.

By strange coincidence, my brother Vincent got involved in broadcasting around the same time I did. Having grown up in the hearing world, where he relied upon lipreading and his hearing aid, in his late twenties he was introduced to the deaf community and learned to communicate by American Sign Language. Initially he felt self-conscious being among other deaf people, because of his hearing aid and his lack of skill with signing. He was as different and set apart from the deaf as he had been from the hearing world. Nevertheless, he continued to participate in the deaf community, quickly mastering sign language to the point where he began teaching it. In group settings he found communicating more efficient and enjoyable with the deaf than with the hearing. He became very involved with the deaf community for many years, participating in social and recreational activities. In the mid-eighties he worked as a volunteer producer/director of the biweekly ASL TV production *The Deaf TV Program,* which was mostly in interview format. He was asked by the Canadian Captioning Development Agency to help promote increased awareness of closed-captioning in British Columbia among both broadcasters and deaf consumers. "This was one of the wonderful experiences I had in connecting the world of sound with the world of silence," he tells me. "I felt that I was involved in an important way in bringing the deaf and the hearing communities closer together through the improvement of closed-captioning on TV."

FOR MY THIRD book I decided to tackle what had for a long time been the impossible dream of writing a novel. Once I'd given myself permission and sucked up a great draft of perhaps illusory self-confidence, I plunged into the writing and eventually muddled my way through to a completed story. In the process I rediscovered a type of passionate engagement with the writing that I hadn't felt in quite the same way since my poetry days. The creation of character, the development of plot, the subtleties of dialogue, and the complexity of connecting themes—all of it was intellectually ravishing. The story in part concerned the campaign to save old-growth forests on the West Coast. I did a fair bit of its writing and revising, following the invaluable suggestions of my Toronto editor, Bernice Eisenstein, while camped out on the beaches of the Pacific Rim National Park Reserve, scribbling away while hunkered down in the sand dunes, hearing the cries of seabirds and the roar of combers breaking across the beach before me. Now here was nature and art commingled to a high degree!

Once again the film world came calling, this time in the person of the respected Canadian filmmaker Mort Ransen. Mort optioned my story and hired me on to assist with his writing of the screenplay. Like the documentary film work, this was an intriguing exercise, learning the distinct requirements of words for the page and words for the screen. The film was never made, but I did cut quite a swath in social circles by announcing that a feature film based on my story was "in production"!

I've written two other novels since then, and with each of them experienced that same intoxicating immersion in another world. My favorite types of fiction usually have a strong sense of place, and that's important in my own writing. I set the second novel in a fictional small town in the B.C. Interior grasslands, where I also did some of the writing, and the third one in Ireland, after spending time there. Don't mistake me: I enjoy writing nonfiction—I've done several subsequent gardening books and still contribute a column to *GardenWise* magazine—but the process seldom carries me to that other place where fiction writing leads, where one enters an imaginative world in which hours sometimes pass without notice, a place where demons are confronted and small fragments of truth unearthed.

By far the best part of the writing life lies in the joy of creation, and the freedom to work when and how one chooses. I do the bulk of my writing in the morning, and then set it aside to get outdoors for gardening, work in the woods, or something else brawny. This often affords an invaluable opportunity for mulling over what I've written earlier, and it's remarkable how many insights and solutions to problems pop into the brain—as is sometimes the case during the transit between sleeping and waking—while the body is more or less mindlessly heaving things around. On Sunday afternoons or warm summer evenings I'll sometimes take a manuscript outdoors and work on editing while occasionally gazing across the gardens. And it's where I belong, with the writing and the earthwork interwoven. I should have known as much all those years ago when, during my momentous summer at Columbia, Thalia Selz assigned us to write a short descriptive piece about a walk through Manhattan. She returned my "Notes on a Walk through Uptown" with the words "trees, grass, birds" scribbled in the margin along with her underlining of nineteen separate references I'd made to them in a one-page piece. Even within the steel and concrete heart of Gotham, I had been preoccupied with things that grew and sang.

I consider this "active mind and robust body" approach an appealing way to spend my days. The icing on the cake comes with doing readings at various festivals, conferences, and other gatherings, and having thoughtful readers approach with words of gratitude for what I've written. A good chunk of my income (after the heyday of the nineties, again reduced to a good chunk of not very much) now derives from giving speeches at gardening or other events. In a peculiar way I've reinvented the Passionist lifestyle of contemplative withdrawal interspersed with periodic forays to distant places in order to speak of a passion and a way of life. I've attempted to substitute humor for harangue, but the message is essentially the same: that redemption is attainable. Then, every once in a while, comes something very special: like the time not long ago when an acquaintance called to tell me that our mutual friend Melda Buchanan, a venerable Vancouver Island environmentalist, had requested that she be read to from one of my books during her final days as she lay dying of cancer in a hospital bed. That alone made the writing, and the long and convoluted pathway to it, entirely worthwhile.

14

GROWING YOUR OWN

The act of putting into your mouth what the earth has grown
is perhaps your most direct interaction with the earth.

FRANCES MOORE LAPPÉ, *Diet for a Small Planet*

MY FATHER LIVED FOR A further twenty years after my mother's death. He remained alone in his little house in Rexdale overlooking the Humber River, continuing to maintain his gardens, which still produced vast quantities of vegetables and fruits, far more than he could eat or fob off on the neighbors. Retired from the TTC, he worked part-time as a maintenance person at a nearby seniors' housing complex. A frequent theme was how lucky he considered himself that he still had his health, something he'd never trade for all the financial and career success previously enjoyed by the ailing seniors he was now assisting. "I couldn't stand to live in one of them places," he'd say. He took special pride in the domestic skills he'd developed doing the chores my mother had formerly done, making delicious orange marmalade as well as multiple pots of jam from his abundance of gooseberries, raspberries, and currants. He'd learned to bake scones that were better than the ones she'd made, and whenever we visited him we'd end up eating an extraordinary number of scones warm from the oven and slathered with butter and jam.

Although he had a bit of the old flirt about him, he seemed to consider remarriage not an option. "I'd never find anyone like your mother," he'd say in full seriousness, which was undoubtedly true but not necessarily an impediment to finding someone quite satisfactory. He had female friends of a sort and took to occasionally attending Blue Jays baseball games downtown with at least one younger woman, but it seemed to be a point of honor with him that he remain loyal to my mother's memory, a depth of affection somewhat more apparent after she'd died than before. "I'd have been a hopeless drunk if it wasn't for her," he told me more than once.

Sometimes my publicity commitments required that I travel to Toronto, and I'd stay with him then for a few days. He was a different man from the irascible and sleep-deprived workaholic I'd known, and resented, during adolescence. He aged into one of those old gents who, rather than getting grumpier over time, lighten up in retirement. He and I now had gardening in common. (My brother Ger, who has degrees in psychology, jokes that this is classic Freudian "identifying with the aggressor," which may "effect an oedipal victory of sorts.") While still vigorous in his seventies, my dad loved to take me through his gardens, and I enjoyed seeing them with him. He was extremely accomplished in his plantings—beds of roses and of irises, long borders of traditional English cottage-garden perennials, and feature specimens of hibiscus with pink, red, and cream blooms the size of dinner plates. The large backyard was still crammed with fruits and vegetables. A grapevine at the back ran for thirty feet or more, expertly trained along wires. "Wouldn't you know it," my dad would grin, "the very day them grapes are just ripe for picking, the old coon gets in and eats every single one of them!" He was forever engaged in a battle of wits with raccoons, groundhogs, skunks, and other invaders from the conservation lands along the river. But now the battle was more of a lark to him, as he didn't really need the food, and he spoke of his adversaries with a curious kind of affection.

Of course the power balance had shifted between us. Where I'd lived for years in dread of his anger, I now towered over him. In his eyes my books and television work gave me a level of prestige inconceivable in his working-class world. During one visit, a television studio dispatched a limousine to pick me up at his place. He stood at the foot of his driveway like a gnarled little leprechaun, beaming proudly as the enormous limo whisked me away to the city. At one point he absolutely floored me with a candid admission: "I was always afraid of you," he told me. Hold on here a second: *He* was afraid of *me?* This was the most bizarre thing I'd ever heard him say. I'd long before let go of my anger and resentment toward him—of how gruff and controlling he'd been with my mother, with Vincent especially, with all of us—but had I known he viewed me with fear, the relationship would have been very different.

Several times he came out west to visit us, staying for a week or so. I didn't rise as early in the morning back then as I do now, and I'd wander fuzzy-headed into the kitchen to find him sitting there, smoking one of his wretched hand-rolled cigarettes. By then Sandy and I had kicked the filthy habit, and I, at least, looked upon smokers with the monstrous disdain of the newly converted. Smoking was absolutely not permitted in the house. But could I tell him to go outside if he wanted to smoke? He was probably the only person on the planet I couldn't say that to.

From the very outset, he had been enthusiastic about our decision to move to Denman, never showing a trace of disillusionment that I was not pursuing a professional career. He had the old Irish notion that getting a piece of land was the wisest possible course of action, and on his first visit to the island with my mum (who was less enthusiastic) he plunged right into helping with the rough work we were doing in the early days. He had all sorts of practical tips about how to rot out a tree stump by drilling holes and filling them with saltpeter, how to clip a chicken's wings, what valuable plants our abundant stinging nettles were (my mother later sent her recipe for stinging nettle beer, which we never did get around to making). "How on earth did you ever find a place like this?" he'd marveled. I sensed that what we were doing on the island was the kind of thing he'd have loved to have done himself had circumstances been different for him. He and my mum regularly sent out packages of seeds and roots and whips of young trees, and many of these still flourish at our place.

In later years, when he came alone, he still loved to get outdoors and do things with us. One time we all went hunting for chanterelle mushrooms in the mossy woods behind our place. He delighted in finding the mushrooms, but had a hard time straddling the many windthrown logs crisscrossed in the forest. "I can't hop around in here like Daddy Longlegs over there," he laughed to Sandy, pointing at me.

I had more meaningful conversation with him during these later times than ever before. He loved to tell old stories of his boyhood. Our goats reminded him of the goats his mother had kept when he was a child. He liked talking about how he courted our mum, over her parents' objections. He and she used to ride a tandem bicycle out through the Lancashire countryside, and he took great delight in how she would leave her house wearing a demure frock, then change into a pair of shorts and a blouse for their cycling adventure, and change back again before returning home. He had several set pieces about experiences he'd had as a footloose young man employed on various farms in Ireland and England, some of which I incorporated into my novel *Climbing Patrick's Mountain*. He told them repeatedly and wouldn't be dissuaded from the retelling. Typically his tales would end with a punchline at which he'd laugh uproariously and then, always, he'd repeat the punchline and laughter. It got so you didn't want to hear any of them ever again, which is unfortunate because, in hindsight, I wish I'd recorded them, as they were genuine snippets from an era now long gone. He was a throwback himself, as was my mum, to an earlier time and a different place. He adapted to life in Canada in a way she never did, but he remained a peculiar little customer "with the map of Ireland all over his face," as people used to say of him. I still occasionally receive letters or telephone calls from people who'd known him in Rexdale. Invariably they speak fondly of him as a genial and generous neighbor.

As age advanced upon him, there came a dreadful time when he sank into ill health and surly reclusiveness. Ger—the only one of us four who lived not far away, and who had spent many years dutifully visiting—had a hell of a time dealing with him. Finally the old boy weakened to the point where he had to be hospitalized. Unaware until then of how severely he'd deteriorated, I flew east, expecting that he might be in his final days. I found him curled up in a hospital bed, shrunken, wizened, and at best semiconscious. I had taken along Frank O'Connor's *A Book of Ireland,* and I sat reading stories from it to him, unaware of whether he was able to hear or understand anything. Seeing his condition, I was quite certain that he'd be dead in short order. But, remarkably, with medical attention and proper nutrition he regained his health, and Ger eventually got him settled at a nursing home in Hamilton, an hour away from Toronto. True to form, he was soon up and about and took on the role, at least in his own mind, of nurse's assistant, helping push wheelchair patients around and the like. Although there was a garden at the facility, he had no interest in it at all.

I visited him there on one or two occasions, but when I flew east for another visit, I came down with a wretched flu picked up on the plane and didn't want to risk taking it into the nursing home. It would have been my last chance to see him. Shortly after, he was unexpectedly visited by a great-niece from Ireland and her husband, whose photos show him holding the young woman's hand with a mischievous glint in his eye and what looks for all the world like a great love of life in his grin. He died peacefully in his sleep that night.

ONLY IN HINDSIGHT did I come to fully appreciate the invaluable inheritance I'd received from him: the gift of growing. Both he and my mum practiced, and passed on, an appreciation of the wisdom of "growing your own" and "doing better with less." The resultant credo by which Sandy and I have lived for many years enjoins us to, as much as possible, eat fresh, eat clean, eat seasonal, and, increasingly, eat raw.

Wildcrafting provides two key ingredients in this diet, stinging nettles and mushrooms, along with a host of lesser ones. Nettles start us off in February or early March, as their vibrant, purplish-green rosettes emerge from cold earth at the first hint of warming. They are our spring tonic, our "Indian spinach" packed with the vital blood juices of the earth. We devour them avidly as a steamed green, or in soup, or folded into mashed potatoes. Later on we dry nettle leaves for use in tea through the winter.

Mushrooms come in two brilliant flushes. In April and May, oyster mushrooms emerge in bracketlike clusters along the trunks of recently dead red alder trees, whether standing or lying on the forest floor. Smooth and pearly white, the mushrooms have a distinctive earthy scent. I slice them cleanly from the trunk, often filling several buckets at a time. We eat them in abundance in season and fry any surplus in a drizzle of olive oil to be put in the freezer for wintertime soups, pizzas, and sauces. Following the first soaking rains of autumn, chanterelle mushrooms, some golden, others white, emerge in the woods. Difficult to detect among the mosses, fallen trees and undergrowth of the forest floor, chanterelles are princely mushrooms and the quest for them a greeny treasure hunt. These too we eat with gusto in season, freezing the surplus for leaner days ahead. There are other types of mushroom to be had as well, but these two come in the greatest abundance and virtually on our doorstep.

Also free for the taking, in the earliest days of spring, are the seasonal wild greens we gather for the salad bowl. Chickweed's among the most generous of these, a cosmopolitan weed that's packed with vitamins and vitality. Miner's lettuce is a slightly later contributor to our salads. These and other wildlings augment a quartet of enthusiastic self-seeders that flourish in the earliest days of the growing year: parsley, chervil, corn salad, and Russian red kale. Throw in the first slender spears of chives and small leaves of sorrel for taste, and for color a sprinkling of the white flowers of rock cress, *Arabis caucasica,* and a few wild pansies, and you've got a salad of gloriously vibrant flavor and healthfulness. The actual gathering of these little leaves is fundamental to their healthfulness, for it gets us out onto the ground, in touch with the warming earth and the surge of its life forces.

Thus the table is set for a three-season succession of gastronomical peak experiences. When the green spears of asparagus appear in April, we take to devouring them night after night, delighting in their delicacy of taste. When the broccoli heads bulge full or the curds of cauliflower swell firm and tight, we crop them and eat them as though they were the only food on earth. For us, variety plays second fiddle to freshness. If you've got fresh asparagus in abundance, eat fresh asparagus, as few things can match its perfection of flavor. When the fava beans reach their peak, before their skins start to thicken, we'll eat them meal after meal, most often blanched quickly, then lightly fried in olive oil with crushed fresh garlic. Heaven! When strawberries or raspberries or blueberries are in full flow, we'll eat an enormous bowl of them for lunch, with a dollop of yogurt. Same thing when the peaches, pears, plums, and figs have ripened—they come straight off the tree and into the bowl, eaten still sensuously warm and sweet from the summer's sun. This is what we mean by *fresh*, that adjective so offhandedly abused by furtive advertisers. *Fresh* entails still possessing the robust wholesomeness of the living fruit or leaf, bursting with sweet juices, crisply delicious with complex subtleties of flavor. You want fresh, go into the garden.

As more and more people seem to be realizing, the best response to the monstrosities of Monsanto is to grow as much of one's own food as possible or, where that's not possible, to acquire food from nearby and trusted sources. I believe there's reason for optimism, seeing the various movements toward developing a local-food culture occurring nowadays—allotment gardens, farmers' markets, Seedy Saturdays, community-supported agriculture, and other direct arrangements between farmers and nearby consumers. Of course there's a tremendous distance still to go before the populace at large has access to healthy and uncontaminated foodstuffs, now widely recognized as a fundamental step away from the culture of obesity and rampant cancers that result from addiction to the foods of convenience and speed.

Throughout winter, we rely for freshness on bean and other sprouts and the leaves of Russian red kale, which endure all but the most severe frosts. One multiseason favorite dish is kale leaves steamed lightly with pressed garlic—we grow about fifty pounds of garlic a year and use it recklessly. We store it, along with sacks of sweet onions, in a cool room. Carrots, beets, rutabagas, parsnips, and Jerusalem artichokes remain in the ground for most of the winter, with a thick newspaper covering to keep off the frost, and are picked fresh as needed and either cooked or grated raw into a slaw. Potatoes are stored in sawdust in a large container in the woodshed, where there's also a big bin of golden russet apples that hold their crispness through winter and well into March. As well,

I plant the unheated greenhouse with mesclun mix early in the new year and we get a sustained cutting of mesclun until the early spinach and arugula can get going outdoors. After the mesclun's done, the greenhouse is planted in tomatoes and basil, those twin stars of the summer eating season.

In winter I brew tea of dried stinging nettle; dried hawthorn blossoms, which I harvest and dry the previous May and consume for a troublesome heart; a bit of green tea; and either grated ginger or fresh rosemary cut from a bush in the greenhouse. As soon as possible in spring, I switch to fresh tea ingredients from the garden, like sweet cicely and lemon balm. In summer I pick fresh mint or peppermint that grows wild along the creek, sometimes adding raspberry leaves or rose petals. Other than when we eat salads and berries in summer, lunch is always a big bowl of soup prepared from our dried beans and stored squash as well as vegetables harvested and frozen the previous year, perhaps augmented with lentils or barley. We sprinkle a heaping spoonful of ground flax-seed and another of Engevita yeast into the soup. Along with that I have a thick slice of Sandy's grain-rich homemade bread, on which I spread a layer of miso and a bean paste made from our fava beans.

For additional protein we rely mostly upon eggs from a neighbor—real eggs, not those pallid, milky abominations extracted from imprisoned chickens—tofu, and inexpensive local wild pink salmon. Special meals often involve barbecuing salmon or tofu and assorted vegetables. Barbecued zucchini strips, lightly marinated in olive oil and lemon juice, have put an end to the perennial dilemma of what to do with excesses of zucchini. I gather red alder chips from around the firewood chopping block for smoking flavor.

Simple and repetitive as it may be, this is a diet for which I count my blessings. I know full well how fortunate I am to live in a place where food can be grown and harvested throughout most of the year, and doubly fortunate to have as a partner someone with tremendous skill for taking basic raw materials and creating from them dishes that are both healthy and flavorful. It's not gourmet or fancy or trendy; it's just darn good. So good, in fact, we now seldom dine out—one in spirit, I suppose, with my dear old mum, whose invariable response whenever I suggested she take a break from her kitchen work by dining out was "Why would we want to go out to a restaurant when we've got all this good food to eat around here?" But, unlike her, I occasionally entertain a singular exception: no matter how fully I recognize its folly, I can't seem to entirely discard the lingering appeal of that monastic indulgence on Sunday morning. Every once in a rare while, especially if I'm off on a speaking tour and staying in fancy hotels, I'll perversely eschew my normal heart-healthy breakfast and instead order up a great whacking big plate of bacon and eggs, hash browns, and toast, finishing up with a cinnamon bun and cup of coffee. Oh, those concupiscible appetites!

ALL THINGS CONSIDERED, I'm grateful to have spent my childhood in what I now think of as beneficent poverty, a condition that excluded luxury and social status but was not so onerous as to paralyze the spirit. My parents' values were those of working-class Britain, sharpened through years of depression and war. Their cardinal rule was to avoid debt at all costs, to make do with what you had rather than hanker for what you didn't have. They grew and preserved enough fruit and vegetables to feed a family of six. They composted religiously. Nothing was thrown away that might be put to later use. They conserved whatever they could: water in which vegetables had been washed wasn't drained away but caught in a bowl, carried outdoors, and poured onto the gardens. Like others of their generation, they were reducing, reusing, and recycling decades before the trilogy became trendy.

Now here I am, years later, doing essentially the same. I consciously chose a career, first in the monastery and then here on the island, in which possessions and social position play insignificant parts. The forest and its creatures, the gardens, the unfolding of seasons, occasional visits to places of great beauty, writing and reading, fine music, the comforts of long-held friendships—these are the "things" we most value and around which we structure our lives. We live conveniently and contentedly below the poverty line. We spend the absolute minimum time at shopping and feel far more at home in a thrift shop than in a department store or boutique. Flashy vehicles, jewelry, and expensive clothing hold little allure. Many of our tools and implements are so old they're almost antiques. Our gardening outfits are a disgrace. Our (my) reluctance to throw anything away borders on chronic hoarding.

I wouldn't be so self-indulgent as to call this way of life "voluntary poverty" or even the "simple living" so in vogue a few years ago. After all, we own acreage in one of the country's most desirable locations along with all the equipment required to live on it in relative comfort. Measured against the standards of North America's consuming classes, our lifestyle is parsimonious to the point of frugality; but compared with most societies on earth, where 40 percent of the world's population lives on two dollars a day or less, we're enviably wealthy.

But I do feel a clarity and rightness about having pursued a life course in which money has played so minor a role. To have never had a mortgage, never been in debt, and never had to worry about where the next payment was coming from is a glorious freedom, something one would wish for everyone. Equally emancipating is the disinclination to have purchasing at the heart of one's being. And beyond that, as the formal discipline of religious poverty taught, lies escape from the habitual placing of attention upon money. I don't mean the anxiety of the truly poor, worrying about where to find money for rent or food, but the slow corrosion that occurs from a persistent and unnecessary obsession with money matters.

We and our contemporaries were, albeit unconsciously, beneficiaries of a certain time and place when cash was to be had for the earning and desirable rural land was ridiculously inexpensive. We were handed a golden key to financial independence in a way that very few people are. Young folk wanting to do today what we did four decades ago face staggeringly high land prices and a relentlessly rising cost of living. "Doing better with less" is a far more expensive proposition than it once was. Nevertheless, at a deeper level, our orientation—through social action, political inclination, and lifestyle—remains more closely aligned with those who have too little rather than those who have too much. And, in several ways, strangely aligned with many of the values my parents held half a century ago.

15

SILENCE AND
SOUNDS

After silence, that which comes nearest to
expressing the inexpressible is music.

ALDOUS HUXLEY, *Music at Night and Other Essays*

AS THE EARTHY WORK OF growing, harvesting, and processing food remains at the core of the undertaking, we still spend a goodly chunk of most every day puttering around the place. We continue to do more than our fair share of arduous and sometimes dirty work—moving big boulders, emptying the compost privy, cleaning the chimney, and the like. I consider it entirely appropriate to get out there, get down, and get dirty every once in a while. Dirty work is like roughage for the soul, scraping off globules of psychic fat. To my mind manual labor requiring physical exertion is something to be actively pursued rather than avoided, so long as there's nobody in charge telling you that you *have to* do it and how. I enjoy the fact that an archaic meaning of the verb *labor* is to cultivate, as in "to labor the ground." Denied that possibility, I suppose I might jog along city streets stylishly attired in colorful, body-hugging spandex or shuffle off to a fitness center to "work out," but really I far prefer to work outside.

Outdoor work is largely determined by the seasons and is subject to a rhythmic seasonal flux in intensity. The days surrounding equinoxes are invariably the busiest while those following solstices seem to subside into a welcome slackening of pace. Spring equinox kicks off a particularly manic stretch because the gardens are then at their most demanding with seeding, transplanting, weeding, thinning, staking, clipping, watering, and everything else, it seems, all insisting they be done *right now!* Simultaneously I usually have an extensive round of speaking bookings—a score or more speeches scheduled for March, April, and May—during which Sandy is left to manage things alone.

Summer solstice, by contrast, is usually followed by at least a month or so of relative calm during which the gardens can be tended and savored at a civilized pace. The tempo quickens again around the vernal equinox when there's a torrent of garden produce to be harvested, processed, and stored, firewood to be brought in, compost to be made, leaves to be raked, and preparations made for winter. But again, after winter solstice the new year's marked by a stretch of relative peace during which far more reading and writing get done, and outdoor work involves doing what's desired rather than demanded. This seasonal ebb and flow of work intensity is, I think, more gratifying than either of the modalities would be on its own, and likely results in untold physical and mental benefits that any day now teams of clever researchers will discover and publicize.

I also welcome the daily give-and-take between intellectual effort and physical exertion. Each constitutes work in its own way and yet neither is what normally might be classified as going to work. There's no getting dressed up, leaving home, commuting, taking directions from management, dealing with coworkers, or collecting a regular paycheck.

Harried as we may be around our place at times, still the intent is to make haste slowly. To meander, to savor, to ponder. When I was young, the epitome of sinful sloth was the person who lay abed late on Sunday morning rather than get up and go to Mass. The late Sunday sleeper was bound for perdition, no matter how hard he or she may have toiled all week, no matter how in need of rest. Nowadays, after six days of early rising and steady work, I find a good Sunday lie-in is precisely what's called for. Then a day given over to old-fashioned leisure—quiet reading, fine music, maybe a special brunch, perhaps a football game on TV or a delicious afternoon siesta in the summerhouse. In such languid repose one is far more inclined to consider the merit of Oscar Wilde's observation that work is the refuge of people who have nothing better to do.

I have come to the conclusion that one of the greatest challenges facing many gardeners is the enterprise of not doing anything at all. Unlike other works of art, the garden is a perpetually unfinished business, which both increases its allure and bedevils its curator. There is always something to be done in it, some imperfection to be addressed, a rearrangement of elements required. The ideal of contemplative repose within this place of tranquillity is repeatedly besieged by the perceived demands of its transience. Plus a host of mighty strictures work against unproductive pensiveness, just as they do against lying abed. Certainly in my own case the earliest classrooms of childhood frequently rang with stern admonishments against "daydreaming." The inquisitive wonderment of childhood was something best abandoned early on, before it curdled into capriciousness. Whimsy was equated with the flighty, erratic, unstable.

Thus the great challenge of the gardening life: to be able every once in a while to set aside all practical considerations and simply allow sensations of delight and wonderment to flood into us for as long as they will. That is why, from among the many possible ways of being in a garden—physically, intellectually, socially—one of my favorites is the refined state of reverie. By this I mean being immersed in a dreamy, musing state in which thoughts, memories, and imaginings play subtly against one another. Warmed by voluptuous sunlight, gently prompted by the sights, fragrances, textures, and sounds of luxuriant vegetation, I wander the garden, entirely given over to sweet abstraction. "It is a good idea," wrote James Douglas in *Down Shoe Lane,* "to be alone in a garden at dawn or dusk so that all its shy presences may haunt you and possess you in a reverie of suspended thought."

This whimsical state of mind is, above all, sublimely unpractical. It is not a time for solving problems, or for focusing on projects that are crying out to be done. It is the very opposite of our workaday bustle and hustle. We will formulate no plans in this fanciful state, nor will we make demands upon ourselves. We will simply let everything be what it is for the moment, entering what the poet Andrew Marvell called "this delicious solitude" that seduces the mind into "Annihilating all that's made / To a green thought in a green shade."

As I think I've by now made abundantly clear, I'm as solidly committed to practicality and proficiency as the next workaholic, but not at the cost of reverie. Not by choking off that part of the spirit that craves the freedom to simply drift and remember and dream, to enter what Gaston Bachelard in *The Poetics of Space* called "the space of elsewhere."

In this regard the gardener is perfectly situated to indulge in what appears to be the lost art of reverie. In a provocative small volume titled *A Philosophy of Gardens,* the British philosopher David E. Cooper argues that "the garden offers precisely the combination of conditions conducive to reverie." While it is certainly possible to attain this visionary state of mind in any number of settings, Cooper maintains that in the garden, reverie finds "a place of special hospitality."

For one thing, we are intimately acquainted with the garden's environment, so the unexpected, the startling, the dangerous are less likely to intrude upon our musings there than they might be in wilderness. The winds and waves of the wild West Coast, for example, while more than capable of inspiring awe and exhilaration, also require that we remain alert for the unforeseen and unpredictable, and thus engender a different state of consciousness than the calm reflectiveness of reverie.

On the other end of the spectrum, indoor spaces often lack the spontaneity of small occurrences—the chirrup of a songbird, the hauntingly evocative scent of a particular rose—that are so conducive to the amalgam of memory, imagination, and thought that constitutes true reverie. In the garden our attention might be snagged for a moment by a particular plant given to us long ago by a loved one now departed. An apple tree heavy with fruit might suddenly stir a childhood memory of having pilfered a couple of apples from a farmer's orchard and been chased by his ferocious German shepherd. These fragments of visions come and go, requiring neither analysis nor judgment. Some induce a state of delight, others one of melancholy, or perhaps a yearning for something elusive that we cannot name.

I believe that it's not only desirable but also necessary to enter into states of reverie at least every once in a while, just as it is necessary to dream, if we are not to become mentally disordered. They take us out of ourselves into other realms in a way that's similar to, but distinct from, the experiences of meditation and contemplation. That the garden is an especially suitable locus for these goings-on adds immensely to the appeal of entering the dreamy, musing elsewhere of reverie.

ACHIEVING THIS REFINED state requires both an inner and an outer silence, and I'm not sure which is easier to access in these tumultuous times. On many occasions Sandy and I will sit out of an evening and remark upon how hushed the soundscape is. It's never absolute silence—there'll be the trickle of the creek, perhaps a rustling of leaves, the chittering of birds among the shrubs. But it's far from the mad cacophony of noise that so many North Americans now accept as normal, the pandemoniacal clangor of demolition and construction, transportation and manufacturing, amplified music, wailing sirens, blaring horns, thudding helicopters, and all the rest. One of the garden's highest purposes is to serve as refuge from the jostle and hubbub of ordinary life, and few things are more inimical to the spirit of a garden than the roar of road traffic or the thundering of aircraft. Over the years I've visited any number of fine gardens made impossible by excessive noise. Peace, tranquillity, contemplative solitude—these are among the primary attributes of the garden, the states of mind it is intended to induce, and they cannot coexist with invasive noise.

Throughout my time of doing television and film work, we were regularly visited by production teams that normally consisted of a producer, one or more camera people, and a sound technician. The sound people were a type unto themselves, headphones clamped to their ears, a portable control panel dangling from a strap around the neck, a big boom mike wielded like a lance. No one knows sounds and silence quite the way a sound technician does. Compulsively fiddling with dials on the control panel and darting looks in odd directions, they could pick up a hint of faraway sound the way a bloodhound will sniff out a scent. During outdoor shoots, if an airplane was thrumming away in the distance, scarcely audible to the rest of us, the sound person would call a halt to proceedings and we'd have to wait until the intrusion was past before restarting the take. Despite their eccentricities, I felt a certain kinship of spirit with the sound technicians concerning the issue of intrusive noise, and most of them appreciated working at our place because of its relative quiet. Frequently they'd comment upon how rare it's becoming to find places as quiet as where we live. Even in the remotest spots, they'd say, it often proved difficult to get out of earshot of vehicles, planes, ATVs, snowmobiles, and other noisemakers as more and more of the natural soundscape is invaded by nonnatural sounds.

But even at our place, the level of background noise, although insignificant by urban standards, has gradually increased over the years. When the wind blows from the west it carries the rumble of semitrailers racing along a new superhighway several miles away on Vancouver Island. Low-flying aircraft are an ongoing annoyance, and certain islanders are partial to perforated mufflers as a preferred method of announcing their passing through.

Whether as a result of tiptoeing around my childhood home so as not to disturb our sleeping dad, or of meditative hours of silence in the cloister, the long and short of it is I've become a bit of a crank on the topic of silence. I particularly appreciate my brother Vincent's perspective on the issue. "I am content with silence," he tells me. "I am happy to live in silence. I prefer silence to sound. I find sound to be distracting and bothersome especially when I'm concentrating on something. Sound is noise to me, uncomfortable and alien, whereas silence is golden, bringing a sense of tranquillity, calmness, and peace."

As the Arabian proverb has it, "The tree of silence bears the fruit of peace," and I wonder how much of human delirium—of war and violence and exploitation—would abate if we all just turned down the volume. Most of the noise can be traced back to the combustion of fossil fuels, and I for one rejoice at the passing of peak oil. I also take heart in the work of noise pollution activists everywhere, like the people who achieved a ban on gas-powered leaf blowers in Santa Barbara, California, and the Right to Quiet Society in Vancouver lobbying against ubiquitous loud music in every public space. I wish every day was International Noise Awareness Day, that every place was designated a "noise-sensitive area."

There are certain silences now haunting the world, ones we do not hear, such as the silence of extinction. Every species of bird that disappears into the black hole of extinction carries away with it a repertoire of songs that will not be heard on earth again. The catastrophic collapse of frog populations occurring around the globe results in wetlands of morbid quiet where once were heard magnificent serenades of throaty croaking. Behind all the noise, Rachel Carson's silent spring is upon us. And human languages too are falling silent. Year by year the number of indigenous languages shrinks, dialects disappear, and with them a particular way of perceiving the world and ourselves. The dreadful silence of their loss is filled, but not really, by the relentless noise of progress.

I suppose a kind of silence will reclaim the earth when our species takes its turn, as every species must, at extinction. In the interim I dream of a world in which silence can exist, like the hush of the garden on a perfectly still evening, the clear crisp quiet of a high mountain meadow, or the deep contemplative silence of the cloister wherein exists the peace that surpasses understanding.

IF THERE HAS to be tone and sonance in the garden, I say let it arise from the sounds of earth or the sweet sounds of music. Our occasional overseas rambles, which generally focus on gardens and landscapes, usually result in a refreshed appreciation of how ingeniously certain musical traditions reflect the landscapes, and perhaps seascapes, of their origin. Several extended rambles through the villages and countryside of Ireland boosted my appreciation of Celtic music into the realms of obsession. The soulful laments of harp and pipes, whistles and bodhran, drenched with longing and loss and love of place, sounded to me inextricable from the high lonesome hills and craggy shores of Ireland. No music lingers more plaintively around the stone walls of our garden or our ancient, brooding trees; none reminds more plangently that all things will pass in their time.

While visiting Yunnan province in southwestern China, we attended a concert of the Naxi Orchestra, several dozen mostly aged musicians playing ancient music on gongs, chimes, wooden clappers, bells, and a variety of ancient string, wind, and percussion instruments. Each of the sacred pieces the orchestra played was a small symphony of rising and falling cadences, a stately layering of rhythmic waves punctuated by the ringing of chromatic bells and the sonorous reverberations of the great gong. Writing in *The Forgotten Kingdom*, Peter Goullart described this classical Naxi music: "It was a recital of the cosmic life as it was unfolding in its grandeur. It was classical and timeless. It was the music of gods and of a place where there is serenity, eternal peace and harmony."

In the old town of Suzhou, "the Venice of the Orient," south of Shanghai, we visited the Master of the Nets Garden one evening. The scent of a two-hundred-year-old wisteria perfumed the mild spring air while the lights of dangling lanterns shimmered in reflection in the garden's central pool. As we sat in a small and exquisitely decorated kiosk overlooking the pool, a lone flute player stood on the opposite shore, the plaintive melody of his bamboo flute seamlessly interwoven through three thousand years of Chinese gardening.

When all else is set aside for the moment, as it was in that lovely interlude, the combination of music and garden can exalt the spirit as close to a beatific state as it's safe to achieve without risking everything. Throughout the warm months of the year, I am in the habit of occasionally wandering our gardens and woodlands for hours while listening to music on headphones. An eclectic program fills the bill, music from all over the globe—the Scottish Highlands, North Africa, India—so long as it's got transcendence in its playing. A lone *shakuhachi* flute will do the job; so will Sufi dervish music or Jascha Heifetz playing a Brahms violin concerto. I wander the gardens and woodlands blissfully transported by the beauty of the playing and the place.

And certainly the garden plays music of its own, as intricate and intriguing as any concert piece. The tricklings and gurglings of a little cascade, the murmuring of leaves and grasses as the breeze combs through them, the cacophony of ravens, the bustling hum of hummingbirds zipping from one nectar source to the next, the electric buzz of feeding bees in summer sunshine, the rustle of falling leaves in autumn, the mournful rain song of tree frogs, the high thin cries of bald eagles, the almost inaudible whisper of spent peony petals or foxglove flowers cascading to the ground. These are the tunes of the garden, songs of the earth, dramatic and sultry, profound and ecstatic and perfectly attuned to the most exquisite music humans have ever written or played.

16

DWELLING PLACE OF
THE GODS

You will find something more in woods than in books.
Trees and stones will teach you
that which you can never learn from masters.
SAINT BERNARD OF CLAIRVAUX, *Epistles*

OUR PROPERTY BACKS UPON WHAT we used to call
Mrs. DeJong's farm. When we first arrived on the island
most of the farm's 160 acres had long since been reclaimed
by forest, with collapsed fence lines threading through mossy
glades and dense stands of timber. Cattle grazed in a few small
remnant fields around the old farmhouse. Well into her eighties,
Mrs. DeJong cultivated Christmas trees on a portion of the farm.
We'd sometimes glimpse her on cold November afternoons labo-
riously cutting small Douglas-firs with a handsaw and dragging
them one by one across the field to a waiting flatbed. The pittance
she made from her trees she donated to overseas orphans.

After her death the farm was broken into three parcels and sold.
The largest parcel—108 acres bordering our place—eventually

fell into the hands of a locally notorious cut-and-run logger. Within days a feller-buncher was gobbling up the trees behind our house. A large machine on treads, the feller-buncher wields an articulated arm that can reach out, seize a tree trunk, slice it free of its stump, strip it of branches, lop off its top, and throw the log on a pile the way you'd throw a faggot on a fire. Each tree dies and is dismembered within moments. The loggers quickly chewed their way right up to our property line, felling trees and spewing slash in all directions. The crew worked day and night. From our bedroom we could see their lights, menacing as troop movements, and hear the cries of dying trees. A more radical break with Mrs. DeJong's gentle ways would be difficult to imagine. When the looters were finished, a great scar of stumps and slash stretched where the woodlands once stood. An area that had seemed endless in its complexities of mosses and lichens, pools and leafy glades, glimpses of Eden, had shrunk to a barren heartache. Viewing the butchery I felt as Anna Brownell Jameson did in her 1838 *Winter Studies and Summer Rambles in Canada*:

> The pity I have for the trees of Canada, shows how far I am yet from being a true Canadian ... Without exactly believing the assertion of the old philosopher, that a tree *feels* the first stroke of the axe, I know I never witness nor hear that first stroke without a shudder; and as yet I cannot look on with indifference, far less share the Canadian's exultation, when these huge oaks, these umbrageous elms and stately pines, are lying prostrate, lopped of all their honours, and piled in heaps with the brushwood to be fired.

After the logging, we spent long and dispiriting afternoons cleaning up the debris strewn along the edge of our property. In late summer we gathered huge armloads of seeding fireweed and foxglove stems from our gardens and carried them into the wasteland, scattering seeds to help begin nature's reclamation work. These wildflowers now turn the scarred earth into a summer garden of sorts. Thistles, nettles, bracken, grasses, and other adventitious pioneer plants have set about initiating the decades-long work of re-establishing a forest. I've transplanted scores of Douglas-fir and western red cedar saplings along the property line.

With the sheltering forest gone, the southeasters that come roaring up the Salish Sea in fall and winter had an unimpeded path to the exposed palisade of trees around our house and gardens. Lashed by the fury of wind, the big conifers would sway and clash against one another, "like tall slim priests of storm," as Archibald Lampman wrote in "In October." Writhing in the wind, they'd hurl branches and large limbs to the ground. Occasionally one of the giants would let go, its roots losing their grip, and come crashing down with a thump on the chest of the earth. For many years on such nights, long before the logging, I'd lain awake in terror, believing a tree was about to come down upon us, flattening our little house and us within it. I'd also experienced a recurring nightmare about the forestland around us being destroyed, our sanctuary ruined. In my dreams, there were huge dead trees lying like beached whales alongside our house, the forest replaced by soulless suburbs crowding up against us. A crushing sense of solitude lost. A feeling of exile from the earth.

After the logging, following each winter storm, we'd walk the property, dismayed at the number of additional trees we'd lost, mostly shallow-rooted hemlocks that readily flip out of the ground, roots and all. Throughout the time we've lived here, I've always cherished working in the woods in wintertime, cutting firewood and making trails through a forest shimmering with green mosses, where a wary deer might tiptoe past or a pileated woodpecker set to jackhammering on a nearby snag. But that work was now degraded to repeated cleaning up of the windthrow each storm created.

Instead of working within the hushed luxuriance of a maturing forest, we were scrabbling on the verge of desolation, constantly reminded of human greed and carelessness. A cold wind whipping up the strait now penetrated into our gardens in a way it never had before.

Eventually the perfect storm struck. In the disastrous winter of 2006–07 our island was caught at the epicenter of colliding storm fronts. At the height of the storm, hurricane-force winds roared down our little valley. Tall conifers whipsawed back and forth in the maelstrom, some snapping like matchsticks. An enormous old Douglas-fir in front of the house crashed to earth. Behind the house a mature hemlock toppled over, levering its root mass out of the ground. With big trees screaming and toppling all around us, we fled the house and took refuge in a safer place. Mercifully our home wasn't hit, though a half-dozen or more buildings on the island were clobbered by falling trees.

We surveyed the damage the morning after the storm. Several dozen big conifers and many more smaller trees lay tangled together like a game of pick-up sticks. A huge limb had been torn off a western red cedar at the back of the garden, dragging down with it the long arms of a Kiftsgate rose that had over the years climbed about forty feet up the cedar and would in midsummer drape a gorgeous cascade of white blossoms. The scene looked uncannily like the recurring nightmare I'd had for so long, the disturbing dream of felled trees, a sense of sanctuary lost, of exile from the place where I belonged.

We took several lessons from this blustery brush with disaster: certainly a heightened sense of awe at the power of nature, as well as renewed empathy for people suffering far worse in other places, and a sharpening of the mind about being adequately prepared for as bad, or worse, to come. It seems entirely likely that these extraordinary storms may in fact become the norm in our increasingly uncertain future. With that in mind, we hired an arborist to examine the remaining trees immediately around the house. He recommended the removal of several, and a crew of skilled loggers worked for most of a week expertly bringing down the trunks in pieces and shredding the branches. Three of the gnarled veterans were rotten and cracked in their heartwood.

After several years of trauma and heavy cleanup work, we have achieved again a sense of relative calm within the woodlands. We no longer lie awake at night dreading the imminent crashing down of enormous trees because the giants that remain pose no threat. There is a lightness and brightness to the yard that was not there before, as rhomboids of morning sunlight sprawl lazily across the lawns and gardens where previously dark shadows ruled. Imposing bald eagles now regularly glide low across the gardens in a way they hadn't previously. And the woodlands still whisper their truths all around us. In the stirring of the breeze, the shriek of the gale, the crackling of dry underbrush in late summer, the forest still communicates its truths.

WINTER BONFIRES HAVE once again become an essential element of our seasonal rituals, in part because of mounting piles of slash from the windthrown trees. Left to its own devices, nature would periodically eliminate dead and fallen branches with quick cleansing fires that would not be hot enough to damage mature standing trees. But wildfire suppression has now eliminated those natural fires. Several consecutive summers of drought and a couple of potentially catastrophic wildfires on the island have sharpened everyone's awareness of fire prevention. When feasible, we've had a chipper brought in to pulverize branches, using the cedar chips on pathways and other types of chips as garden mulch. When chipping's not feasible, winter bonfires are in order, and that's not an altogether unwelcome thing. Gathered for an ancient fire festival, our ritualistic forebears undoubtedly knew that nothing quite lifts the spirits like a great roaring bonfire when autumn to winter resigns the pale year.

I take a few pieces of dry firewood from the woodshed and split a handful of dry cedar for kindling. I lay two of the faggots about a foot apart, crumple newspaper between them, and cross-hatch the kindling on the paper. It is a point of honor that only one match be used to ignite a fire, whether in the woodstove or at a campfire or bonfire. The flame of the struck match suckles greedily at the newspaper's edge and spreads like an insurrection through the paper and kindling. Gingerly I lay on the remaining pieces of dry firewood as the cedar crackles and sparks. Now the crucial transition point comes, from igniting dry materials out of the woodshed to getting storm-soaked branches and limbs to burn. Quickly I break off small clusters of twigs from dead and dried-out hemlock branches and feed them to the hungry flames. Then a few dead sticks broken from the undersides of cedar trees, followed by gradually bigger and bigger sticks until the fire's hot enough to ignite branches of cedar and fir fronds. Their green needles hiss and scorch on the little fire and I keep layering on dry branches and fresh fronds, the heat building so that twigs as well as needles now catch and burst into flame without smoking.

It is a slow and great ritual, the building of a bonfire from a single match to a roaring cone of blazing branches. This is the ingenuity of humankind at a primal level, the power to command the elements, to manipulate the world for our own purposes. Slowly I work the heap up, careful neither to smother the fire with excessive wet material nor to let the branches dome up so that there's insufficient fuel down among the coals. Then the moment occurs, as it does with every conflagration, as it did in that summer meadow of childhood, when fire declares itself independent, capable of devouring whatever comes its way. Sparks spiral skyward, and the voices within the fire become a choir of hissings and pops, cracklings and, under all, a feral roar. Sandy and I begin working together, throwing branch after branch onto the insatiable flames. Once the heat is intense enough we begin casting on detritus from the garden that cannot be composted—soggy peony stalks blackened by blight, rose canes cancerous with galls, the roots and seed heads of pernicious weeds like creeping buttercup and trailing blackberry.

Typically we'll run a bonfire for about five hours, by which point we're physically exhausted and darkness has crept up around the fire circle. We fetch a couple of chairs and a bottle of wine to celebrate the beauty and warmth of the fire. Surrounded by the looming dark shapes of conifers, with the querulous barking of sea lions away off in the distance, and with moving curtains of cold air brushing against our backs, I'll stare into the mound of incandescent embers. I'm gazing into the glowing coals of childhood, into the flames of Hell and Purgatory, those imaginary monsters that devoured my youth. These same coals have smoldered since the times of ancient bane fires, the fires of woe. Or medieval bone fires on which human bones were burned in order to repel dragons. Or further back in our race's long relationship with fire to the Celtic fire festival of Samhain and the Nordic *nod-fyr,* and the festival fires of Thor and Woden.

We light them to ward off the onset of chilling darkness this time of year, to burn off the diseased and evil, to cleanse, to celebrate, to conjure the sun's return. There are dragons still to be repelled, heretics and witches to be burned. They live inside us, among us, in memory and in desire. They are burned and still return. Their laughter is in the voices of the fire. Their lamentations too. I listen for them, staring into the embers, until Sandy exclaims, "Oh, look up at the stars!" The sky above is a dome of polished jet in which the distant fires of countless galaxies are burning.

HAND IN HAND with bonfires, the cutting of each winter's firewood remains one of the year's bigger and more satisfying projects, and a welcome counterpoint to the soily work of the gardens. The right trees must be selected and felled, the branches cut away and the boles bucked to suitable length. For splitting the rounds I use an eight-pound maul, swung overhead like a barbarian's battle-ax. The noisy and oily chainsaw part of felling and bucking is short on aesthetic appeal, but there's a tremendous rightness about the primitive physicality of splitting blocks of wood by hand: judging the grains of the wood, the complications of gnarly knots, the arc of the swung maul, and its solid clean cleaving of the block so that the severed sections leap apart. The simplicity of the action, its repetition, produces a physical strain and mental clarity, like that of the long-distance runner or cyclist, when mind and body unite in rhythmic common cause.

I stack the split pieces in the woods to dry through spring and summer, and in autumn I wheelbarrow the dried pieces from the woods and restack them in the woodshed. When the last load's finally in and the shed chockablock with prime dry wood, I take an honest satisfaction in a lengthy job completed, and always there's a tinge of regret that this gratifying occupation is done for another year. Any suggestions that I hire a young buck to do the work for me, or bring in a gas-powered log splitter that can do as much in five minutes as I can in an afternoon, get quickly rebuffed for the heresies they are.

Heating by fire is not without its problems, but economically and aesthetically it has enormous appeal. Considerably evolved from the wood-devouring and smoke-belching old stoves of the past, the heater has baffles and secondary combustion features that reduce fuel consumption and smoke emission and maximize fuel efficiency. A water coil inside the firebox provides hot water all winter.

Still, it's a primitive and polluting method of heating a space. I soothe my conscience with the reflection that it's solar heating in a way—the energy of the sun being temporarily stored in the tree, then released again by fire. But it's an indulgence nevertheless, this having a fire at the heart of the house where one can linger for a while on a dirty winter's day, backside to the burner, feeling the glorious warmth of summer glowing again in the fire. And perhaps recalling in a maudlin moment the sensuous heat of the coal fires of childhood in Woolton Village.

ANOTHER LEGITIMATE EXCUSE I've developed for getting into the woods in winter is to lift big trees. Not the Herculean labor it sounds, this involves removing branches from the lower parts of tree trunks so as to open up the woods near ground level, for both aesthetic and fire-prevention reasons. The Douglas-firs have more or less self-pruned their trunks; starting out as bushy seedlings when clustered together, they gradually discard their lower limbs and at maturity stand with bare columns like those of a cathedral, clad in roughly textured bark. Western red cedars are more inclined to hold on to their lower limbs. With sufficient sun, they'll form a solid curtain of deep green needles from the ground to treetop. Even in shade they'll produce lower branches that twist a thin fringe of needles toward whatever shafts of sunlight penetrate the forest canopy. It's mostly these ambitious but unwanted lower limbs I engage myself in removing.

The chainsaw makes quick work of the larger limbs near ground level. Then I lean a ladder against the trunk and, balancing somewhat precariously, take the chainsaw to slightly higher limbs. At the height where I no longer feel secure wielding a chainsaw (my childhood fear of heights at least partially overcome), I switch to a bow saw. Oftentimes I'll be near the top of the ladder working the saw with one hand while clasping a branch with the other. Taking a breather from vigorous sawing, I sometimes hug the trunk with both arms for balance and rest. It's an exhilarating sensation to perch high above the ground with your body and face pressed against the flesh of the tree, to feel it as a living thing, ancient and vibrant with life.

I believe in the voices of trees. Stephen Crane wrote in *The Red Badge of Courage*, "There was silence save for the chanted chorus of the trees." And Thomas Hardy wrote in *Under the Greenwood Tree*, "To dwellers in a wood almost every species of tree has its voice as well as its feature. At the passing of the breeze the fir-trees sob and moan no less distinctly than they rock; the holly whistles as it battles with itself; the ash hisses amid its quivering; the beech rustles while its flat boughs rise and fall."

Oftentimes when I'm sitting in the garden on a summer afternoon, my attention will drift away from the effusions of roses and poppies up to the high crowns of the trees, vivid green against blue summer sky. The forest possesses a strength and rightness and timelessness that the garden, for all its charms, cannot hope to duplicate. Nor are the trees my dependants, the way the peonies and clematis are. They were here before us and, with luck, will still be young long after we're gone. I don't believe with absolute certainty that trees are sentient beings or in any way conscious of my being among them. But I have no doubt that ancient forests are places of spiritual significance, mystical precincts beyond human— at least modern human—comprehension. I acknowledge the existence of sacred groves and the enlightenments to be obtained within them.

I started off long ago hankering for a mythic cabin in the clearing, and although instead I answered what I believed to be God's call to priesthood, in the end, the call of the trees proved stronger and truer. At this point the greater part of my life has been lived among trees and in intimate relationship with them. Sandy and I have spent time among ancient bristlecone pines of the High Sierra, among timeless twisted yews in Ireland and Joshua trees in the Sonoran Desert, with mighty English oaks and beech trees, with California redwoods and in the olive groves of Greece and the remnant great podocarp forests of New Zealand. All of them lovely, all under siege. But mostly we are here at home in the great coniferous forests of the Pacific Northwest, attempting all the while to be open to rediscovery of their secrets, to a personal recreation of the purity of humankind's primeval relationship with trees. The oldest writing, the epic of *Gilgamesh,* tells us: "They stood still and looked at the forest. They beheld the height of the cedar. They beheld the entrance to the forest . . . They beheld the mountain of cedar, the dwelling place of the gods."

Trees have given us the wood from which our house and outbuildings are built as well as our fences and arbors and garden structures. Wood from their bodies keeps us warm all winter. And being among them so long has given us something else, something much more elusive: an answer, perhaps, to the sense of rootlessness that so pervades modern consciousness, the sense of estrangement from ourselves that besets some who have wandered too far from the trees.

In summertime, at the end of the day we'll often walk down a twisting footpath through our woods and into the adjacent conservation lands that we helped preserve twenty years ago. We'll sit along the bank of a gorgeous small pond entirely surrounded by a mature fir and cedar forest. It is a place of surpassing beauty and serenity, rich in movement and mysteries. A place of sanctuary. An undeniably sacred place in which to ponder the salvific power of life systems.

17

REDEMPTION

The salvation of this human world lies nowhere else
than in the human heart, in the human power to reflect,
in human meekness and human responsibility.
VACLAV HAVEL, addressing the U.S. Congress in 1990

"OH, THIS IS *just* LIKE the Garden of Eden!" Two visitors
approach me along the path, male and female, she
exclaiming effusively. Respectably attired, Bibles in hand,
they are instantly identifiable as Jehovah's Witnesses, come to
save our souls. They're infrequent callers at our place, rare as solitary thrushes, and I can tolerate their occasional well-intentioned
intrusions, so long as they've mastered the art of brevity. Our
gardens provide them with an apparently irresistible segue into the
Garden of Eden, and from that sure starting point they endeavor to
carry me off on largely incoherent rambles through the thickets of
Holy Writ.

A century ago William James wrote in *Pragmatism*: "The
most violent revolutions in an individual's beliefs leave most of his
old order standing. Time and space, cause and effect, nature and
history, and one's own biography remain untouched. New truth

is always a go-between, a smoother-over of transitions. It marries old opinions to new facts so as ever to show a minimum of jolt, a maximum of continuity." But it would require a mighty act of prestidigitation for me to marry my visitors' solemn dogma, so like my own from years ago, to what I now experience as truth.

Throughout the transition period I'd spent in Vancouver, after leaving monastic life, and for our first several years on the island, I had clung to the remnants of my faith. Partly this was from a love of ritual and its seasonal implications. Sandy and I fasted in Lent and Advent, celebrated with friends on Easter morning at dawn and on Christmas at midnight. But, gradually and ineluctably, the reservoir of belief trickled away and eventually was gone, lost to another time and place. I ceased believing that there existed a conscious deity who created Heaven and Earth and now sits in observation of humankind. I ceased believing that Jesus Christ was the literal Son of God, born of a virgin, who by His passion and death redeemed humanity from a state of original sin inherited from Adam and Eve. I no longer believe that there exists elsewhere a literal Heaven, Hell, Purgatory, and Limbo to one of which the soul of every human is consigned at death. I no longer expect to stand trembling before God Almighty and all His heavenly host on Judgment Day at the end of the world.

While deploring many of the reactionary and obtuse teachings of the Catholic church, I continue to appreciate the holy men and women I encountered in my formative years—Sister Rosalie and Fathers Norbert Dorsey, Augustine Paul Hennessey, and other of the monks. These were admirable individuals who had entirely devoted their lives to the set of beliefs I have now abandoned as untenable. I have lost no affection for the brilliant artistic achievements this spiritual tradition has inspired, the splendid works of art, sublime music, astonishing architecture created in its service. The majesty and beauty of the conception, the elegance of its theology, its extraordinary influence over the course of two millennia can't be denied. But to believe literally in any of it now seems preposterous. It is a story, a brilliant compilation of metaphor, allegory, myth, and tradition to which I can no longer possibly ascribe literal truth. Nor do I feel inclined to replace it with any other old story framed in a world that no longer exists. All sacred traditions have essential truths to teach, but none alone encompasses the self-emergent universe of the new epoch that human civilization is entering. As Thomas Berry, the Passionist visionary I met long ago, pointed out, the passion of Christ in ancient times has been replaced by the passion of the earth in our own times. I too needed a new story, one that would grow over the years in this place we now call home. The new truths, which I discovered in my relationship with Sandy and in the woodlands and gardens and community of our new island home, would in the final analysis manifest a peculiar continuity with, as well as a radical break from, the orthodoxy I previously knew.

Listening to my visitors' enthusiastic explication of biblical truths, I hear familiar echoes from long ago. And, yes, a part of me can regret the loss of bedrock certainty that's the perquisite of an unquestioning faith. All these years later, I retain some residual hankering for the uplifting rituals of monastic life: the antiphonal chanting of matins and lauds in a candlelit chapel in the middle of the night, the splendors of the Easter Week liturgy, the hours of contemplative silence in chapel and on solitary walks. Certainly I regret the loss of that angelic little chap I was on the day of my First Holy Communion. He is gone forever. So is the cowed adolescent kneeling in the dark confessional, weighted with the guilt of innocent sins.

The chubby little fellow with curly red hair, dressed in short pants, a baggy shirt, and scuffed boots, standing in a meadow where birds and butterflies flutter above a moving sea of grass—I scarcely think of him as myself, but rather as some distantly remembered other self, almost the self of a dream. I see the same lad, slightly older, on an outer deck of a transatlantic liner on a warm May evening, watching the lights of Liverpool slide away into the darkness as the great ship plunges forward toward the open Atlantic and the brave new world of Canada. His innocent expectations, his trembling with excitement at all that lay ahead, are pure states of being, undiluted by the compromises and diminishments of experience. I can almost, but not quite, still smell the leafy heat of those first years in Canada when summer holidays lasted forever, warm and golden days of games in the schoolyard across from our house, and neighborhood girls to have a crush on while Pat Boone crooned "Love Letters in the Sand." Or the shocking cold of winter when icicles hung like stalactites from the eaves and creeks froze solid and everything seemed locked in ice that might never melt.

The remembered self draws closer during the time of the great divide, when I leave the sunlight of childhood fields and trees to enter the dark confessional, the morbid gloominess of monastic life, the darkness that settles around my spirit from denial of the real world, postponement of the possibilities of paradise. Then eventually, mercifully, a complete self begins to emerge as I find my balance with Sandy here on the island, achieving something of a full circle back to the remembered, or perhaps imagined, peace and beauty of Knowle Park.

NOT LONG AGO a young friend commented that to his way of thinking Sandy and I were reminiscent of Helen and Scott Nearing, the American patron saints of enlightened self-reliance. While I would like to think that his comparison centered on the intelligence, commitment, and rigorous self-discipline of the Nearings, I suspect it may have had more to do with our advancing age. Helen and Scott continued working away at "the good life" until she was well into her eighties and he into his nineties. As my old dad used to allude to, there's nothing quite like robust longevity to put a definitive exclamation mark upon your life choices.

Unaccountably, this year I am eligible to begin receiving the old age pension, a development that has already elevated some of our friends from relative penury to opulence. I've become accustomed to glancing casually around a foyer or bus and realizing that I'm probably the oldest person present. Slender young clerks in stores inquire considerately if I need a hand carrying out my purchases, dainty bags that are far lighter than the loads I regularly trundle around at home. On several occasions I've had brawny young guys shoulder me out of the way lest I damage myself by performing some task. And I've reluctantly ceased being perplexed by character descriptions from brilliant new voices in fiction in which some hoary old fossil, addle-headed from an atrophying mind, creaks about on arthritic limbs for several pages before it's revealed that the character is fifty-nine years old. As the great Moms Mabley said about old age, "You just wake up one morning and you got it."

I've long felt the appeal of the old Confucian maxim that the first fifty years of life should ideally be spent in activity, the second fifty in measured application of all that has been learned in the first. The sense is of eventually withdrawing from the hubbub of what we call daily life in order to ponder what has gone before, what lessons have been learned, and how these might best be applied, along with what yet remains to be mastered.

Sandy and I, and many of our friends, had the great good fortune to put down roots here long years ago and, through our collective efforts, to create a special community. Scarcely more than kids ourselves at the time, we have witnessed the birth of children and their growing and eventual leaving and frequently returning. We now gather to celebrate the weddings of kids we remember being born, to commemorate the passing of aged friends. There remains a pervasive sense of identity and continuity.

Meanwhile, the long-ago hippie–redneck conflict has been replaced by a more nuanced contest between the island conservation community and recently arrived upscale advocates of a developer-friendly Chamber of Commerce approach. The skyrocketing land prices of recent years have had developers drooling over the windfall possibilities of what they think of as "undeveloped" land. Like many other places, we are struggling with issues of community sustainability: how to prevent astronomical real estate prices from driving off everyone but the well-heeled. How to control what on other islands has been identified as "destructive gentrification," in which wealthy people install themselves in trophy homes and set about demanding urban-style amenities. How to ensure affordable housing for a diversity of age and income levels while still retaining the rural nature of these special places. I still believe this is one of the great contests of our times: the struggle to maintain the power of community, the values that bind us together, against the onslaught of mobile capital and an ethos of exploitation divorced from any concern for the human community or the integrity of ecosystems.

As the community has grown—there are now about twelve hundred permanent residents—new voices and new ideas have arisen, and this is as it should be. While I keep an oar in the local political waters, I find it less necessary nowadays to attend *every* meeting on every issue, but relinquishing the illusion of control involves frequent practice of transcendental tongue biting, and I'm reminded of one old-timer I overheard in the early days describing us "new people" as "bearded know-it-alls." My instinctive love of solitude is reasserting itself, in a way that it wasn't permitted to do previously, and I take delight in the additional time and tranquillity available for writing and gardening, both of which frequently got sidelined in more turbulent times.

And thus perhaps there comes at last a slackening in that life-long tension between the active and the contemplative life. The act of writing this memoir has in a way involved a touch of that Confucian wisdom, because it has compelled me to look back upon the fantastic stream of data, ideas, memories, dreams, interactions, emotions that floods across the decades of a lifetime, and to try to compose at least some portion of the torrent into a pattern of coherence.

As for the future, I have absolutely no illusions about the global environmental crisis—an acute awareness of it has informed my lifestyle choices and activism for most of my adult life—and I'm convinced that there's a hard rain going to fall, that it has indeed already begun to fall. Nor do I have any enthusiasm about the inescapable discomforts, inconveniences, and indignities associated with the body's gradual breaking down.

Nevertheless, I don't see that pious young monk, or that strapping young back-to-the-lander sporting outrageous hair and beard, as representing a personal apogee of any sort, a point from which everything thereafter was disappointingly anti-climactic. Those young fellows were merely earlier forms within a personal evolution. And while part of me would avidly embrace being that age again—to be experiencing the exhilarations and heartaches of young love, the vigor of a powerful young body, the bonds of youthful friendship that promise to last a lifetime; to be miraculously relieved of my chronic limp and gimpy heart and weakening musculature; to have once again a lifetime of possibilities awaiting—nevertheless, I would not trade the perfections of the present for illusions of the past. Longing to do so is to confuse the seasons, to believe that only springtime, the age of promise and expectation, has value. It is a misguided hankering for what cannot be, what time will not bestow, no matter what wonders the geneticists might perform. It is the ultimate folly of the aging tycoon pathetically accompanied by a succession of trophy mistresses young enough to be his daughters; he fails to recognize, or perhaps refuses to accept, that we are on a pilgrimage of sorts, a journey along which every point, every aspect, has its own particular resonance and meaning.

Seasoned gardeners, like other artists, know full well the potency of framing. Plants, buildings, landforms, or other elements are artfully employed to frame a particular feature so as to focus the viewer's attention upon it within an informing context. A single large urn or statuary located at the end point of an allée of clipped yew or beech is a simple and common example. A moon gate is typically situated in a classical Chinese garden so as to frame a featured stone or specimen plant, creating both a composition to be appreciated from without and an enticement to enter into what lies beyond. The creation of artificial hillsides and water bodies and the grouping of large trees in specific locations in the English landscape garden represent framing of viewscapes on a grand scale. The point is to focus awareness upon precise relationships so as to leave open the possibility of perceptions that might not otherwise occur. To see beyond what is seen. One of age's greatest gifts is the art of framing, the putting into perspective, the realization of depths and relationships among what had seemed unrelated entities.

Although in one sense nothing about my reality today has substantially changed from what it has been over the previous four decades, in another sense everything has. A cycle of life has in fact run its course and brought me full circle to another beginning; it is time to start learning the language, the skills, the great art of growing old. Part of the art involves continuity, the carrying on with unfinished business. For myself, only now entering the first days of young old age, I trust that means many more seasons of getting the gardens and woodlands to where we would like them to be. This impossibility has both motivated and confounded us since the beginning, and I see no sound reason to abandon it yet. And I look for more years too of writing and speaking, as the words have not yet run out nor begun to repeat themselves like aging rockers sadly reduced to a nostalgia act. A writer lives with the knowledge that the muse may at any moment depart. It comes with the gift, and the bargain is not a bad one. I shall lament the day, if it does arrive, when there are no further words, but I hope not to fight against it, not to deny it.

Other aspects present themselves in the retrospective reflection Confucian wisdom suggested. There is a profound joy, for example—a joy unknown to youth, and only hinted at in middle age—in the appreciation of lifelong fidelity: to have bonded fully in loyalty and love, to have spent decades weaving two separate sets of conscious and unconscious desires into a single undertaking, to have in some way achieved the abandonment of self for the sake of the other that was the object of my monastic rigors. I don't mean to suggest that monogamous bonding is appropriate for everyone, or inherently more virtuous or praiseworthy a choice than others, only that there is an exquisite sweetness and felicity derived from having pledged lifelong commitment to another and then having done the necessary work over the years to ensure that the arrangement was more than habit or convenience, that it remained an evolving relationship of perpetually renewed affection, creativity, and joy. I give full credit here to Sandy's early and enduring adherence to the principles of feminism as crucial in alleviating some of the worst aspects of the masculine and misogynist orthodoxy of my education.

I like to think that we've also remained loyal to the youthful ideals that inspired us and many of our generation. From the outset, the object of the undertaking was to live close to the earth, to be respectful of its processes and our fellow creatures, in touch with its seasons, fed by both its bounty and its beauty. We would impose ourselves upon it as gently as possible, proceed with care, slowly, and with mindfulness. We would maintain awareness of the plight of the planet and of the poor, making what contributions we could to their well-being. We would work within community to try to incorporate similar values into its deliberations and decisions. We would, when necessary, mount the barricades in defiance of those who would pollute and exploit and destroy through ignorance or for selfish purposes. None of those values seem less apposite today than they did forty years ago.

THE JEHOVAH'S WITNESSES have departed. Rather than the fixed and unchanging universe of their Bible, and of my own upbringing, I have come to believe in a perpetual unfolding of life on earth, a cosmogenesis, in Thomas Berry's description. He taught that the human story is merely the latest installment in an evolutionary process that stretches back for millions of years. We humans do not exist as a completed species, the pinnacle of all life-forms in an unchanging cosmos; rather we are among a host of participants in an ongoing developmental process, a cosmogenesis. I believe this life process includes both the cyclical patterning of the seasons and the evolutionary unfolding of the cosmos, the two intertwined, seasonal circle and evolutionary helix, female and male, spiraling together through a vast infinitude of space. The basic mood of the future, Berry speculated, might be one not of gloom over environmental collapse, but rather of confidence in the ongoing revelation that occurs in and through the earth. He considered that a sense of wonder, of enchantment and amazement, might be the fundamental virtues of the New Story.

Alone now in afternoon sunshine, I'm turning the compost heaps, a chore that on good days combines the best of muscular vigor with prayerlike devotion. The heaps themselves, though composed of decaying plant material, kitchen scraps, and excrement, in their own way manifest a paradigm of redemption. Through the transformative power of bacteria, fungi, nematodes, and swarms of other decomposer organisms, garden detritus is transubstantiated into the priceless medium from which new life will grow. The process is strangely analogous to the transformation sought through prayer or contemplation.

I try to make a meditation of the turning. With each deep plunge of the manure fork I unearth congregations of wondrous creatures. An occasional big brown ground beetle emerges grumpily from the disturbance and clanks off like a Sherman tank across the dark terrain. The elongated bodies of large centipedes seem to flow over the surface on a hundred small legs of magnificent coordination. A deadly hunter and killer, the centipede commands respect even in retreat. Each turned forkload of compost exposes scores of red wrigglers, small pinkish-red worms that, when disturbed, rapidly coil and uncoil themselves like frenzied dancers. I recall a visitor from the American Southwest describing how she'd started a compost heap at her new home in the desert, and how in very short order the heap was seething with red wrigglers. Where did they come from, she wondered. How did they find their way out into the middle of the desert? Nobody knew. Compost heaps are as rich in mystery as any other liturgy. The turned heap, infused with fresh oxygen, will support even more life in a week or two.

My worldview includes the belief that working the earth is a prayer to divinities whose names we do not know. The deities of growing things bestow blessings we have not thought to ask for because, as Mohandas Gandhi put it, prayer is not asking; it is a longing of the soul. I like the ancient Taoist belief that the spiritual life is at its core "a longing for mountains and waters." With mindfulness, the act of gardening becomes an extenuated exercise in soul-longing. We fumble with words like peace, tranquillity, contentment, with which to describe the benefices found here, but even as we say or write the words we know they are insufficient. Far closer to the essence of the thing is that old definition of biblical Jehovah: I am who am, "that which is ever coming into manifestation."

The garden is a place in which to simply be, in essence less a certain place in time than a state of being. Like the unspoiled places of nature, the garden subsumes us into itself so that we are in a way dissolved, our individuality lost. The interstices between self and not-self, between present as experienced and past as remembered, between sensation and imagination, decompose and are gone, leaving garden and gardening self as one. That which is.

We laborers in the earth study the sacred texts, perform the solemn rituals of seeds and ablutions. Acolytes at a temple of earth and stone, of petals and pistils, our prayer is for moments of the ineffable, glimpses of the divine. Occasionally we are rewarded for our faithfulness. Perhaps by a winter wren perched amid the brilliant tiny fruits of a Red Jade crabapple tree, chirping its plaintive haiku. And for just a moment all else is hushed, the background becomes monochromatic, the turning world suspended, while the little wren sings its minimalist song of love and death. This is what we're here for; this is who we are.

From the admittedly limited vantage point of my green age, I suspect the true art of aging lies outside time. We gaze back upon time past, maybe contending with feelings of satisfaction for what we did well and regret over what we failed to do, certainly with gratitude and affection for those we knew and loved along the way. With sufficient purity of heart perhaps we come to experience what Marcel Proust described in *Remembrance of Things Past* as "privileged moments," when past and present seem to fuse and the timeless essence of the two creates a transcendence within which there are no moments. There we enter the garden of the soul, the place we have sought for so long, the landscape of spirit we have labored to create. It is where our unconscious selves, our multiple forms of self through time, are manifest. The garden of spirit, and that is every garden, is a dreamscape created from all that is precious in this world, all that we have seen and heard and loved and remembered and forgotten. They are all here in this place of beauty. The voices of trees and children, the songs of birds and the laughter of lovers, the unfurling of perfect leaves and impossible petals—all are here. And so are we, out of time, beyond time, lifted up in wonderment and awe.

ACKNOWLEDGMENTS

M Y THANKS TO VISITBRITAIN, BRITAIN'S national tourism agency, for generous assistance with travel and accommodation. Also, heartfelt thanks to Julia Guest, the talented travel consultant who organized our recent tour of great British gardens, as well as previous garden tours to China and New Zealand. Special thanks to Heather MacAndrew for her encouragement and insightful observations on the manuscript. And great appreciation to the editor Susan Folkins, whose deft touch significantly helped in shaping and polishing the final product. Thanks to Carol Pope, my editor at *GardenWise* magazine, as a small portion of chapter 15 originally appeared in its pages. And a tip of the hat to the photographer Allan Mandell, who managed to catch me between the roses and the forest.

My brothers, Ger, Brendan, and Vincent, showed considerable generosity of spirit in allowing me to tell my version of a story that is partly theirs. The same for my companion, Sandy, who, as always, assisted and inspired in both the doing and the telling.